Approaches to Meaning in Music

MUSICAL MEANING AND INTERPRETATION
Robert S. Hatten, editor

EDITED BY

BYRON ALMÉN

AND

EDWARD PEARSALL

Approaches to
Meaning
in Music

INDIANA UNIVERSITY PRESS
Bloomington and Indianapolis

This book is a publication of

Indiana University Press
601 North Morton Street
Bloomington, IN 47404-3797 USA

http://iupress.indiana.edu

Telephone orders 800-842-6796
Fax orders 812-855-7931
Orders by e-mail iuporder@indiana.edu *

The paper used in this publication meets the minimum requirements
of American National Standard for Information Sciences—Perma-
nence of Paper for Printed Library Materials, ANSI Z39.48-1984.

Manufactured in the United States of America

Library of Congress Cataloging-in-Publication Data

Approaches to meaning in music / edited by Byron Almén and
Edward Pearsall.
     p. cm. — (Musical meaning and interpretation)
   Includes bibliographical references (p.) and index.
   ISBN 0-253-34792-0 (cloth : alk. paper)
   1. Music—Philosophy and aesthetics. 2. Music—Semiotics. 3. Music
theory—Criticism and interpretation. I. Almén, Byron, date II. Pearsall, Edward, date III. Series.
   ML3845.A67 2007
   781.1'7—dc22
                                                2006006217

1 2 3 4 5   11 10 09 08 07 06

For Sarah

For Ludim

Contents

Approaches to Meaning in Music

1   The Divining Rod: On Imagination, Interpretation, and Analysis

Edward Pearsall and Byron Almén

Musical meaning has become a seductively compelling topic for music scholars over the last few decades, with works by Lawrence Kramer, Daniel Chua, Jean-Jacques Nattiez, Robert Hatten, Kofi Agawu, Carolyn Abbate, and countless others pushing the question of signification to the forefront of the discipline. That this is so can partly be attributed to the semantic slipperiness of the term "meaning," which we fill with so many hopes and expectations. It suggests a special kind of knowledge, a privileged insight into our fascination with the experience of music. Indeed, explorations into musical meaning lay claim to embodying the central core of our discipline, justifying its very existence by revealing the source of music's power, by translating its implicit message.

And yet that source is as opaque as it is compelling. Philosophers, artists, and theorists from the time of Pythagoras have wrestled with the concept of musical meaning, always to come up short. There are so many intractable problems to be solved. Is meaning entirely mediated by culture, or are there identifiable universals? Is meaning communicable from one person to another, given the vagaries of subjective response? For music to communicate, must it also be beautiful? Does music convey anything at all beyond its play of sounds? What, indeed, does "meaning" mean? What methodological tools are appropriate? Is music like a language, a natural object, an article of faith? Or is meaning more like a subjective confession, an idiosyncratic recognition of meaningful patterns? Is there any common ground at all on which to lay a foundation for a theory of meaning?

In the title of this chapter, we allude to an unusual metaphorical analogy between the study of meaning and the traditional folk practice of dowsing for water, analytical method being correlated with the dowser's tool—the *divining rod*. This analogy fruitfully illuminates the unusual character of musical meaning as an object of inquiry in several respects:

1. The object of search is, in both cases, precious and fundamental: water is essential for life, and music exists only through the significance we give it.
2. The mechanisms through which either is achieved are opaque and mysterious. Just as there is no apparent effective relationship between wood and

water, so, too, is there no indisputable connection between our theoretical tools and their object of interest.

3. There is some question whether either process actually works, or whether something akin to a magical sleight-of-hand is involved. Approaches to musical meaning have often been rejected as being products of wishful thinking, not amenable to proof.

4. In both cases, the difficulty lies not with the object but with the means of apprehending it. Meaning, like water, is manifestly present—although some might even question this position—but it may be that we can have no access to it unless it is immediately apparent.

5. The practice of dowsing, as with the discovery of meaning, seems to involve the complicity of the seeker's personality. Meaning in music appears only through the processes used to construct it. Hence musical signification is emergent, contingent on researchers and their methods.

This analogy would likely appear unwelcome to a researcher interested in establishing the legitimacy of musical meaning as a scholarly subject. Yet this is the situation facing us today: the mystification surrounding musical meaning as a subject is a great stumbling block to research. For a theory of musical meaning to succeed, it must attempt to demystify the mysterious without robbing it of mystery. Further, if it cannot place the entire phenomenon within one frame, it must attempt to identify that portion of the phenomenon which can be comprehended, and reveal it in the face of seeming arbitrariness, self-contradiction, and contingency. This book, featuring a variety of voices from our contemporary musical community, is intended to display the rich variety of ways in which musical meaning is today being divined.

In this collection of essays, written by theorists, musicologists, and cultural scholars, we present a survey of the problems and issues inherent in pursuing meaning and signification in music, one we hope will take into account the instability of the interpretive landscape as well as the complicity of the researcher in generating the content of his or her scholarship. Within these pages a provisional taxonomy emerges for mapping the terrain of current approaches to meaning, with a sufficiently large sample so that significant landmarks within that terrain are revealed. Within these pages a range of positions, ideas, and approaches representing both established and emerging scholars are displayed. More than this, however, the collection embodies an ideal of cross-disciplinary and intra-disciplinary collaboration that is a hallmark of the hermeneutic standpoint shared by all its contributors.

As we have indicated, music is a complex phenomenon, one involving a host of cultural, phenomenological, cognitive, cultural, and music-artistic factors. To understand music in its fullest sense, then, is to be willing to entertain a variety of perspectives. But the nature of academic inquiry resists such an approach. How can one give equal emphasis to all aspects of a problem without losing focus? Indeed, how can we even identify all the influences that might apply? It is out of practical necessity, therefore, that each perspective concentrates on a particular interpretive feature of music. This does not preclude, however, the existence of multiple viewpoints, even ones that are equally tenable. Nor are multiple perspectives necessarily mutually exclusive. Rather, each can be seen to contribute to some aspect of our total understanding without claiming to have arrived at a conclusive, once-and-for-all understanding of music.

Viewed in this way, meaning in music resembles the elephant in the Buddhist parable in which three blind men, together, come upon an elephant: the first man grasps the elephant's tail and thinks that the elephant is a rope; the second feels the elephant's trunk and believes the elephant is a snake; the third touches the elephant's foot and imagines that the elephant is a tree. Like the blind men in the parable, we music scholars, in our analysis of music, grope around the various aspects of music and then, as William James observed, we "substitute the aspect for the whole real thing" (1977: 100). Like the elephant, however, music is not understood so easily.

By taking a few steps back, we can begin to identify certain methodological similarities in the approaches used by scholars who address the problem of meaning in music. Among other things, we see that many scholars—including those already mentioned and those whose work appears in this volume—often discover meaning through a dialogic process, via the interaction of contrasting ideas. Indeed, that so many theorists and musicologists, independently of one another, have employed this approach gives credence to the idea that the dialogic process lies at the core of the hermeneutic enterprise and arises from a psychological imperative.

These contrasting ideas that give rise to "meaning" arise both within and among scholarly works. The former, "intra-essay" approach is more typical, occurring when an author counterpoises multiple perspectives in a single essay or treatise. The latter process—the bringing into contact of disparate approaches through multiple treatments of a single subject—is, in our view, less frequent but equally fruitful. We have chosen to model this "inter-essay" approach: by juxtaposing a variety of perspectives in our volume, we hope to promote a more diversified environment for the study of music. In doing so, we propose a methodological middle ground between presumed and unquestioned orthodoxy, on the one hand, and dogmatically centrifugal relativism, on the other. We proceed from a shared assumption that the articulation of meaning—whether sanctioned through tradition and conventional usage or emerging from the unique dynamics of the work or the cultural milieu—is possible and realizable. Indeed, it is only on the basis of shared assumptions that a cross-disciplinary discussion might take place at all. It is our intention, therefore, to balance a healthy respect for traditional hermeneutics with a desire to avoid sealing off theoretical discourse from fresh ideas and approaches.

The various chapters in this volume cover a broad spectrum of approaches to musical meaning, involving issues of gesture, narrative, discursiveness, temporality, symbol, association, collage, and social utility. These topics offer a wide variety of perspectives and cut across disciplinary boundaries, but they share a common intent: that of showing how music is informed by its cultural, political, and artistic influences. On one level, then, the volume functions as an introduction to various approaches to music analysis, and, on another level, it draws these approaches together to form a more complete picture of the interpretive landscape and the possibilities inherent in collaborative discourse.

Toward a Multidimensional Approach to Music Analysis

It is probably impossible at this point to articulate an entirely satisfactory taxonomy of musical meaning. For one thing, neither of the most appealing organizational options—logical or conventional divisions—is without its problematic features. Logical division lends itself to a certain elegance of presentation and, potentially, a greater degree of comprehensiveness, but its success depends on the willingness of a significant proportion of musical meaning scholars to adopt a single terminology and epistemological paradigm. More important, the criteria through which the domain might be organized are not obvious: should one classify according to parameter (melody, harmony, etc.); scope of application (global, medial, local); sign type (icon, index, symbol); degree of idiosyncrasy or consensus; level of simplicity or complexity; degree of universality; relation to a particular style or time period; paradigm (cognitive theory, sociology, semiotics); range of application (personal, interpersonal, cultural); or something else altogether? Perhaps a classification system combining some or all these criteria is necessary. The more features we include, however, the more we trade elegance for comprehensiveness.

Conventional groupings, by contrast, have the advantage of deriving from relatively cohesive communities of scholars who work with a shared terminology. A classification system based on traditional terminology has a self-evident and ready-made efficacy. But there is no guarantee that these communities, taken together, are adequately accounting for the full range of signifying phenomena. Further, without a universally agreed-upon set of principles, advances in one area may not filter through to inform advances in other areas. Indeed, disciplinary barriers and mutual distrust often prevent the clear exchange of ideas.

Perhaps, at this stage, it is too early to force a solution to this problem. The proliferation of approaches and methodologies in the area of musical meaning, though perhaps working against the immediate likelihood of a unified field, has the advantage of drawing in a larger interested audience. A critical mass of material is accumulating which may itself provide the nucleus for a diverse yet coherent subdiscipline. In such a climate, scholarly anthologies of the sort represented by this volume are one way to move this process forward. While largely adhering to a variety of traditional or conventional approaches to meaning, then, we hope to provide the impetus for a more focused and barrier-free disciplinary community to emerge.

Among the primary musical parameters, melody has the longest history as a locus of meaning. The ubiquity of its association with the human voice has indelibly marked it as the premiere embodiment of expressive communication, even when, in instrumental music, the voice is mute. Jean-Jacques Rousseau (1981 [1825]: 95) hints at the connection between melody and human agency when arguing for the primacy of melody: "everyone takes pleasure in listening to beautiful sounds, but if the experience is not animated by *melodious* and familiar inflections it will in no way be delightful or sensually pleasing."[1] Modern treatises on melody have continued in the same vein, often emphasizing the fundamental cognitive or psychological features underlying it. Eugene Narmour (1977: 7) asserts that the basic principles of his implication-realization model "operate independently of any specific style structures, of any learned, replicated complexes of syntactic relations." Narmour bases melodic perception on Gestalt categories, in some quarters thought to lie at the root of human perception. These categories include similarity, proximity, and common direction, the latter derived from the common-fate principle in Gestalt psychology (1977: 6). Leonard Meyer (1973) cites a similar premise in his well-known book *Explaining Music*—although, for Meyer, stylistic conventions also play a role. Meyer expresses melodic perception in terms of a single overriding principle: "*patterns tend to be continued until they become as stable as possible*" (130). Building on this principle, Meyer identifies a number of specific melodic types, axial melodies, gap-fill melodies, neighbors, and the like. In Meyer's paradigm, these melodic gestures form the foundation for melodic structuring in music.

To Meyer's basic melodic gestures, Patrick McCreless, in chapter 2, "Anatomy of a Gesture: From Davidovsky to Chopin and Back," adds another. McCreless's gesture is a four-part melodic idea consisting of (1) increased intensity in the highest register (increase in rate of events, thickening of texture, crescendo); (2) suddenly, at the peak of this increase, a quick, precipitous drop to a low register; (3) a "thud" at the bottom of the second part of the gesture; and (4) a "rebound" in the middle register. McCreless traces the origins of this gesture to Romantic piano music, where it constitutes a closing pattern in works by Chopin, Liszt, and their contemporaries. He then traces the gesture and its modifications through musical history, culminating with a discussion of modified four-part gestures in the music of such disparate twentieth-century composers as Tatum, Copland, Messiaen, Boulez, and Davidovsky. In this way, McCreless's essay incorporates a two-level analysis centering on both the structural properties of the gesture and its development as a cultural-historical object.

The concept of gesture—a class of musical events sharing common morphological and, by implication, semantic features (often, but not exclusively, including aspects of melody and register)—is also one of the traditional categories used by music scholars to approach the issue of meaning. Its genesis might be traced back as far as the early seventeenth century, when rhetorical *Figuren* began to be associated with certain musical phenomena. The term has since acquired various resonances from similar but non-overlapping concepts: *leitmotiv,* Schoenberg's *musikalische Gedanke,* and various semiotic entities. McCreless's four-part gesture is thus also *meaningful:* it has a psychological component that motivates its historical propagation and accounts for its compelling quality. McCreless appeals to the physicality of this gesture for an understanding of its semantic content, correlating the motion between registral, dynamic, and timbral extremes with corporeal motion. This in turn suggests dramatic content, as we come to imagine "action sequences" that might correspond to this gesture. And, of course, the more precise content of the gesture depends on how it fits into specific networks of sound. The resulting spectrum of possibilities is amply fleshed out by the numerous examples McCreless provides. Even within a limited scope, complexities of meaning emerge from a single gesture through its acquisition of contextual associations, the extent to which it invokes historical predecessors (see also chapter 5, J. Peter Burkholder's essay on associative meaning), and its strategic deployment in a given work (see chapter 4, by Robert S. Hatten, for a discussion of stylistic and strategic coding).

The notion that music can make use of dramatic patterns, as suggested above, is likely a product of another primary characteristic of music: its temporality. The potential for dramatic unfolding in music, explored by Abbate (1991), Maus (1988), Tarasti (1994), and others, is only one of the ways in which the temporal qualities of music inflect aspects of meaning. Many authors have noted the fundamental salience of temporality as a musical characteristic. By contrast, composers such as Stockhausen, Feldman, and Ligeti, among others, have attempted to create "music that has nothing to do with time, but which instead is strictly static in character" (Sessions 1970: 38). For our purposes, this debate is interesting in two respects. First, it suggests that our experience of temporality in music might be altered by the manner in which it is organized (see chapter 4 for a treatment of this issue involving the positing of an unmarked "ongoing present"). Second, it implies that meaning might emerge from the strategic deployment of various degrees of perceived temporality or its opposite, staticism. This is the subject of Edward Pearsall's essay, "Anti-Teleological Art: Articulating Meaning through Silence" (chapter 3).

Previous discussions of musical stasis have typically characterized music in terms of its "nonlinear" or "anti-teleological" effects.[2] Such approaches have met with criticism, because they generally attempt to justify the *structural* role of musical events on the basis of a *feeling* or effect. As a result, discussions of linearity and nonlinearity in music often veer off into philosophical debates over the nature of time; music becomes a mere example of a temporal phenomenon rather than a rich and robust mode of expression in its own right. Pearsall attempts to renegotiate the problem of nonlinearity in music by couching his discussion in terms of discursive and non-discursive categories, thus redirecting attention away from linearity with its attendant cultural bias. (Meyer [1967] and J. Kramer [1988], for example, associate linearity with Western tonal music and nonlinearity with music of tribal cultures and post-tonal music.) For Pearsall,

> discursive events in music are those that manifest themselves primarily as functional or purposeful transactions, whereas non-discursive events are those whose aesthetic impression is their most prominent feature.

In providing these definitions, Pearsall recognizes the essentially subjective nature of any musical experience. Discursiveness and non-discursiveness depend on context and the manner in which musical relationships are interpreted, not on immutable properties thought to reside in music itself. This approach broadens the concept of nonlinearity beyond music traditionally considered nonlinear to include a wider range of music including the compositions of Mozart, Vaughan Williams, and Ives.

Robert S. Hatten's essay, "The Troping of Temporality in Music" (chapter 4), also addresses the critical relationship between temporality and meaning, in this case on the expressive effects created by disjunctions between the expected and actual locations of musical events relative to a constructed dramatic sequence (a sequence that differs conceptually from the moment-to-moment unfolding of notes in time). Hatten calls this process the "troping of temporality," which involves playing against an unmarked "ongoing present" in which the phenomenal and dramatic sequences share essentially the same ordering—initiatory gestures occur in initial locations, closural gestures occur in terminal locations, anticipatory gestures prepare other events, and so on. Troping only emerges when the "ongoing present" is contradicted by events that appear to be out of place. The idea that stylistic temporal codes can be used strategically in unusual contexts is not entirely new: Kofi Agawu (1991), for example, has previously discussed the rhetorical consequences of employing beginning, middle, and ending gestures in unexpected locations. What Hatten signally contributes to this discussion is a recognition that troping creates expressive effects beyond an awareness of sequential disjunction. Such moments also engage their specific contextual environments to further specify semantic content in ways that would not otherwise have been possible. Just as narrative theorists like Gerard Genette (1980, 1988) (with respect to literature) and Vera Micznik (2001) (with respect to music) track differences in temporality between *story* and *discourse,* so, too, does Hatten explore the effect of troping on the semiotic codes that contribute to the meaning of a musical work.

Several paradigms, not intended to be exhaustive, are identified by Hatten in the process of exemplifying his thesis. These include (1) passages in which closural functions appear in initiatory locations; (2) the unfolding of an "evolving theme," analogous to Burkholder's "cumulative form" strategy, in relation to the emergence of topical elements; (3) the breaking off of an idea or a motion toward a goal; and (4) the parenthetical insertion of an unexpected idea into the musical discourse. Hatten goes beyond identification to discuss the strategic expressive effects that derive from their specific contexts. For example, individual parenthetical interpolations are shown variously to suggest the suspension of time, premature developmental activity, and "timeless oscillation," depending on the particular musical events they inflect. Hatten's approach to temporal manipulation particularly highlights the way these phenomena participate in a larger web of significations.

McCreless, in his discussion of gesture, has already hinted at the role played by memory, quotation, and association in the formation of meaning. In that instance, more recent variants of the four-part gesture derive part of their significance from the composer's/listener's/analyst's awareness of previous variants—these earlier variants influence and concretize the possible range of new, strategically emergent meanings. It is possible, of course, to push this principle much further: in one sense, *every* kind of meaning is dependent on association and memory. Semiotics and postmodernism have taught us that the text is endlessly signifying, that it acquires meaning only through the relationships it makes with every other text. This signifying process is continually in flux, impossible to circumscribe and define, and is crucially dependent on the observer's interpretive lens.

Burkholder's "A Simple Model for Associative Musical Meaning" (chapter 5) foregrounds these issues, subjecting inter-subjective experience to a meta-stylistic analysis. He identifies five stages of associative perception: (1) recognizing the familiar; (2) being aware of more immediate, denotative associations; (3) being alert to less immediate, connotative associations; (4) accounting for what is unfamiliar or "new" in the music; and (5) interpreting "all this information, including the associations aroused and the changes or new elements that are introduced."

Burkholder's model is meant to reflect what *happens* when we listen, not what the outcome of the listening activity might be. In Burkholder's words, "this model will not do our interpretive work for us." Through his model he acknowledges, with Pearsall and Hatten, that interpretations can vary with their interpreters, although he does refer to several musical signs whose associations are less subject to interpretive variation (military bugle calls such as *Reveille* and *Assembly* communicate, for the knowledgeable listener, in a manner similar to language). Burkholder's model, with its recognition of both the familiar and new features that accompany its reuse, also implicates Hatten's distinction between stylistic and strategic codes. It is noteworthy that the emphasis on association in Burkholder's discussion highlights a kind of intertextuality that also underlies this collection of essays: familiarity with music and with the cultural artifacts surrounding it can significantly inflect (enhance?) the hermeneutic process.

The associative principle also informs Nicholas Cook's contribution to this volume, "Uncanny Moments: Juxtaposition and the Collage Principle in Music" (chapter 6). Cook suggests that, in tandem with more traditional modes of analysis, meaning may arise from the juxtaposition of a work with other works of a similar nature. This approach recalls the film-theoretical concept of montage in which the juxtaposition of images or sounds gives rise to emergent meanings—meanings that are not inherent in the images or sounds, but generated through their interaction within a unique compositional context. Thus Cook foregrounds what is implied by Pearsall, Hatten, and Burkholder, namely, that meaning arises through a dialectical process involving a play of interrelated ideas and images.

One consequence of understanding meaning as endlessly negotiating the totality of texts is that the composer does not occupy the interpretive center; that is, meaning is reliant on many other factors—sociological, political, historical, cognitive, and so on. The essays by Byron Almén and Jann Pasler (chapters 7 and 8, respectively) centralize this aspect of our study; they reveal that the contributing factors to the meaning of a work are much more varied and extensive than typically imagined. Almén challenges the priority of the composer and the immediate cultural environment for constructing an interpretation of a given work. He argues that interpretation need not confine itself to the cultural milieu of the composer but can be informed by connections not necessarily accessible to the composer. Almén recognizes that listeners may attach *new or historically prior* meanings to the music based on their particular cultural perspectives, thus participating in the web of signification and actively engaging in the formation of meaning. Such an act, though apparently idiosyncratic, is no less arbitrary than a composer-centered interpretation. The analyst, as much as the composer, is involved in the creative process of artistic communication, which is effective insofar as it is *persuasive* to the community to which it is directed. As an illustration of this process, Almén analyzes the received corpus of symbols, as determined by the scholarly community, associated with Mahler's first four symphonies. Using these symbols as raw material, he constructs a narrative interpretation of the whole, taking into account their historical and mythical resonances and constructing a coherent interpretation derived from their perceived interconnections. Such a narrative, itself a creative act, reveals the broader landscape within which these symbols are enacted.

Jann Pasler also expands the interpretive compass in her essay, "Contingencies of Meaning in Transcriptions and Excerpts: Popularizing *Samson et Dalila*," by suggesting that meaning frequently emerges from cultural factors outside the composer's control. She interrogates the notion of the musical "work" by examining the early performance history of Saint-Saëns's *Samson et Dalila*. Early audiences heard this work in many different forms: various subsets of its movements were performed and published with different orderings and scorings, in the guises of orchestral concerts, piano recitals, and outdoor wind performances. Each of these "versions" arose from a particular configuration of social circumstances and reflected differing and shifting views of women, national identity, and musical practice, among other factors. On the other hand, the variants gave rise to contingent meanings based on their individual orderings, omissions, and configurations, and these meanings influenced subsequent versions of the material. It is inappropriate, then, to speak of "the" meaning of *Samson et Dalila* or even of "the" work, given the multiplicity of its manifestations. Under these conditions, Pasler maintains, meaning is contingent, "conditioned by certain frameworks, and affected by a sometimes disjunct, sometimes cumulative layering of meanings." The opera thus functioned as a constantly shifting tableau—both agent and object—participating in the negotiation of cultural identity and values in contemporary French society.

The essays in this volume incorporate interdisciplinarity by approaching music from various perspectives, all of which account for some detail of our total experience. Thus individual chapters model in the particular what the entire book models in the abstract. Patrick McCreless does not take the universality of his four-part gesture to be a given but, instead, sets out to provide evidence for such a claim by following the gesture's historical trajectory. In so doing McCreless creates a more *rigorous* study (not a more *superficial* one) by including multiple perspectives based on structural and historical paradigms. The same can be said of the other essays in this volume. Both Hatten and Pearsall describe temporality in terms of linguistic categories, thus calling attention to the ways in which extra-musical domains can impinge on one's interpretive behavior. In addition, both allow for multiple interpretations, albeit within the confines of certain stylistic norms and conventions. This perspective is also reflected in the meta-theoretical essay of Peter Burkholder. Rather than shying away from the complexities inherent in the hermeneutic position, these essays address the issue of complexity head-on while supplying constraints that can be generalized to a wide variety of situations, thus demonstrating that different perspectives may emerge through a similar process. Byron Almén and Jann Pasler build on a similar premise by broadening the cultural milieu—often spoken about with respect to the composer alone—to include that of listeners, both those of the composer's generation and beyond. All these authors, moreover, have independently constructed arguments centering on dialogic processes, elevating the idea of dialectical structuring to a principal position in their research on music and meaning. Nicholas Cook's essay directly involves dialogic processes to the extent that he advocates an approach to analysis based on the juxtaposition of several works within the same interpretive frame and also because his model refers to other domains of experience including museum collections and film montages. As a whole, then, these studies demonstrate that in entertaining multiple perspectives, one does not necessarily have to sacrifice depth in the interest of breadth. Rather, breadth can sometimes lead to an even more profound understanding of the subject at hand.

Among the specific conclusions one may draw from the insights offered in this volume are that music is a complex phenomenon, one that involves many interacting factors on many levels; that musical meaning is emergent, subject to inter- and intra-subjective experience; and that music is experienced in relation to culture. Clearly music cannot be expressed in simple terms or as one entity apart from its many manifestations. At the same time it is probably unrealistic to expect that any one study can fully explore the ramifications of even a few of music's features with respect to the specific topic under discussion. We can acknowledge, however, that the subject of musical meaning cannot be constrained by a single domain of experience even when our research paradigms are. This, too, can become a part of our ongoing search for meaning in music, for the sustenance that, still hidden, flows beneath our feet.

Notes

1. Interestingly, Rousseau goes on to say that "harmony in its strictest sense is even less favourably placed. Since its beauties derive only from convention, it gives no pleasure to the ear that is unaccustomed to it" (1981 [1825]: 96).
2. See, respectively, J. Kramer 1988: 20; and Meyer 1967: 73.

2 Anatomy of a Gesture: From Davidovsky to Chopin and Back

Patrick McCreless

The composite gesture that constitutes the climax of the first section of Mario Davidovsky's *Electronic Study No. 1* (1960) begins with a soft, sustained beam of sound that emerges, high in the frequency spectrum, out of some unruly brassy sounds in the middle of the spectrum. The sound begins to grow in intensity and harmonic richness, and soon we hear superimposed upon it an increasingly hurried pattern of crystalline high sounds. What brings this crescendo in the sustained sound, combined with the growing activity around it, to a climax is, first, a sudden cascade of loud, aggressive buzzes that starts high in the spectrum and immediately falls down into the lower registers; and, second, a similarly descending, though slower, succession of metallic crashes—all culminating in the low, reverberant gong-like structural downbeat that is the climactic moment itself. The climactic "thud," however, not only reverberates; it also generates a "rebound," in the sense that the middle-register brassy sounds return, to absorb and dissipate the considerable energy that still remains.

As it turns out, this four-part gesture—high-register crescendo with an increase in activity, precipitous plunge, low-register crash, and rebound, visually represented in figure 2.1, is both thematic and form-determining for the *Electronic Study*. The *Study* is structured in four sections: the second and fourth are loose variations of the first, and the third functions as a contrast to the other three. It is almost as if the piece is a sonata form with repeated exposition and a development of different character. The composite gesture described above provides the climax not only for the first section but for the second and fourth sections as well. As seen in figure 2.2, the dynamic curve of sections 1, 2, and 4 of the *Electronic Study* crescendos from a soft beginning to a point of maximal intensity articulated by the four-part gesture (G), the rebound of which initiates a diminuendo to the end of the section. Only section 3, which remains quiet throughout, lacks this large-scale dynamic shape.

The climax of the second section is even more straightforward, if also louder and more boisterous, than that of the first. Amid increasing activity, suddenly a strident, high, foghorn-like sound emerges in the higher register. The sound cre-

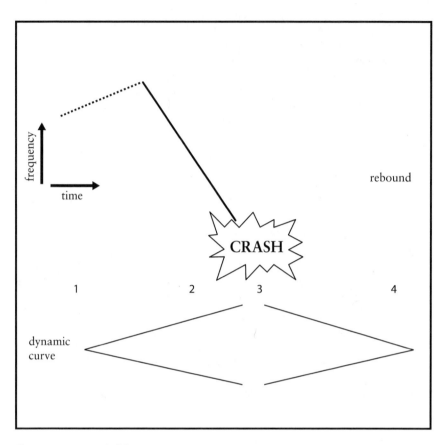

Figure 2.1. Prototypical four-part gesture

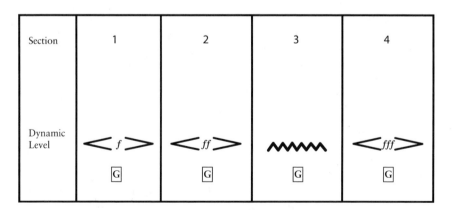

Figure 2.2. Davidovsky, *Electronic Study No. 1*, large-scale dynamic shape

scendos as activity gathers around it, and then the whole texture focuses itself in a single, raspy electronic voice that "dives off" the foghorn and plummets instantly to a low crash, again with reverberation and rebound.

The gesture is predictably expanded and intensified in the fourth section, so that it works as the climax not only of the section but of the whole piece. Now, in addition to a high-pitched sustained sound, an ascending sequence of low but pitched rumbles is counterpointed against faster-paced descending cascades of bell-like sounds. The music crescendos toward the cacophonous climax through the addition of brittle, high-pitched trills, of fast patterns of mechanical sounds that suggest impossibly quick returns of a typewriter carriage, ever faster and more compressed streams of sounds darting up and down the pitch spectrum, and finally a last precipitous plunge of buzzes to the loudest crash in the piece. The stronger structural downbeat here generates even more reverberation, as well as a longer, louder rebound of muffled brasses that eventually dovetails into the quiet echoes that bring the work to a close.

What makes these three climaxes so compelling? Surely it is at least in part the sheer physicality of the gestures that binds us to them. We can imagine tossing and turning in an upper bunk bed with dreams that are more and more disturbed, a beam of light boring in harder and harder upon our consciousness, until suddenly we fall out of the bed, crash upon the floor, limbs flying in all directions before we settle in a semiconscious heap. Or two film stars fight to the death on the highest walkway of a large warehouse; the fight intensifies in pace and violence, but at the critical moment the hero strikes the telling blow and the villain falls to a crushing death. Or a fight takes place on a bridge, and the victim falls far below into the water with a resounding splash.

The technique is perhaps a musical version of what is referred to as "suture" in film theory—placing the camera in such a way that it functions as the eye of the protagonist of the film, thereby drawing us, as unwitting spectators, to become the "subject" of the film ourselves, since we share the same visual field and same point of view.[1] Davidovsky's music captures us by drawing us into the sounds of what we can imagine as action sequences that imitate experiences from our own lives (or, in contemporary culture, our vicarious lives, as experienced in the movies). He even chooses timbres that subtly encourage us to hear the music in this way: the penetrating, high sustained sounds that one cannot listen to for too long; the increasingly harsh and metallic sounds just before each climax; the thuds, crashes, or splashes of the climax itself; and especially the dull, muffled sounds of the rebounds, which sometimes sound vaguely human in a way that suggests the curses of the person who has fallen or the comments of spectators.

There is a delightful paradox, of course, in our experiencing the gestures in the *Electronic Study* so physically, since performances of the piece involve no human physical action whatsoever. As a classic electronic work, composed in a "classic" electronic studio in 1960, it now exists as a piece of recorded history: inasmuch as concert performances (that is, playing the tape to a live audience) of such early works in the history of electronic music virtually never happen now, the only way to hear it is by listening to the long-playing album on which it was released in the

Anatomy of a Gesture 13

early 1960s, along with works by Milton Babbitt, Bulent Arel, Vladimir Ussachevsky, and others.[2] Thus the physical actions suggested by the climactic gestures of the *Electronic Study* are but virtual actions to be experienced in our minds and in our own living rooms.

It was not always so with this gesture. Another reason why the gesture pulls us in, and also why we experience it so physically and describe it with such physical metaphors, is that it has a long and distinguished history in repertoires more familiar (and perhaps more beloved) to our ears: in Romantic piano music, in jazz, and even in contemporary art music—all sites in which the gesture does take on a real physical presence in the actions of a real performer. The gesture is quintessentially one for the Romantic piano. Indeed, in no other medium does it work better; in this medium it has its source, and from this medium it extended its tentacles into jazz and contemporary music. The buildup to a high pitch of intensity in the upper registers of the piano, culminating in a sudden plunge to a resounding low note or chord in the resonant depths of the instrument, rebounding with a series of concluding chords: what more familiar gesture is there in the Romantic piano literature? Consider, for example, the final cadence of Chopin's Waltz in E Minor, Op. posth. (example 2.1), where all four parts of the gesture—preparation, precipitous descent, crash, and rebound—are present (although the *diminuendo* in the descent renders the third part of the gesture less a crash than a mere arrival at the lowest register).

Or, for a more complicated example, consider the concluding cadence of the finale of the Sonata in B Minor, Op. 58 (example 2.2). Here, the end of an entire sonata calls forth more virtuoso filigree and a richer contrapuntal texture, as well as a final descent that metaphorically suggests, since it is not a single quick gesture plunging from the high to the low register, less a free fall than, say, an avalanche.

What gesture could be better suited for the new Erard and Broadwood pianos of the 1830s and 1840s, with their increased power and fuller bass resonance, in comparison with the Walters, Steins, and Grafs of previous generations? The new pianos, as it were, were made for it, just as the gesture itself was invented for the new pianos. The new pianos could better withstand the force of pianists throwing themselves from one end of the keyboard to the other, landing with their full weight on a single bass note, and rebounding with a series of crashing chords. And what could be better suited to the new virtuoso pianist, who relied on grand, almost palpable gestures to draw in audiences to become one with his or her heroic self? Again, there is a certain reflexivity here: between the virtuoso subject and the gesture, the gesture and the virtuoso subject. Foreign to the keyboard works of Haydn, Mozart, Beethoven, Schubert, and their contemporaries, the gesture comes into its own with the works of Chopin, and later in those of Liszt, Grieg, Rachmaninoff, and others. It is from the piano music of these composers that most of us probably have the schema embedded in our unconscious musical minds, and that Davidovsky taps into in the *Electronic Study*.

Of course, Chopin did have his models. Beethoven, for example, often closes the finales of piano sonatas—particularly early sonatas—with a long arpeggio to a

Example 2.1. Chopin, Waltz in E Minor, Op. posth., conclusion

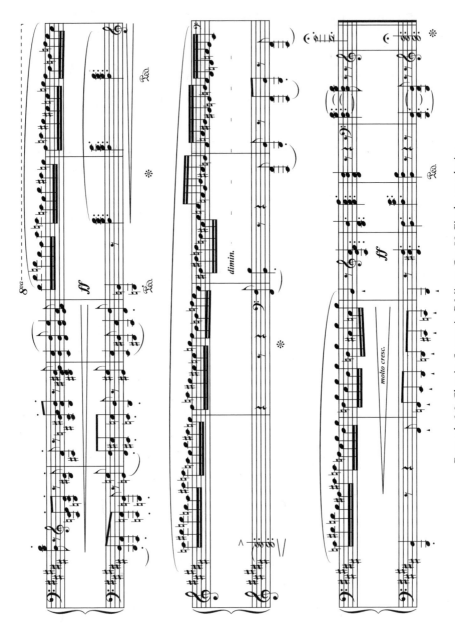

Example 2.2. Chopin, Sonata in B Minor, Op. 58, Finale, conclusion

Example 2.3. Beethoven, Piano Sonata excerpts
  a. Piano Sonata in F Minor, Op. 2, No. 1, Finale, conclusion
  b. Piano Sonata in A Major, Op. 2, No. 2, Rondo, conclusion
Continued on the next page

single low note. Such is the case in the sonatas in F minor, Op. 2, No. 1; A major, Op. 2, No. 2; D major, Op. 10, No. 3; and D minor, Op. 31, No. 2 (example 2.3). But the sense of this gesture is quite different. There is no sequential or other buildup of intensity in the high register, so the sum of energy to be released is much less. More significant, Beethoven's gestures end *softly:* there is a decrescendo over each descending arpeggio, and the goal note is not accented. And since there is no accent, no crash, there is nothing from which to rebound, and so the sonata movements characteristically end on the low note itself; the effect is that the music disappears into the depths instead of making a concluding grand rhetorical flourish. Again, the instruments of Beethoven's time would not have suggested such a gesture, and his closest approximations to it have an entirely different musical meaning.

Example 2.3. Beethoven, Piano Sonata excerpts
  c. Piano Sonata in D Major, Op. 10, No. 3, Rondo, conclusion
Continued on the next page

Chopin occasionally uses Beethoven's gesture at the end of a piece, though usually with a characteristic Romantic buildup to precede it. The Waltz in A♭ Major, Op. 64, No. 3, is a good example: not only is there no rebound but the arpeggiated fall is marked *decrescendo,* and thus vanishes into the low register as in the early Beethoven sonatas (example 2.4).

But Chopin more frequently changed Beethoven's gesture into a dramatic grand Romantic flourish, and he is infinitely resourceful in varying it subtly according to the expressive character of the pieces he uses it to conclude. A particularly beautiful

Example 2.3. Beethoven, Piano Sonata excerpts
 d. Piano Sonata in D Minor, Op. 31, No. 2, Finale, conclusion

example—and one that gives the sense of being an apotheosis or triumph—is that from the Ballade in A♭ Major, Op. 47 (example 2.5). Here the use of the repetition, inversion, and foreshortening of the arpeggiated figure from C down to E♭, the precipitous descent, and especially the rebounding chords (V⁷/vi–vi–V⁷–I) are all intriguingly reminiscent of the gestures in the Davidovsky *Electronic Study* (or, better in a chronological sense, the Davidovsky is reminiscent of the Ballade). The arpeggiated figure itself is, of course, not only conventional but also thematic, since it brings back the theme of the central section of the piece (mm. 116–36). (The motion from C down to E♭ in the arpeggio is also an inversion of the motion of the opening melody, which moves scalewise from E♭ up to C.) And the physical experience of the gesture—for the pianist or for us, vicariously through the pianist— is as much a part of its musical meaning as the notes themselves: intensification through the repeated figures preparing the F7; a forceful attack on this note, as a momentary receptacle for the surge of energy that will plunge to the bottom of the keyboard; landing with the pianist's full weight on the low A♭; then rebounding from this point of arrival, as the remaining energy flows, in tempo, through the chords leading to the final cadence.

   In some works of Chopin essentially the same gesture has a different effect, be-

Example 2.4. Chopin, Waltz in A♭ Major, Op. 64, No. 3, conclusion

cause one or more parts of it are varied. For example, the thunderous conclusion of the Etude in A Minor, Op. 25, No. 10, has the same sequence of sub-gestures, but the descent to the lowest register of the piano, like that at the end of the B minor Sonata, is accomplished through an alternating sixteenth-note figure that embeds a chromatic scale in eighth notes, so that the rush to the bottom note is slowed down, thus giving the impression less of a free fall than of an onrushing flood (example 2.6).

The Ballade in F Minor, Op. 52, similarly complicates matters in that it builds, through a sequence of repetitions far more complex than in any of the examples thus far, to F7, which initiates a precipitous downward scale; but the trajectory of the scale is interrupted at middle C, and a sweeping arpeggio takes the right hand almost as high as before, to D♭6, from which point the left hand joins in an octave lower, and both hands play a jagged descending figure in octaves that reaches a structural downbeat on the lowest F octave of the piano before the rebounding chords bring the work to a close (example 2.7).

Perhaps the most spectacular use of the convention in all the works of Chopin is the conclusion of the D minor Prelude, the last of the preludes, Op. 28. Here, yet another variant of the four-part conventional cadential gesture functions as a coda (mm. 65–77) and lends an unusually bitter, tragic character to the end of the work

Example 2.5. Chopin, Ballade in A♭ Major, Op. 47, conclusion

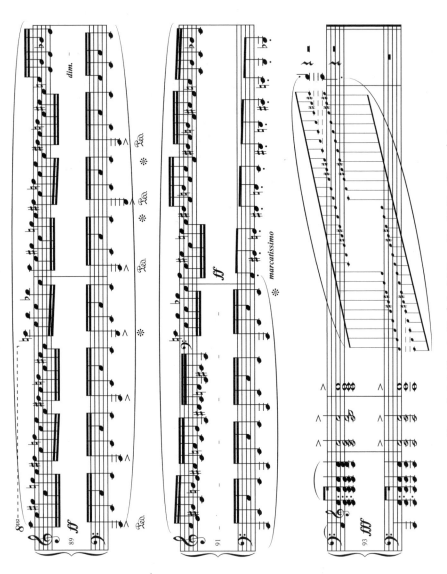

Example 2.6. Chopin, Etude in A Minor, Op. 25, No. 10, conclusion

Example 2.7. Chopin, Ballade in F Minor, Op. 52, conclusion

(example 2.8)—an ending that inspired André Gide (1949: 48–50) to write the following:

> I have elsewhere strongly protested against that reputation for nostalgic melancholy which is given, usually without discrimination, to all Chopin's music, in which I have so many times encountered the expression of the highest joy. But really, in these two preludes [the A minor and D minor] I find only the most somber despair. Yes, despair; the word "melancholy" is no longer pertinent here; a feeling of the inexorable, twice cut through, in the last measures of the Prelude in D Minor, by a harrowing moan, spasmodically taken up a second time in a twisted, jolted, and, as it were, sobbing

Example 2.8. Chopin, Prelude in D Minor, Op. 28, No. 24, mm. 49–end

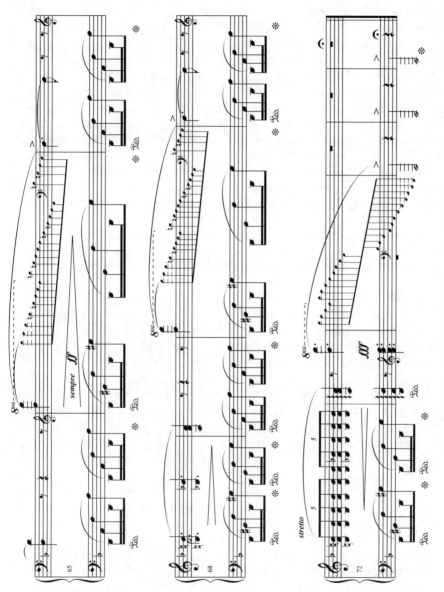

Example 2.8. Chopin, Prelude in D Minor, Op. 28, No. 24, mm. 49–end

rhythm; then swept by the implacable final run, which concludes *fortissimo* in the frightful depths where one touches the floor of Hell.

In this final, morbid Prelude, the long, unmeasured, scalewise or arpeggiated flourishes, both ascending and descending, assume a motivic role early in the piece, so the precipitous falls in the cadential gesture are thematic as well as conventional. The Prelude shares this overt thematicism of the descending figure of its climactic gesture with the A♭ major Ballade, although the character of the two pieces is utterly different: the same four-part gesture that articulates triumph in the Ballade brings tragedy in the Prelude. In the D minor Prelude, the sweeping ascending gestures—two of which are introduced by comparable descending gestures—that crescendo to the downbeats of measures 15, 19, 33, and 37, provide emphatic melodic cadences at phrase endings, and each concludes on the tonic of whatever key is tonicized at the time (F major, A minor, C major, and E minor, respectively). In the final third of the piece—from the return of the opening at measure 51, to the end—there are four sweeping descents to match the ascending ones earlier in the Prelude. The first is a virtuosic right-hand descent from F^7 to A^4 in thirds, spread over two measures, above a sustained German sixth (mm. 55–56) in D minor. This descent occurs early in the long, extended phrase that begins with the return of the opening melody and ends with the structural cadence (or, in Schenkerian terms, the close of the *Ursatz*) at measure 65. The remaining three we will look at in greater detail as components of the coda.

At the cadence in measure 65, the harmonic energy of the piece seems to be spent, but the rhythmic energy is not; the accumulated force of the incessant ostinato rhythm and the final jagged flourish in octaves in the right hand demands a coda to dispel its charge. The situation at measure 65 here in the D minor Prelude is exactly parallel to that of measure 230 in the A♭ major Ballade. Both these measures begin with gigantic structural downbeats that in a sense absorb the cumulative energy that has accrued since each work's main thematic return in the tonic (m. 51 in the Prelude, m. 212 in the Ballade). In both cases, the theme, rather than leading to the cadence which it did upon its first appearance, avoids cadencing at the expected time and instead extends through a long process of intensification and crescendo, gathering, as it were, the energy of the whole piece together, to spill into the structural arrival on the tonic. Thus it is the task of the coda—that is, an extended version of our four-part cadential gesture—to discharge the rhythmic energy of each piece after the structural harmonic cadence, and to conclude with a rhetorical flourish.

The four-part climactic gesture at the end of the D minor Prelude properly begins with the resolution of this cadence, and the whole gesture (m. 65 to the end) constitutes the coda. How is this coda configured expressively to lend to the conventional gesture such an unrelenting sense of bitterness, and what is responsible for its communicating a sense of desperation or hopelessness, whereas virtually the same extended gesture in the Ballade projected a sense of triumph?

A close comparison of the two codas is instructive. The contrasts between the two are striking, and the points of opposition between them, despite their gestural similarity, clarify their radical difference in expressive effect. Of course, the difference in mode—major for the Ballade, minor for the Prelude, plays a predictably important role. But a number of both surface and formal features contribute as well. The work of the left hand certainly does its part. Compare the driving ostinato bass here, with its stark alternation of minor and diminished triads over the pedal D, and the obsessive end-accented left-hand rhythm, to the left hand of the coda of the Ballade. The relentlessness of the D pedal, and the fact that there is no harmonic motion whatsoever, suggests less an intensified motion to a goal than the hammering in of a goal that has already been attained. Or, better yet, the inevitable harmonic goal has arrived, and we cannot escape it. In the Ballade, by contrast, despite an apparent tonic pedal, there are two harmonic motions to the dominant and back so that the harmony is not completely static. Only the F♭s of measures 231 and 233, which twice generate a taut augmented triad when combined with the right hand, disturb the sense of diatonic security. In measures 231 and 233 of the left hand, a gentle cadential gesture, E♭3–C4–B♭3–(A♭), in a "tenor" voice gracefully complements each bass move to the dominant—a tension-releasing gesture that creates a vastly different effect from the constantly churning uneasiness of the left hand of the Prelude. (A lovely detail here is that the ascending sixth, E♭–C, of this gesture is a rhythmically compressed inversion of the grander two-measure gesture from C down to E♭ in the right hand, just as it also recapitulates in a single ascending leap the E♭–C motion of the opening theme of the work.) Furthermore, the long-short, beginning-accented rhythms of the left hand of the Ballade have an altogether more benign effect than the nervous, end-accented ostinato of the Prelude. And the relaxed, rollicking motion of the left hand in the Ballade imparts a far greater sense of resolution than the physically demanding traversal of an octave and a half of registral space that the left hand of the Prelude requires in every beat.

There is a subtle but important macro-rhythmic difference between the two codas as well, one that reaches back to the structural thematic return in the two works. In both the Ballade and the Prelude the long phrase extending from the thematic return to the structural cadence is rigidly constructed in two-measure units (beginning with m. 212 in the Ballade and m. 51 in the Prelude). In the Ballade the first measure of the coda is elided with the jubilant cadence of the prolonged buildup of measures 212–30; the surge to the apex of the coda begins with the two two-measure descending flourishes in measures 230–31, which thus continue the momentum of regular two-measure groups initiated back in measure 212. Even when the descending two-measure gestures from C down to E♭ are compressed and inverted into two one-measure gestures from C up to E♭ in measures 234–35—the foreshortening in the approach to the climax is, of course, entirely characteristic of the conventional four-part gesture—these two measures work as a group and, accordingly, continue the already established macro-rhythm and the rhythmic momentum. Measures 236–39 then function as a four-measure group, thereby preserving the higher-level regularity and turning the final measure into a strong hypermetric downbeat.

By contrast, in the Prelude the two-measure descending flourishes contradict the

Table 2.1. Comparison of Gestural Elements

Ballade in A♭ major (11 mm.) (beginning m. 230)	*Prelude in D minor* (13 mm.) (beginning m. 65)
	one-measure "vamp"
two-measure descending gesture	two-measure descending gesture
	two-measure response
two-measure descending gesture repeated	two-measure descending gesture
foreshortening: two one-measure gestures	two-measure response; high chord
	(anticipates plunge)
five measures: plunge, low A♭, rebound;	four measures: plunge to low
final cadential chord arrives on a	Ds; no rebound; ends
strong measure	on a strong measure

larger hypermeter. As in the Ballade, the drive to the structural cadence (m. 65) is in two-measure units (beginning at m. 51), and these groupings proceed uninterrupted through the end of the coda, as is clear from the harmony in measures 65–77. However, the right-hand descending gestures and the responses to them in measures 66–67, 68–69, and so forth, cut across the regular hypermeter projected in the left hand. The difference, in contradistinction to the comparable place in the Ballade, is subtle, but it obscures the rhythmic regularity that has obtained since measure 51, and it allows us to hear one measure of the churning of the left hand before the right hand begins its conflicting two-measure flourishes. The cadential schema that begins in measure 66 also works in a way that is strikingly different to that of the Ballade. Table 2.1 compares the two codas.

Whereas the Ballade immediately repeats the initial descending two-measure flourish and then presses on to the climactic plunge by compressing the unit to one measure (2 + 2 + 1 + 1), the Prelude rejects this means of gathering steam and, in fact, undercuts the momentum by answering both initial two-measure descents (mm. 66–67 and 70–71) with the haunting melodic fragment B–B♭–A, a figure never heard in the piece before. The expressive effects of these two enigmatic responses are entirely different, since the first is a decrescendo in dotted quarter notes and the second an anguished crescendo in *stretto* quintuplets. Leaving aside for the moment the hermeneutics of these strange gestures, we can still note that, after a clangorous D-minor triad in the high register anticipates by a half-measure the four-measure phrase that contains the plunge to the low D, the final plunge and cadence are, in two formal respects, markedly different from that of the Ballade: as noted above, the two-measure gestures conflict with the hypermeter; and, most striking, there is no rebound—the low D is simply repeated three times.

These formal and rhythmic factors, along with what we have already noted about the differences in the left-hand parts of the Prelude and Ballade, interact with other surface features to account for the expressive contrast between the two codas. Let us summarize the differences by making a final, detailed pass through the coda of the Prelude, using the Ballade as a foil. The structural cadential measure (m. 65) of the Prelude continues the established hypermetric regularity, but the delay of the first two-measure descent isolates a measure of the passionate vamp. The descents themselves are curious: not only are they unmeasured, unlike those of the Ballade, but they are far more gnarled harmonically, since the modal g^7 chord of the right-hand descent grinds against the D–F–G♯ sonority of the left hand. They thus seem wilder and more out of control. Moreover, these descents plummet to the tonic, not to the dominant; the accented melodic Ds—note that each descent concludes with 3–2–1—especially over the strong-beat Ds in the bass, impart a grim sense of melodic finality that the similar descents, which conclude on 5, in the Ballade, do not. And the rhetoric is different in the two codas: in the Prelude, rather than two successive descents and a foreshortening pressing toward the climax, the initial plunge has a conclusiveness that suggests not an immediate repeat but rather a gesture (the figure B–B♭–A) that is simultaneously a resigned response (because of the descending chromatic motion, in a decrescendo) and a question (because of the end on 5 rather than 1). But upon the recurrence of the pair of gestures in measures 70–73, the second gesture becomes more assertive: the stretto quintuplets and crescendo counteract the "yielding" effect of the chromatic descent, and instead push the rhythmic energy forcefully ahead into the final four measures.

The most breathtaking effect is reserved for the end. The fortissimo chord on the second half of measure 73 is like a shriek at the top of the precipice, a last look before the leap into the abyss. The plunge itself bears striking similarity to that in the Ballade: each is a six-octave descent based on the arpeggiation of scale degrees 6, 5, 3, and 1. The only difference, other than the crucial one of mode, is also telling in its musical meaning and expressive effect. At the bottom of the gesture, rather than leaping from 5 down to 1, thereby leaving an open space above the tonic, the descent in the Prelude obsessively repeats the 3–2–1 of the flourishes in measures 66–67 and 70–71, even in the lowest register of the piano—an effect that is not only gruff and grotesque but that reinforces the sense of utter finality communicated by the previous gestures. And, finally, from these depths there is no rebound: as if the repeated landings on the tonic thus far were not enough, the last two measures repeat the violent D twice more, and the piece ends with this single note reverberating, for as long as the pianist dares to let it ring.

With Liszt, who may well have learned the schema from Chopin, it accrues an even flashier level of virtuosity and piano sonority, as well as a greater freedom of structural usage. First and foremost, Liszt made the gesture harder to play, as he does at the end of his arrangement of the "Miserere" from Verdi's *Il trovatore*, by placing the cataclysmic plunge in double octaves rather than in single notes (example 2.9).

In the manner of Haydn, he also took an ending gesture and converted it into an opening one, as he does in the introduction to "Mazeppa," from the *Etudes*

Example 2.9. Liszt, arrangement of "Miserere" from Verdi's *Il trovatore*, conclusion

Example 2.10. Liszt, "Mazeppa," *Etudes d'Exécution transcendante*, introduction
Continued on the next page

d'Exécution transcendante (example 2.10). Here there is no rebound from the bottom note of the long descending scale; instead, the beginning of the main tune coincides with the structural downbeat at the scale's end.

"Eroica," the seventh etude from the same set, problematizes and thematicizes the gesture, and continues to return to it throughout the piece. As in "Mazeppa," the schema is used in an introduction to an etude (example 2.11). This time a mere

Anatomy of a Gesture 31

Example 2.10. Liszt, "Mazeppa," *Etudes d'Exécution transcendante*, introduction

four quarter notes, F♭ octaves alternating with diminished seventh chords, constitute the repetitive ascent to the highest chord.

The plunge that follows is subverted at the very end to give not a full-weight thud but a question—note the reversal of direction in the last two notes. The ascending quizzical chord pairs that ensue are both a rebound from the low point and a preparation for a sequential repetition of the whole pattern a semitone higher in measure 5. In what promises to be a third leg of the sequence (measure 9), the high chord and precipitous descent are excised, and the introduction proceeds to the main march tune at measure 20 by other means. But the schematic gesture recurs frequently throughout the march (see, for example, mm. 27–31, 40–43, and 56–62 [not shown]), thereby integrating the introductory bravura passages with the much different material of the march itself. This integration comes to fruition at the end (see example 2.12, m. 112; the nine measures leading into this passage are included in the example in order to establish the musical context of the return). Here a tonic recapitulation of the opening gesture—now with all four quarters that lead to the high diminished seventh chord being octave E♭s—brings the ascending chromatic melodic line of the march in the bass contrapuntally against the right-hand plunge, so that both conclude on the downbeat E♭ of measure 114 (example 2.12).

The chords from measures 3–4 are now omitted, so that this E♭ begins a restatement of the same gesture, this time at the same pitch level rather than a semitone higher, as at the beginning. The coup de grâce comes in the last five measures, when the change of harmony (to V^7/♭II) at measure 115 forces the next downbeat, at which the march tune and the plunge again coincide, up to an E, so that the triumphant rebound chords are in the wrong key, E major. The sleight of hand that saves the day is the suppression of the expected chord on the downbeat of measure 117 (an E major chord on such a strong downbeat would virtually force the etude to end in the wrong key) so that, from out of all the fury in the extreme registers, the hero suddenly walks out of the deafening silence in the middle register, his march tune safely intact in (what else?) E♭.

Example 2.11. Liszt, "Eroica," *Etudes d'Exécution transcendante*, beginning

Example 2.12. Liszt, "Eroica," *Etudes d'Exécution transcendante,* conclusion

Together with many other gestures that had their roots in the eighteenth- and nineteenth-century tonal repertoire, the four-part cadential schema lives on in various corners of twentieth-century music—especially piano music. One place in which it found fertile soil was in the brilliant virtuoso piano improvisations of Art Tatum, who, as is well known, was trained as a classical pianist before devoting himself exclusively to jazz. Given his grounding in the works of Chopin, we should not be surprised to find examples such as the final cadence from Tatum's arrangement of Duke Ellington's "Don't Get Around Much Anymore," which presents a stride version of the same gesture so familiar in the earlier composer's piano music (example 2.13).

Despite the transference to an entirely different idiom, the four-part schema—

Example 2.13. Art Tatum, arrangement of Ellington, "Don't Get Around Much Anymore," conclusion

sequential ascent to a peak, rapid descent, hitting bottom, rebound—is preserved in all particulars.

In the Tatum arrangement, as in most of the nineteenth-century examples, the schema goes hand in hand with tonal structure, in the sense that, as a final cadential gesture, it affirms the tonic. But the gesture is hardly dependent upon tonality. For, just as, say, Schoenberg's atonal music preserved a number of gestural and rhythmic qualities of tonal music in his atonal and twelve-tone music, so is our four-part schema sufficiently detachable from its tonal moorings that it can function in posttonal contexts as a rhetorically heightened cadential gesture. As such, it is most likely to appear in the work of composers who have not consciously severed their connections to nineteenth-century gestural rhetoric: Messiaen, Copland, and Davidovsky, for example, but not Stravinsky, Webern, and Babbitt.

A characteristic example from the piano music of Messiaen articulates the end of the first half of the fifteenth movement of the *Vingt Regards sur l'Enfant-Jésus* (1944), "Le baiser de l'Enfant-Jésus" (example 2.14). The tonal language is new—the excerpt is built entirely on a single octatonic collection, except for the final chord—but the rhetoric is the familiar gesture from the nineteenth century. All the performance indications highlight precisely the shape of the conventional schema: "Pressez" and "Pressez encore," with *crescendo,* in the buildup; *forte,* with accent, and "Vif" at the peak; a crescendo to the bottom with *fortissimo* and the first indication of pedal on the lowest note; and a direction to hold the pedal through the rebound.

Messiaen uses the same gesture to a rather different expressive purpose at the end of the final movement, "Sortie," of the *Messe de la Pentecôte,* for organ (example 2.15). The ecstatic, almost uncontrolled rush of jagged thirty-second notes refers to the wind invoked in the scripture ("And a mighty wind rushed through the house," Acts of the Apostles 10:10) cited underneath the title. The fall to the low perfect fifth in the pedals occurs suddenly, after a brief rest, and is almost instantaneous—the gesture is not continuous as it is in the piano piece. Furthermore, on the organ the effect is different: the low crash is not a percussive attack that immediately decays, as it would on a piano, but a thunderous roar that maintains its intensity while the "rebound" chord adds a complex new color in the upper registers.

In an entirely different idiom the schema is recognizable in the Piano Fantasy

Example 2.14. Messiaen, "Le baiser de l'Enfant-Jésus," from *Vingt Regards sur l'Enfant-Jésus,* mm. 54–63. Music: Olivier Messiaen. © 1947 by Editions Durand.

Example 2.15. Messiaen, "Sortie," from *Messe de la Pentecôte*, conclusion. Reproduced by permission of Alphonse Leduc owner and publisher, Alphonse Leduc, Paris, France.

(1957) of Aaron Copland (example 2.16). Again, the rhetorical intensity of the gesture dictates that it be used only at a critical moment in the structure. In the Piano Fantasy the gesture brings the first long section of the work (mm. 1–186) to a crashing climax at measure 181, while the rebounds in the measures that follow prepare a transition to the more restrained second section that begins at measure 205. Many details here are different from the Messiaen examples—for example, it is a right-hand ostinato rather than technical filigree that accomplishes the buildup to the peak, and the descent slows down, gathering weight as it goes, rather than falling quickly and precipitously to the bottom—but the schema is unmistakable.

A final example for piano occurs in a recent work of Pierre Boulez—improbably, since it was Boulez (1999 [1952]: 145–51) who wrote perhaps the most famous twentieth-century polemic against the preservation of nineteenth-century gestures in the new music. The entire little second piece of the *douze notations* (1985) is a relative of our cadential schema (example 2.17).

After three violent measures of ascending glissandi and double-note trills, a rhythmically irregular right-hand ostinato begins, against which a more melodic left-hand part climbs from B♭2 up to A7 and back down to B♭2. The sudden left-hand ascent that follows is coordinated with an ascending glissando that absorbs

Example 2.16. Copland, Piano Fantasy, mm. 168–84. © Copyright 1957 by the Aaron Copland Fund for Music, Inc. Copyright Renewed. Boosey & Hawkes, Inc., Sole Publisher & Licensee. Reprinted by permission.

2.

Example 2.17. Boulez, *douze notations*, No. 2. © 1985 by Universal Edition A. G., Vienna. All Rights Reserved. Used by permission of European American Music Distributors LLC, agent for Universal Edition A. G., Vienna.

the accumulated tension built up through the right-hand glissando, and both peak with a double-note trill on the highest notes of the piano. A precipitous descending glissando falls to an accented cluster chord in the middle register, followed in quick succession by a cluster of the lowest three notes on the piano, the chord, the low cluster, and a final rebounding ascent to the brusque chord for the last time. Now removed from even the faintest trappings of tonality, the four-part schema exists as pure gesture, indeed, as gesture in caricature: the violence of the piece, the deliberate use of the highest and lowest notes of the piano, the glissandi rather than articulate pitches—all combine to suggest a modernist parody, a parody of excess.

From the Boulez it is but a small step to come full circle with a return to the

Davidovsky *Electronic Study*. For if Boulez removes the last vestiges of tonality from the gesture, Davidovsky removes from it the whole notion of tempered pitch. Even more than with the Boulez, the Davidovsky piece embodies the gesture *as* gesture, as abstract musical motion disembodied from the moorings of pitch. What began its life as a rhetorical articulation of tonal content ends up as rhetoric pure and simple: the rhetoric *is* the content.

Notes

1. See, for example, Kaja Silverman 1983.
2. *Electronic Study No. 1* is available only on a long-playing record, Columbia ML 5966 (1964). The sounds of the piece, which was composed with the "classical studio" equipment of the Columbia-Princeton Electronic Studio of the early 1960s, will undoubtedly seem primitive and dated to listeners familiar with the digitally produced electronic music of the past twenty years.

3 Anti-Teleological Art: Articulating Meaning through Silence

Edward Pearsall

One of music's most distinguishing characteristics—indeed, perhaps its *most* distinguishing characteristic—is that it is, as Roger Sessions (1970: 39) once remarked, "inevitably, a temporal art." Yet scholars of more recent vintage have challenged this idea, noting that music, though it unfolds through time, does not necessarily constitute a temporal gesture on the semantic level.[1] One of the first theorists to have made such an observation is Leonard Meyer (1967: 72):

> music of the avant-garde directs us toward no points of culmination—establishes no goals toward which to move. It arouses no expectation, except presumably that it will stop. It is neither surprising nor, once you get used to its sounds, is it particular startling. It is simply *there*. And this is the way it is supposed to be. Such directionless, unkinetic art, whether carefully contrived or created by chance, I . . . call *anti-teleological* art.

Jonathan Kramer (1988: 44) has expanded on Meyer's views, going so far as to assert that anti-teleological events essentially "suspend a composition's forward momentum through time." For Kramer, anti-teleological events—or "nonlinear" events as he calls them—resist the sense of progression in music whereas linear events amplify music's temporal unfolding. Nonlinear events, that is, seem to coalesce into a unitary object suspended in space, one whose component parts can be scrutinized in any order like the objects in a painting. This seems compatible with our cognitive experience of nonlinear music; as the repetitive features of the music come into focus, we begin to understand how its beginning connects to its end. This, in turn, enables us to peruse the music forward and backward by means of prospective and retrospective hearing.

Jonathan Kramer (1988: 23–25) and Leonard Meyer (1967: 73–74) associate nonlinearity on the semantic level primarily with what they perceive as an attempt on the part of avant-garde composers to assimilate cyclical conceptions of time characteristic of many non-European cultures. Conversely, they associate *linearity* with the progress-oriented perspective of time peculiar to Western civilization. As intriguing as these distinctions are, they do not necessarily reflect either the intentional or derived meaning of all music that incorporates linear and nonlinear structuring. Indeed, as Yayoi Uno Everett (2004: 10) has observed, "whether a musical element is perceived as 'Western' or 'Eastern' by an individual listener depends on the situated differences in cultural attitude—[the] localized, embodied meaning and references we attribute to music." This suggests that, as important as cultural perspectives on time are in the discussion of nonlinear music, they are not as self-evident as one might at first think. As with all forms of cultural appropriation, avant-garde music can only reflect, at best, a Western *perspective* on Eastern culture.[2] Ascribing transcultural attributes to music that follows the Western model with regard to its instrumentation, note set, and mode of composition may lead to the false impression that linearity and nonlinearity are universal principles rather than analytical constructions based on a particular way of conceiving music.

The problem in this case is not with the observations Kramer and Meyer make but rather with the limitations they place on musical expression. Not only are events nonlinear in terms of their formal construction, but they are also expressive of nonlinearity on the semantic level. To be sure, temporality is one of music's most distinctive features. But music is also capable of making references beyond its own syntax and structure. John Tavener, for example, creates textures that conform in every way to the parameters of nonlinearity; they are exceptionally repetitive and contain nonfunctional harmony. Yet Tavener's music does not represent an attempt to signify cyclic time but rather one's "longing for God" (Tavener 1999: 157). Tavener associates what he characterizes as the "over-proliferation of notes" (158) in contemporary music with the failure of modern composers to recognize the omnipotence of God and, consequently, the limitations of the human mind. To counteract such modernist tendencies, he seeks to "strip the music bare" (158), providing an opportunity for God to make himself known. Hence Tavener's redundant textures represent a form of reverent quiescence, not a perspective on time.

Tavener's compositional premise has important implications because it suggests that nonlinear music might in some cases represent silence rather than arrested temporality. But what if we were to interpret *every* case of nonlinearity in music as silence? The term "nonlinearity" focuses attention specifically on temporality along with both its syntactic and semantic features. On this view music becomes inexorably linked to time, both as a signifier and as to what it signifies. Silence, on the other hand, implies only the suspension of an utterance. It does not specify what this suspension refers to. Describing music in terms of silence and discourse, then, while no less metaphorical than temporal portrayals of music, allows for the kinds of distinctions Meyer and Kramer confer without restricting musical meaning to certain types of cultural representations regarding the passage of time.

In this chapter I explore this idea, treating silence as an extended metaphor for non-discursiveness in order to emphasize its opposition to discursive events in music.[3] Just as silence implies the absence of sound, so, too, does non-discursiveness imply the absence of form and structure. Patterns in non-discursive music do not immediately transmit the sense that they are part of a global structure[4] whose dimensions exceed the boundaries of the "present now of consciousness."[5] Under these circumstances, music, although acoustically active, may seem to fall largely silent, reflecting our inability to describe it using the traditional tools of structural analysis. When music's structure becomes less than self-evident, it can be tempting to dismiss the music as incomprehensible and hence inconsequential; like an impressionistic painting, sounds in such music do not cohere into sharp, unmistakable images and forms. Yet, also like an impressionistic painting, there is no absence of structure in the absolute sense. Rather, the structural aspects of the music remain elusive and hidden.

In my view, concealed structures are not expendable components of music. On the contrary, they are part of the design of a piece and hence integral to one's experience of it. Non-discursive music is silent, not inoperative. Silence not only clears the way for utterance by implying the presence of something not yet fully determined but also makes room for contemplative reflection, thus constituting an interpretive space within which meaning can emerge.

Understood in this way, silence in music is not only conveyed through the absence of sound or even the pause at the end of a musical statement or phrase (although pauses may take on this role in some instances) but also by means of a musical texture that lacks discursive intent. Silence of this kind is *performative*, enacted through sound rather than by the curtailment of sound. This description conflicts with the usual definition of silence. In the parlance of everyday language, silence nearly always indicates the absence of sound.[6] Yet, as John Cage (1961: 8) reminds us, absolute silence is nearly impossible to achieve. Even in the anechoic chamber—a room constructed in such a way that there is no reverberation—one still hears sounds, specifically those of the nervous and circulatory systems.[7]

Just as absolute silence is impossible to achieve, so, too, is the suspension of signification on the semantic level. Music in particular magnifies the importance of silence as a semantic construct because its meaning is almost never absolute.[8] Musical meaning arises, that is, *primarily* from acts of interpretation.[9] The composer contributes to, and to some extent directs, the listener's interpretive activities by creating a context that requires a response.[10] With performative silence, however, it is almost entirely up to the listener to supply meaning. Under these circumstances, silent contemplation on the listener's part is elevated to a principal role. No longer is the listener required to recover the *intentional* meaning of a piece. Instead, music has been liberated from its stylistic moorings, becoming almost wholly a space for intra-subjective reflection.[11]

At the same time—because the composer is responsible for composing the music in the first place—the composer (or the composer's persona) remains implicitly present in the music.[12] As Bernard P. Dauenhauer (1980: 55) has observed, silence is intentional; it is "the positive abstinence from employing some determinate expression." In other words, the composer suppresses his or her voice, thereby transforming silence into a form of expression.[13] This, in turn, has the effect of making room for the listener by opening up a broad indeterminate space for creative contemplation. Thus the composer continues to play an active role, not by communicating directly but by inviting the listener to participate more fully in the creative process. Neither discursive events nor non-discursive events communicate absolutely. Nor does non-discursiveness in music categorically oppose discursiveness. Both, though different, can therefore be conveyed through the same medium—that of musical sound.

Discursive and Non-Discursive Properties in Music

Having described what I mean by performative (i.e., articulated) silence, I now turn to a discussion of the qualitative differences between discursive and non-discursive elements within musical structure. Discursive events in music are often associated with what Célestin Deliège (1989: 107) has referred to as the "process-oriented" aspects of a work. These include "melodic continuity" and "thematic function" (Deliège 2000: 220–21). In discursive contexts, events follow one another in a logical manner so that events seem to lead to other events on progressively higher and higher levels (218–19). Discursive features, then, have to do with those properties that govern music's hierarchical organization. In many cases, these properties parallel those of spoken language. Indeed, similar ways of constructing music and language have led to similar ways of describing them; we frequently analyze music in terms of phrases, statements, questions, answers, and—on a higher level—expositions and narratives, for example. When connections between successive events become tenuous, music may lose some of its discursive impact. Thus non-discursive music hypostatizes silence—or, more specifically, the active role silence plays in spoken dialogue—inasmuch as music can continue to sound even when its discursive strength or rhetorical unfolding falters.

Given these constraints, we may construct the following broad definitions: *discursive events in music are those that manifest themselves primarily as functional or purposeful transactions, whereas non-discursive events are those whose aesthetic impression is their most prominent feature.* This does not mean that non-discursive events have no actual function or purpose but rather that their aesthetic impact is more perspicuous than their formal or syntactic role. Conversely, discursive events may have an aesthetic impact, but their structural role remains their most defining attribute.[14] Although, by this definition, non-discursive events are less overtly purposeful than discursive events, they are no less expressive. In fact, non-discursive events typically convey important, if indirect, information about a passage or composition and can therefore intensify whatever musical or referential meaning it has.[15]

Non-discursive textures manifest themselves mainly in terms of qualitative attributes such as timbre and intervallic saturation; it is their surface attributes, that is, that create the greatest interest. The relations between events (especially large-scale relations), on the other hand, are de-emphasized. As Leonard Meyer (1967: 74) explains,

> The more one perceives the relationships among things, the less one tends to be aware of their existence as things in themselves—as pure sensation. You may, at some time, have heard a radio or television set go haywire so that the sound was completely distorted. If so, you may recall that when the syntax and grammar became obscured and meaning was lost, you became very aware of sound qua sound—you became conscious of the bleeps, bloops, and squeaks.

Meyer's description reinforces the point of this discussion; when syntax is obscured, sound itself becomes the center of attention. Steve Reich's *It's Gonna Rain* provides a case in point. In this piece, the phrase "It's gonna rain" is presented via a tape loop. As the piece unfolds, phonetic fragments are detached from the phrase and presented in rapid succession. By isolating these vocalizations, the piece draws attention to their sound quality rather than their rhetorical content. This heightened importance of sound qua sound is essential to the experience of silence in music.

Silence in Context

Because nonlinearity, like non-discursiveness, is a qualitative property of music—and hence attributive—it is difficult to generalize about the form it will take.[16] Rather, as Jonathan Kramer (1988: 20) has pointed out, "linearity and nonlinearity hinge on the expectations of the listener." One of the problems with incorporating subjective responses into analysis, of course, is that analytical outcomes may vary widely depending on one's perspective. Célestin Deliège's discursive category, for example, corresponds in every way to its opposite, the lyric category, in Raymond Monelle's discussion of music and temporality. Whereas for Deliège (1989: 102) phrase and thematic structure always result in a "linear-type logic," for Monelle (2000: 99) these are largely nonlinear phenomena.[17] Indeed, Deliège completely inverts Monelle's categories—using Monelle's own terminology—when he advocates "a return to the elementary level of *syntactic* articulation, since it is a question of restoring the *discursive* process" (112; my emphasis).

The determination of what constitutes a discursive or non-discursive event is clearly based on each individual's familiarity with stylistic conventions. Thus it would appear that categorizing musical events in terms of their qualitative attributes is not purely a matter of identifying structural properties but also one of ascertaining how such properties function within a particular musical context, while also taking into account the interpretive mechanics that have gone into their construction. Musical events are not inherently linear or nonlinear, discursive or non-discursive, rhetorical or aesthetic. Rather, these properties are derived on the basis of criteria external to the events themselves.

This suggests that the assignment of events to discursive and non-discursive categories is fundamentally a dialectical process; meaning arises through an oppositional interplay. Jean-Jacques Nattiez (1990b: 9) outlines a similar approach to meaning in his oft-quoted passage on referential modalities in music:

> An object of any kind takes on meaning for an individual apprehending that object, as soon as that individual places the object in relation to areas of his lived experience— that is, in relation to a collection of other objects that belong to his or her experience of the world.

Nattiez's discussion of music and discourse emphasizes the relational aspects of the musical experience and thus takes into account both formalist (Hanslickian) and referentialist views. Indeed, in Nattiez's view, music is more recondite than

Example 3.1. Ives, *The Unanswered Question*, melodic descent in mm. 1–12

either of these two perspectives typically allow.[18] Instead, "music as a symbolic fact is characterized by the presence of complex configurations and interpretants" and is therefore contingent on political, historical, artistic, cognitive, and inter-subjective factors, all of which coalesce within the act of interpretation (102–103).[19]

These observations drive home the notion that interpretive acts are based largely on the ways in which concepts interrelate. This principle applies to silent articulation as much as it does to other aspects of musical experience. In the words of Susan Sontag (1966: 11),

> "Silence" never ceases to imply its opposite and to depend on its presence: just as there can't be "up" without "down" or "left" without "right," so one must acknowledge a surrounding environment of sound or language in order to recognize silence. . . .
> [T]he artist who creates silence or emptiness must produce something dialectical: a full void, an enriching emptiness, a resonating or eloquent silence.[20]

This is not to say that musical communication is either absolute or arbitrary but rather that whatever meaning there is emerges on the basis of a conceptual dialectic. Applied to the present discussion, this means that the content of any specific instance of silent articulation in music depends on the ways in which discursive and non-discursive elements intermingle within a specific passage. While discursive and non-discursive events can be defined with a high degree of precision for any given piece, then, the particular structures that constitute such events over a broad spectrum of styles cannot be strictly identified because these change from one musical context to another.

Charles E. Ives's *Unanswered Question* (1953) provides an excellent proving ground for testing these ideas. The piece begins with a slow descent from G^6 to C^6 in the first violin part as shown in example 3.1. In terms of its melody alone, then, the passage seems to embody a sense of motion. The underlying harmony and voice leading, however, conflict with this interpretation. While the first few chords of the piece outline the key of G, for example, the leading tone (F♯) veers uncharacteristically downward in measure 5, thus weakening the tonal effect of G. Even the promising discursive move from G^7 to C in measures 6 and 7 fails to restore a clear sense of harmonic continuity because the passage ultimately ends on A minor.

The intense pointillistic chromaticism of the "question"—which enters around measure 16—intrudes sharply on the serene diatonic terra firma of the string parts.[21] To the extent that the wind parts incorporate metrically accented rhythms, motivic variation, and a gradual increase in dynamic level over the course of the piece, they reveal a gradually unfolding large-scale structure and therefore assume a more discursive demeanor than the strings. Indeed, the string parts may even *literally* disappear from our conscious awareness for a moment or two, so unanticipated are the wind entrances.

Once the winds enter, the strings shed whatever vestige of discursiveness might remain and thus take on the characteristics of silence. The phenomenal silence of the strings parallels the expressive silence assigned to them in the foreword to the piece; as Ives (1953) stipulates, the offstage strings are meant to "represent 'The Silences of the Druids—Who Know, See, and Hear Nothing.'" The strings in this case do not lapse into silence because they are *inherently* non-discursive, however. Rather, their silence results from the way they are heard in relation to the wind parts. Context, then, plays a critical role in the determination of the relative discursiveness of the instrumental groups in the composition.

This analysis suggests that the decision regarding what constitutes a discursive or non-discursive event (as well as what these events represent) depends on the ways in which the oppositions between certain types of musical events play out. As the following examples reveal, such decisions may involve *structural, stylistic,* or even *sociopolitical* criteria. Furthermore, non-discursive events themselves may occur *intermittently, pervasively,* or *concurrently with discursive events* over the course of a given composition.

Not every instance of silent articulation is corroborated by the composer's own word as it is in the pieces by Ives and Tavener discussed so far. In such cases, the analytical judgments of the observer become especially important. In the analyses that follow, the silence I attribute to the excerpts by Vaughan Williams, Mozart, and Debussy is substantiated by the analysis of the events themselves rather than by references to correspondence in letters and books. Such an approach amplifies the importance of subjectivity, which, of course, accompanies all interpretive acts.[22]

Concurrent Discursive and Non-Discursive Events

Measures 118–42 of the fourth movement of Vaughan Williams's Symphony No. 3—the *Pastoral* Symphony—contain a subtle example of a texture in which discursive and non-discursive events intermingle, producing a powerful expressive statement on the semantic level. In measure 118, the first and second violins—having just reiterated the main theme—languish into the repetitive descending eighth-note pattern shown in example 3.2a, while the winds and low strings take over the principal melodic role. This falling *pianissimo* pattern continues through the next ten measures, during which time it seems to dissolve into the texture, becoming nearly, if not completely, inaudible owing to the melodic and harmonic richness of the other instrumental parts in the passage.

Because of its redundant rhythm and the exuberance of the principal theme, the stream of eighths in the passage seems to lapse into silence.[23] Yet without this eighth-note pattern, the music loses much of its pathos and sense of drama. Whether or not it penetrates our conscious awareness, the relentless struggle of the descent to endure in the midst of overpowering melodic and harmonic forces man-

(a)

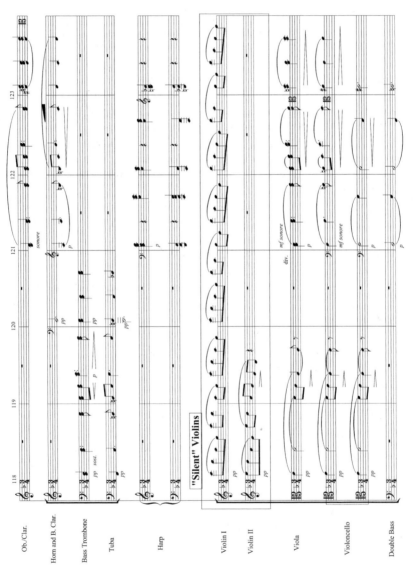

Example 3.2a. Vaughan Williams, Symphony No. 3, "Pastoral," fourth movement, mm. 118–23. © Copyright Faber Music Ltd., c/o Boosey & Hawkes, Inc., 35 East 21st Street, New York, NY 10010.

(b)

Example 3.2b. Reversal of eighth-note descent in Vaughan Williams's Symphony No. 3, fourth movement, mm. 138–42

ages to make itself known, thus conveying the sense of a courageous struggle for survival on the semantic level. Indeed, the eighth-note pattern changes direction in measure 139 (example 3.2b) after which it climbs with renewed vigor, finally joining with the principal melody to create the triumphant climax that arrives finally in measure 142. To the extent that it conveys the bleak isolation that accompanies many of life's most oppressive challenges, the tenacious stream of eighth notes in the passage imparts meaning just as much as the more discursive events it accompanies.

Intermittent Non-Discursiveness

While non-discursiveness is, perhaps, more pervasive in music written after the advent of the twentieth century, it is by no means confined to music of that period. Consider the first movement of Mozart's Symphony No. 40 in G Minor. This familiar movement would seem, on first consideration, to be a perfect example of the discursive archetype in music. Certainly this is true with respect to the opening measures, which form what William Caplin (1998: 17) would refer to as a "tight-knit" theme. In measures 72–76, however, the principal theme is dismantled, leaving only its motivic stepwise descent.[24] In these measures the stepwise descent, bracketed in example 3.3, repeats at various tempi and pitch levels in a number of different voices. While tonic and dominant chords alternate throughout the passage, the sense of progression is weak. This is, in part, because the leading tone is left hanging with each iteration of the dominant. When the tonic arrives on the following downbeat, moreover, it is accompanied by a suspended non-chord tone. Thus the passage becomes caught in a potentially endless pattern of repeating motives. The redundancy of the passage is reinforced by invertible counterpoint; the Eb–D and Bb–A suspensions are exchanged upon the return of the passage in measures 80–84 without changing the overall effect. The temporal displacement of the gestures in these measures arrests the discursive unfolding of the piece. As a result, the music seems to hesitate, taking time for a brief catch of breath before resuming its progress.

The repeating motives in Mozart's Symphony in G Minor do not by themselves produce non-discursiveness in the passage. The way the suspensions overlap also influences this perception. A similar passage heard in measures 58–61, for example, maintains its discursiveness because the Eb^7 chord, elaborated by a series of caden-

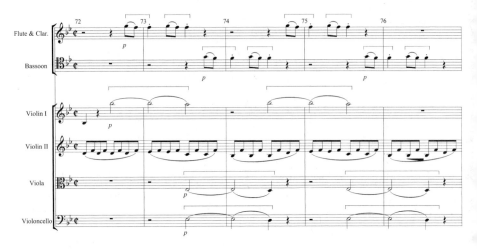

Example 3.3. Mozart, Symphony No. 40 in G Minor, first movement

Example 3.4. Debussy, *Iberia*, third movement ("Le matin d'un jour de fête"), mm. 15–16, with bracketed whole-tone motives

Example 3.5. Bloch, Sonata No. 1 for Violin and Piano, first movement, mm. 1–3. Copyright © 1922 (Renewed) by G. Schirmer, Inc. (ASCAP). International Copyright Secured. All Rights Reserved. Reprinted by Permission.

tial six-four chords, functions as the dominant throughout the passage despite the presence of a number of repeating stepwise ascents and descents.

The performative silence that occurs in Mozart's G minor Symphony is intermittent because it is sandwiched between more discursive events in the music. Another instance of intermittent silence involving a motivic breakdown occurs in the third movement of Debussy's *Iberia,* demonstrating that the techniques leading to non-discursiveness can be applied, with similar results, to music of different styles and periods. The passage in example 3.4 comprises a number of motives heard elsewhere in the piece. These motives are altered in measures 17–20 so that they consist only of pitches drawn from a whole-tone scale. This has the effect of causing the motives to blend together so that their individual melodic identities become less evident. In this case, the whole-tone collection itself creates the greatest sonic impact in the passage. As a result, the music manifests itself as a mesmerizing wash of sound punctuated by various instrumental timbres whose specific melodic content remains largely concealed.[25]

Ernest Bloch's Sonata No. 1 for Violin and Piano adds an interesting dimension to the discussion of silence and discourse, because it engages silence on stylistic and political grounds in addition to purely intra-musical aesthetic grounds. The first movement begins with an interplay between the violin and piano parts, as shown in example 3.5. The two parts together outline a D♯ diminished seventh chord. This chord, however, does not function, or "sound like," a diminished seventh. Rather, the two parts fuse into a compound melodic entity, one that produces little sense of harmonic expediency despite the frenzied energy created by the syncopated rhythms in the passage. This music incorporates the notion of contextual contrast not on the basis of opposing textures, then, but based on two independent melodic fragments. The mixing of these fragments masks their functionality and thus weakens their rhetorical impact.[26]

In the second movement of the piece, diatonic fragments combine to create a similar sensation. The movement begins with an ostinato in the piano part. This ostinato, shown in example 3.6, can be broken down into two parts, a right-hand descent and a left-hand alternating E/B pitch cycle. Each of these parts taken in-

Example 3.6. Bloch, Sonata No. 1 for Violin and Piano, second movement, mm. 2–3. Copyright © 1922 (Renewed) by G. Schirmer, Inc. (ASCAP). International Copyright Secured. All Rights Reserved. Reprinted by Permission.

dividually belongs to a different diatonic collection, E (either major or minor) in the left hand and E♭ major (spelled D♯) in the right hand. Playing the two fragments together obscures the sense of key, producing instead a diaphanous overlay of undifferentiated sound.

An almost miraculous move along the discursive/non-discursive continuum occurs at the end of the third movement, where a melodic pattern similar to that in example 3.6 occurs. The music for this passage appears in example 3.7. The melody in these measures, like that in the second movement, begins with gently oscillating triplets above E and B in the left hand. In this case, the right-hand triplets intone harmonically ambiguous—and, hence largely non-discursive—E/B fifths and B/F tritones. Beginning in measure 228, however, the texture begins to take on a more discursive demeanor. This is owing to the arrival of F♯ and D in measure 228. These pitches fill in the missing thirds in the 5/7 interval cycles that occur along with F♯ and D in the right hand, and thus lead to the construction of two triads in the second half of the measure. The first of these, D major, conflicts somewhat with the B pedal, but nonetheless points the passage in the direction of tonal harmony by introducing a complete triad. The tonal—or, perhaps more correctly, modal—characteristics of the passage gradually come into focus as the music continues. B, though minor, takes on a dominant function, while the chord succession in measures 229–31 fills in the pitches of an E minor scale. Hence the passage seems to move, in a literal and perceptible way, from non-discursiveness to discursiveness in the final moments of the piece.

Despite its neo-Romantic exterior, Bloch's Sonata for Violin and Piano, No. 1, resists categorization along stylistic lines because its harmonic content is distorted. As a result, the music seems aloof, foreign, dispossessed—in a word, silent. Seen in this light, the piece as a whole conveys a sense of estrangement reflective in a broader sense, perhaps, of Bloch's rejection of mainstream musical modernism. The following quote expresses Bloch's intense views on this subject:

"Serious" composers persist in the obsession with technique and procedure. They discuss and argue; they laboriously create their arbitrary, brain-begotten works, while the emotional element—the soul of art—is lost in the passion for mechanical perfection. Everywhere, virtuosity of means; everywhere, intellectualism exalted as the standard.

Example 3.7. Bloch, Sonata No. 1 for Violin and Piano, third movement, mm. 225–33. Copyright © 1922 (Renewed) by G. Schirmer, Inc. (ASCAP). International Copyright Secured. All Rights Reserved. Reprinted by Permission.

This is the plague of our times and the reason for its inevitable death. (Quoted by Eric Johnson 1976: 32)

With this statement, Bloch alienates himself from what he sees as the excesses of musical modernism based on his deeply felt belief in art as "an experience of life, and not a puzzle game . . . or icy demonstration of imposed mathematical principles" (quoted by Olin Downes 1976: 23). To the extent that Bloch's music reflects his devotion to such ideals, it may also project a general sense of otherness and emotional distance as well.

Pervasive Non-Discursiveness

Other composers have incorporated the tenets of non-discursiveness in an even more self-conscious way. Non-discursiveness in works by these composers is often *pervasive* and usually takes the form of thick textures in which notes cluster together, thereby losing their identity as individual tones. The redundancy of the musical events in these compositions is the result of a purposeful effort to produce a static, spatial quality in which the texture itself becomes the focus of attention. Under these conditions, music becomes completely non-discursive, silent, an embodiment of pure sound perceived primarily in terms of its timbre or, to use Ligeti's characterization, its "iridescent tone colour."[27]

Example 3.8 shows the first few canonic entries in measures 23–25 of Ligeti's *Atmospheres.*[28] The voices in this piece—like those in several other pieces by Ligeti, including *Apparitions* and *Requiem*—proliferate to such a degree that the individual parts eventually blend into an "atmospheric plane of sound."[29] As Ligeti (1983a: 14–15) observes,

> you cannot actually hear the polyphony, the canon. You hear a kind of impenetrable texture, something like a very densely woven cobweb. I have retained melodic lines in the process of composition, they are governed by rules as strict as Palestrina's or those of the Flemish school, but the rules of this polyphony are worked out by me. The polyphonic structure does not actually come through, you cannot hear it; it remains hidden in a microscopic, underwater world, to us inaudible. . . . All in all, you cannot hear my music as it appears on paper.

This music not only embodies the principle of silence by means of its blurred, atmospheric texture, then, but does so also because the canonic structure of the piece itself is inaudible. Hence Ligeti's music of silence takes on figurative as well as aesthetic connotations.

The third movement of Barbara Kolb's *Appello* also incorporates a largely inaudible compositional structure with similar results. Example 3.9 illustrates how the first two measures unfold. The first measure contains a four-note pitch set that repeats four times. The apparent randomness of the pitch succession in this measure, however, is misleading. In fact, each note of the pitch set occurs once, and only once, on each quarter-note beat-class as the chart below the excerpt reveals. This process repeats in measure 2 and in each successive measure as the piece unfolds. In this case, the length of the pitch set governs the number of repetitions, and hence the length of each large measure. New pitches are introduced in consecutive measures until all the pitches of the complete aggregate have occurred, after which the process begins again. In this movement, the redundancy of the pitch set produces an ethereal, floating effect similar to that of Ligeti's *Atmospheres*. Like Ligeti's *Atmospheres,* moreover, the structure that gives rise to this effect remains largely hidden.

By referring to Samuel Beckett, Morton Feldman's *For Samuel Beckett* also calls attention to the aesthetic of silence as it applies across a broad artistic/generic range. Speaking of his music in general, Feldman (2000 [1984]: 181) observes that "silence is my substitute for counterpoint. It's nothing against something. The degrees of nothing against something. It's a real thing, it's a breathing thing."[30] With these words, Feldman plainly asserts his commitment to silent articulation in music. Silence in *For Samuel Beckett* takes the form of a redundant, spellbinding texture created by repeating the same music over and over again. Individual instruments in the piece tend to articulate one or two pitches using simple repetitive rhythmic patterns. The pitch material gradually changes over the course of the

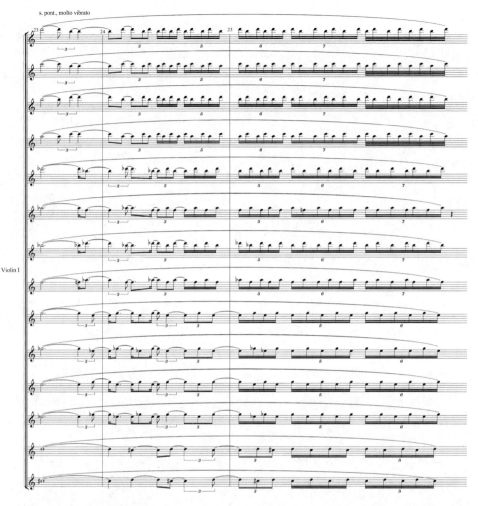

Example 3.8. Ligeti, *Atmospheres,* mm. 23–26, canonic entries. © 1963 by Universal Edition A. G., Vienna. © Renewed. All Rights Reserved. Used by permission of European American Music Distributors LLC, agent for Universal Edition A. G., Vienna.

composition but without any real sense of progression, since many of the principal ideas presented at the beginning of the piece remain prominent throughout the entire composition. Thus, as Catherine Laws (1998: 77) observes with respect to another of Feldman's compositions, "the reiteration and variation of limited material enhances the self-referentiality of the work."[31]

Measures 1 and 2, shown in example 3.10, contain what may be considered the main content of the piece. As the example illustrates, this material—with the addition of a few new pitch classes—remains largely intact eighty measures later. The original pitch classes have migrated to different instruments and octaves in meas-

Example 3.10. Feldman, *For Samuel Beckett,* common pitch classes in selected measures.

ures 85–86 but maintain their pairings and timbral associations as the arrows in the example indicate; B♭, for example, continues to be paired with A♭, while C is paired with A in the high woodwinds and piano part. The bassoon pairing also remains prominent despite the half-step change from F to F♯ in measure 85.

Feldman's *For Samuel Beckett* is not rich in content; it conveys little new information—musical or extra-musical—after the first few measures. This dearth of content has the effect of highlighting what is omitted or underdeveloped in much the same way Beckett's literary works focus attention on what is left unspoken. Indeed, this is a hallmark of Feldman's style. For Feldman, it is what is hidden within the shadows that is most interesting, not that which is already exposed to the light. On the other hand, as Feldman (2000: 179) himself observes, "Shadows are not really shadows." Silence, that is, has its own peculiar way of communicating.

Relative to traditional contexts, pieces like *Appello, For Samuel Beckett,* and *Atmospheres* seem silent—unobtrusive and taciturn. The non-discursive elements in these pieces, moreover, have been expanded to the point that the music has become *primarily* a silent space. Silence, that is, is pervasive and total. The context for making such an assertion is a very broad one in that it comprises tonal repertoire in general.

It is easy to characterize music that downplays traditional formal relations as an affront to coherence and musicality. Such music, because it does not contain familiar melodic and harmonic constructions, seems to go nowhere, to present itself, instead, as a static, nonfunctional mass of sound whose trajectory in time and space cannot be predicted. Thus the music becomes silent both in terms of its projected meaning and its structural content.

On the other hand, performative silence, that which occurs in and through sound, does not necessarily oppose signification altogether. Just as in spoken discourse, silence can be a powerful means of communication. What is needed to uncover this meaning is simply a different set of tools than those used to analyze traditional, goal-oriented music. In this chapter I have relied on contextualized events interacting within a dialectical frame to tease out meaning in non-discursive music. Such an approach provides the analyst with the means for identifying the precise attributes that lead to the perception of silence and discourse within a particular passage while also allowing for interpretive flexibility in the semantic domain.

What music communicates under these circumstances is somewhat more difficult to pin down. As the analyses in this chapter suggest, music whose texture is its most conspicuous feature is not necessarily reflective only, or even primarily, of Eastern conceptions of time, although in certain circumstances it may take on such a connotation. Rather, non-discursive music is capable of conveying a host of cultural, political, stylistic, and narrative ideas depending on the specific ways in which discursive and non-discursive elements unfold. I do not dispute the idea that what I describe as non-discursive or silent music may also embody a sense of timelessness but rather that conceptualizing music in terms of its temporal characteristics alone severely limits the range of narrative expressions it is capable of generating. In a sense, characterizing events as having no motion even reinforces the idea that nonlinear music is relatively powerless as a means of communication, because it implies the music is deficient or lacking in some way. Calling attention to the non-discursive nature of such music opens up a new space for generating meaning, one that is capable of embracing multiple modes of representation.

As I have attempted to demonstrate in this chapter, both discursive and non-discursive events contribute to meaning. The strings in Ives's *Unanswered Question* convey a powerful message by demonstrating that the query posed so insistently in the wind parts is, in fact, unanswerable. The silent struggle of the eighth-note stream in Vaughan Williams's *Pastoral* Symphony deepens the sense of personal triumph we feel as the piece nears its end. Intermittent silences, like those that interrupt the progress of the themes in Mozart's Symphony No. 40 and Debussy's *Iberia,* provide a pause in the action, so to speak, allowing the music to embark on a brief liminal exploration before returning to its original path. Pervasive silent textures in pieces such as Ligeti's *Atmospheres* and Feldman's *For Samuel Beckett* challenge aesthetic complacency based on traditional progress-oriented harmonic conventions and formal structures. On an even broader scale, the silent articulation of the unusual harmonies in Bloch's Sonata No. 1 for Violin and Piano expresses the ideological distance that separates the neo-Romantic Swiss-Jewish composer from his modernist Franco-German peers.

Events in music are not inherently discursive or non-discursive. Rather, they take on these characteristics by means of an active, ongoing exchange of ideas. The perception of discursiveness and non-discursiveness in music, moreover, may change from listener to listener. Heard as primarily tertian, even the most intricately structured tonal piece may lapse into silence. This does not mean, however, that the music for a listener who hears the piece in such a way is meaningless. Silence is more than a void. Silence constitutes a dramatic presence in music similar to that of music at its most overtly discursive and plays an important, if not indispensable, role in the production of meaning.

Notes

1. Raymond Monelle underscores this distinction by drawing a sharp line between music's syntactic and semantic features. For Monelle (2000: 83), syntactic features in music involve formal processes. Hence their temporality is a "temporality of the signifier." Musical events, on the other hand, can "sometimes acquire indexical force" and thus "signify time on the semantic level" (84). To the extent that music seems to represent time as a general concept rather than an intrinsic aspect of its own construction, then, it can convey information of a semantic, rather than a purely syntactic, nature.

2. For a more thorough investigation of the ways in which the perception of Eastern culture has influenced Western music and musicians, see John Corbett 2000.

3. Eero Tarasti's (1994: 42) modalities of "doing" (discursive) and "being" (non-discursive)—based on ideas first introduced by Greimas (1983)—closely resemble these categories.

4. Whether a pattern manifests itself as a non-discursive event stems at least in part

from the listener's familiarity with discursive conventions in music. The less one knows about structure in music of a certain type, the less the surface patterns convey a sense of the music's large-scale coherence.

5. The notion of a "present now of consciousness" is Edmund Husserl's (1991 [1893–1917]: 31). Husserl maintains that memory allows past aural events to be united with those in the present to create a "total formation" (22). This explains how listeners are able to recognize and remember melodies and other sound constructions that unfold through time.

6. The sound/silence opposition lies at the root of explorations into the role of silence as a border or frame for music undertaken by Edward T. Cone (1968) and Richard Littlefield (2001). Toru Takemitsu (1995: 5) incorporates the framing aspect of silence as a compositional premise by treating "sound as something to confront silence."

7. For Cage, too, silence is made up of sounds, those that occur along with music but are not written down. Unlike Cage's unintentional silence, performative silence is deliberate, an active form of expression.

8. There are, of course, exceptions. Military bugle calls, for example, convey very specific messages to their hearers.

9. As Adorno (1992b: 3) once put it, "To interpret music means: to make music."

10. For a more in-depth exploration of the composer/listener dialectic, see Pearsall 2003.

11. This idea has been explored by Ludim Pedroza (2002: 91) in conjunction with the solo recital. Pedroza suggests that the solo recital has become a rigorous exercise in contemplation. Therefore any music featured in it becomes "primarily an object of contemplation." Kevin Barry (1987: 3) theorizes that the contemplative approach to music is grounded in eighteenth-century philosophy: "Given that a piece of instrumental music must appear, according to Lockean principles, to be empty of signification, its enjoyment is evidence of the necessity for an aesthetic complex enough to include the pleasures of uncertainty in interpretation and of some free subjectivity."

12. Edward T. Cone's work on the subject of musical personae in German lieder is well known. Cone (1974: 17) suggests that it is through the guise of three personae—the vocal, the instrumental, and the complete musical persona—that music finds expression. In a later revision of this concept, he collapses his three original personae into one "unitary vocal-instrumental protagonist that is coextensive with the persona of the actual composer of the song" (1992: 181). In all his work on this subject Cone maintains that it is the composer's voice which speaks most clearly, and argues that this voice, although it may be a "composite" voice, represents the composer's persona, albeit a fictional persona the composer takes on in order to communicate a particular musical idea (181).

13. The affront to stylistic norms that occurs when a composer writes non-discursive music can, in fact, mark conventional ways of structuring so that they become even more poignant (less silent) than when they are used pervasively. As Susan McClary (1998: 13) has remarked, "During the period of a convention's reign . . . we may fail even to notice its presence. . . . Only when it breaks down does a convention become a marker that distinguishes 'their beliefs' from 'ours.'"

14. To better understand the differences between functional and aesthetic categories, we may turn to Tzvetan Todorov's discussion of symbolic language. Todorov (1982 [1977]: 62) associates function with rhetorical intent: "[Rhetorical] speech is above all functional; to be functional is to be fitting. . . . The key notion of rhetoric is therefore the notion of suitability." In Todorov's view, "Any speech may be efficacious; it must simply be used toward an appropriate end" (61–62). Thus, for Todorov, rhetoric is language best suited to communicate a particular idea. Beauty plays a minimal role in this process. "Aesthetics cannot come into being until its object, the beautiful, is recognized as having autonomous existence, and until

this object is judged irreducible to neighboring categories such as the true, the good, the useful, and so on" (111–12). Hence rhetorical speech embodies "efficaciousness" whereas discourse that can be "appreciated for itself, for its intrinsic qualities, its form and beauty" entails aesthetic values (67).

Cast in terms of Todorov's discussion, discursive events in music are those whose most prominent attribute is their rhetorical functionality. Such events bring the syntactic aspects of a passage to the forefront. Discursive events manifest themselves primarily as vehicles for formal structure, melodic development, metrical organization, and harmonic continuity. Functionality plays a less important role where non-discursive events are concerned. This allows their aesthetic quality or sonic signature to become more pronounced.

15. In this regard, music again parallels spoken discourse; Bernard Dauenhauer (1980: 5), for example, observes that silence is "an utterance of a peculiar kind, a way of 'saying' something determinate."

16. In this case I am using the term "attributive" in the same sense that Benjamin Boretz (1977: 104) does, that is, to refer to acts of interpretation which "ascribe properties to and thereby determine what there is."

17. While Monelle (2000: 99) recognizes that the motion to the dominant in the first phrase of a period constitutes a "syntactic move," it does not, in his opinion, produce the "feeling of a progression" on the semantic level.

18. Nicholas Cook (2001: 174) also recognizes the slippery nature of these categories, noting that a careful reading of Hanslick's *Vom Musikalisch-Schönen* might lead to an interpretation of Hanslick's book "as an exercise in aesthetic categorization, not denying music's expressive power but drawing a clear line between expression and beauty."

19. Lawrence Kramer (1990: 15) adopts a similar position, noting that an "interpretation unhesitatingly seizes on any association, substitution, analogy, construction, or leap of inference that it requires to do its work."

20. Bernard Dauenhauer (1980: 24) makes a similar observation, noting that "silence always appears in connection with an utterance."

21. The dissonance of this gesture has become even more pronounced for me after living for a number of years in Mexico. There one sometimes hears a vulgar insult delivered in the form of a whistle whose rhythm and contour resembles that of the spoken insult as well as Ives's musical question.

22. Many authors distinguish between meanings that can be objectively verified and those that are self-derived. John Kaemmer (1993: 113), for example, distinguishes between what he refers to as denotive and connotative meaning. For Kaemmer, "denotive" meaning in music is "formulated . . . by the [person] creating it" whereas "connotative meaning [is that] which is inferred by the listener." Benjamin Boretz (1977: 242) makes a similar distinction, referring to connotative meaning as "attributive" and denotive meaning as "descriptive." In his discussion of music and discourse, Lawrence Kramer (1990: 15) goes so far as to assert that "interpretation cannot stabilize key concepts—or if you prefer, cannot afford the illusion that concepts are stable in the first place. On the contrary: interpretation can only proceed by intensifying conceptual mobility." Such a perspective not only allows for subjective freedom but suggests that, for meaning to be viable at all, it must take subjective slipperiness into account.

23. The inclination to filter out a constant sound reflects a perceptual phenomenon known to psychologists as *habituation* (see Burghardt 1973: 329). Habituation occurs when a non-fluctuating sound, such as the hum of a refrigerator or fluorescent light fixture, disappears completely from one's conscious awareness as time passes. Cognitive scientists have demonstrated that this phenomenon is not merely an illusion. After a period of time, neu-

rons in the brain can actually stop transmitting signals associated with hums and other repetitive sounds (see Solomon and Davis 1983: 351).

24. See Hueß 1933: 54–66 for a more complete description of this motive and its transformations.

25. My thanks to Judith Lang Zaimont who, after hearing a presentation of an earlier
version of this paper, pointed out that while the motivic content of this passage may engen-
der silence, the passage as a whole builds steadily toward the climax that arrives in measure
29. Hence the music exhibits both discursive and non-discursive tendencies depending on
whether one attends primarily to dynamics or pitch groupings. These hearings do not necessarily conflict with each other. Indeed, the crescendo provides a clue regarding the representational content of the non-discursive events; the silence of Debussy's *Iberia* is an un-
comfortable silence, one that grows gradually more agitated until it becomes intolerable, at
which point it gives way to the principal theme.

26. Bloch (1976 [1933]: 11) himself acknowledges the performative silence that occurs
in the third part of his *Sacred Service*, noting that "first there is a Silent Meditation which
comes in before you to take your soul out and look at what it contains." Bloch also speaks
of silence in reference to the final epilogue: "Then in the enormous silence, outside of space,
comes an impersonal Voice, with the Law of Eternity, that everything was and will be; that
He Is, He Shall Be, without beginning, without end."

27. Ligeti used this phrase to describe the texture of the *Kyrie* from his *Requiem* in answer to a query by Marino Lobanova. See Lobanova 2002: 135.

28. While all the parts enter together, they articulate similar melodic contours (or their
inversions) and follow one another imitatively.

29. See Ligeti 1983b: 98.

30. Also quoted in Feldman 1985: 166.

31. This quote, while constituting a fitting description of the piece discussed here, refers
specifically to Feldman's opera *Neither*.

4   The Troping of Temporality in Music

Robert S. Hatten

I begin with an important distinction between time and temporality in music. When we think of musical time we generally think of meter, rhythm, tempo, rubato, or pacing—elements of great structural and expressive significance for music. By temporality, on the other hand, I refer to the ways in which we might characterize temporal experience in music.[1] In this chapter I examine four presuppositions of temporality in the music of Western composers: (1) that we subjectively experience a kind of temporal flow which in its unmarked form might be considered an ongoing present; (2) that the flow is comprised of musical events which have *stylistic* temporal coding of their own (anticipatory, retrospective, ongoing) and take on *strategic* sequential coding when individual events imply their own kinds of continuation; (3) that musical events at this level have dramatic roles to play in an overarching expressive genre; and (4) that composers can play with their ordering, possibly signaling a narrative agency, but at least creating a dramatically marked reordering as distinguished from a normative, and hence unmarked, dramatic sequence. I claim that this reordering of temporally coded events affects the ways in which we interpret them when they do appear and that an emergent meaning results. I call this process the *troping of temporality:* the complex syntheses created when composers explore unexpected relationships between the expected location of musical events and the actual location where they appear, relative to one another and to their plausible dramatic sequence.

I begin by reviewing how Western composers achieve rough analogues to the linguistic categories of *tense* and *aspect* (Hatten 1997; Hatten and Pearson, forthcoming). The typical ways that time may be experienced in a dramatic flow of events (with or without the higher agency of narrative direction, reaction, or commentary) include categories akin to *tense* but which, for music, I prefer to call *temporal perspective* (Hatten 1997). The most common examples are familiar to everyone: anticipatory or prospective (as in introductions), and reflective or retrospective (as in codas). Other characterizations of temporality include the categories of *aspect*, which Charls Pearson (Pearson and Hatten, forthcoming) has defined for all semiotic systems as "the syntactic coding of the relation between the time of interpretation of the sign and the relation among the times referred to by the proposition of the sign."

An example from language will illustrate the variety of possible *aspectual perspectives:* "I [was playing] the first movement and I [would have finished] it, but Mary [interrupted] me [just before] the coda." The words in brackets all imply temporal relationships between events, as well as the temporal character of the events themselves. We are cued linguistically to the status of each event, from (1) *progressive* (/was playing/) = *iterative* or *durative* without specified termination, to (2) *perfective* (/would have finished/) = durational but with an implied goal or completion, and (3) *non-durative* (/interrupted/) = an event that happens at a single point in time. We also know (4) when each event happened in relation to the others (/just before the coda/), along a time line that, in this case, involves events in the past relative to the time of the speaker's utterance of the sentence. I ignore still other elements of *mood* (for example, the conditional "would have") and *voice* (action relative to the speaker as agent or patient) in this brief orientation to temporal perspective and character.

Theorists are familiar with many of the cues for temporal perspective in music. For example, we know that in classical works a move to V^7/IV at the point where we expect a final cadence can launch a retrospective coda. The reversal of the leading tone to the seventh of V^7/IV aptly symbolizes not only the avoidance of closure but also the compensatory move to the subdominant side that is more relaxed and hence more suitable for reflection and reminiscence—and balancing earlier, intensifying moves to the dominant in a major-key sonata movement. We are also familiar with the various ways that a slow introduction can build a sense of impending expectation, as when a prolonged dominant finally resolves to the initiatory tonic in a structural downbeat that launches the Allegro of a first-movement sonata form. Furthermore, when we hear what we identify as a passacaglia or ground bass, we know that an *iterative* process is being projected as a consequence of the variation genre. We may further appreciate the way that Brahms avoids the implied closure at the end of each variation unit, as in the finale of the Fourth Symphony, in which he creates larger temporal units and thereby creates something akin to the expressive trajectory of the sonata cycle itself.

But there are more complex ways in which composers can manipulate our understanding of the temporal, as in language, by reordering various musical events in ways that challenge our (unmarked) expectation of a continuous, present experiencing of events. For one might argue that, even in cases of prospective introductions or retrospective codas, we are *presently* experiencing an anticipation of future events or *presently* enjoying a reminiscence of past events. Indeed, this is no different from the present, experienced time of a speech act in which one employs the future or past tense. Instead, it is the temporality of the *events referenced* in speech acts or *expressed* as musical performative acts—specifically, how they relate to one another and to the temporal location of the experiencing agent—that is crucial to our understanding of a play with temporal experiencing. Of course, interpreting reordered events is possible only with reference to a time line of events for which we have some temporal expectation. The dramatic trajectories that are stylistically encoded in what I call *expressive genres* (Hatten 1994) provide one regulative guide; the Schenkerian-conceived stylistic patterns of normative harmonic progression

Example 4.1. Brahms, Violin Sonata in G, Op. 78, second movement, mm. 1–11

and voice-leading (at all levels of structure) provide another. And, strategically, the individual exigencies or internal logic of a thematic discourse imply still a third. Against these interactive backdrops of expectation that create a generalized temporal flow, a composer can reorder events to achieve rather remarkable temporal (and expressive) effects, when examined from an aspectual perspective.

I begin with two related examples (discussed more exhaustively in Hatten and Pearson, forthcoming).[2] In the first (example 4.1), Brahms begins the slow movement of his Violin Sonata in G, Op. 78, with what Leonard B. Meyer (1973: 214–16) analyzes as a closural gesture used for an opening theme.

In that paper I argued that the situation was more complex, that one could interpret this opening as a positively resigned acceptance of some problem situation yet to be presented. The listener is thus led to expect something worthy of such a magnificent gesture of abnegation, and it is not long in appearing—the subsequent phrase thrusts us into a tragic realm of experience marked by minor mixture and *empfindsamer* sighs (or, perhaps, a remembrance of that experience—music is not as determinate as language in its specification of temporal experience, even when we can detect the differences that cue what we sense are contrasting temporal per-

b: ii⁰⁷₄ – 5   V⁷₆–₅   i

(as plagal extension)

Example 4.2. Berg, Piano Sonata, op. 1. © 1926 by Schlesinger'sche Buch-u. Musikhdl. Reproduced by permission of Robert Lienau Musikverlag, Frankfurt/Main (Germany). All Rights Reserved.

spectives). When Brahms uses the opening gesture to close the movement, its dramatic role as an outcome "delivered too early" is confirmed, although its expressive effect at the opening goes beyond mere contradiction of location. In the expressive genre from which this movement departs, the problem situation would normally appear before the emotional outcome. When it doesn't, the prematurely delivered outcome influences how we hear the problem—here, how we interpret the tragic events that intervene. Anthony Newcomb (1987) has explored the narrative consequences of reordering in a work of Schumann's. What I wish to explore here is the *motivation* for such reordering—not only its potential for affecting our sense of temporality but also its expressive consequences.

Berg's Piano Sonata, Op. 1 (example 4.2), is aspectually similar to the Brahms, but a different outcome is adumbrated.

Here the first phrase ends with a terribly tragic and final cadence in B minor. As listeners, we are cued to wonder what events might have led to such a fateful result. Since this phrase is varied to end the single-movement work, there is the implication of a framing level of discourse (as, for example, in Schumann's "Fabel," from the *Phantasiestücke*, Op. 12, No. 6). But as in the Brahms, the opening phrase clearly initiates the thematic discourse, and Berg's notated repeat of the exposition confirms its initiatory thematic status. I suggest that the expressive effect is akin to that experienced on hearing a tragic Scottish ballad, in which the dreadful outcome is already stated at the beginning and our interpretation of subsequent events is haunted by that knowledge.

As illustrated by these two examples, there is a creative yield—an *emergent* expressive meaning—from their unusual negotiations of temporal expectation. They are, I would argue, *tropes* (Hatten 1994: 161–202). Examples of this type of troping, expressed simply as a contradiction between closural function and initiatory location, have already attracted attention (see Meyer 1973; J. Kramer 1973; and Lochhead 1979). For example, Haydn's witty use of the trope of function contradicting location occurs in the opening of the finale of the Quartet in E♭, Op. 33, No. 2, affectionately nicknamed the "Joke" Quartet.[3]

A related kind of trope, one that also depends on an established expectation that is reversed, is the "evolving theme." Typically a theme is stated in its complete form, and development takes off from there. But a composer may reverse the process, beginning with pieces of a theme that only gradually come together into its definitive form. A clear example is the third-movement march from Tchaikovsky's Sixth Symphony, in which the motto opening of the main theme appears imitatively and leads through an enormous buildup to the definitive statement of the theme in the clarinets, far into the movement (at Rehearsal H). Charles Ives extends this technique, resulting in what Peter Burkholder (1983: 385–407) terms "cumulative form," to structure entire movements. Burkholder defines cumulative form as "a thematic, non-repetitive form in which the principal theme is presented, not at the beginning as in traditional forms, but near the end, and is preceded, not followed, by its development" (1995a: 137).

Beethoven's introduction to the fugal finale of the *Hammerklavier* Piano Sonata, Op. 106, offers a spectacular example of cumulative formation, although the evolution toward a theme here is not predicated on its motivic elements but on its emerging topic (Baroque-derived "learned style"), and the evolution is meant to suggest the process of composition itself.[4] As shown in example 4.3, Beethoven tries out three ideas, pastiches of Baroque counterpoint, but cuts off each after only a few bars.[5]

The increasingly contrapuntal progression leads generically toward fugue, but there is no clear derivation of the ultimate fugue subject in these ideas—rather, the subject emerges from the descent in thirds that *surrounds* the pastiches. Charles Rosen (1997 [1971]: 428) observes:

> The sketches for this movement show that Beethoven copied out little phrases of Bach's *Well-Tempered Keyboard* along with his work on the themes. It is evident that he wished here for an effect of the gradual creation of a new contrapuntal style, arising from the improvisatory structure of the transition.

In interpreting the implied temporalities of this introductory transition, one notes several *prospective* cues:

Example 4.3. Beethoven, Piano Sonata in B♭ Major, Op. 106 (*Hammerklavier*), transition to the fourth movement, mm. 1–5

1. The ordering of pastiche allusions is increasingly contrapuntal.
2. The descending third motion between the quotes might be heard as anticipatory (as if ruminating on a possible future idea).
3. The entire transition functions as an anticipatory anacrusis to the structural downbeat of the fugue proper.

Several *retrospective* cues are also evident:

4. The pastiches allude to an earlier style, which may symbolize an ideal as
   grounded in the past, while also conveying the sense of venerable authori-
   tativeness which was a typical correlation for Baroque-learned styles when
   they appeared in classical works (Hatten 1994).
5. The descending thirds between the pastiches allow time for mystical reflection upon these elements of the past.
6. After the quotes there is a reference to a fermata-like moment of reflection
   from the first movement (mm. 81–84; see Hatten 1994: 201), doubly retrospective here in that it involves a moment remembered from the work's
   own past, as well as a fermata-like expansion (stepping out of piece time)
   that marks the moment as one of reflection.

But the ultimate *tropological* effect comes from a blending of the prospective
and retrospective, captured in Rosen's image of the "gradual creation of a new contrapuntal style":

7. The pastiches come at separated intervals, interrupted by the descent in
   thirds, suggesting a back-and-forth temporal play, and exemplifying the
   act of *Phantasierung* as a stream of consciousness in which new ideas suddenly emerge, only to be broken off just as abruptly, as the mind rejects
   them.

A third type of trope involving temporality is related to the Beethoven example.
When a presumably continuous idea is broken off, or its clearly projected goal is
evaded, as in certain rhetorical gestures or shifts in level of discourse, then there is
also a sense of shift in temporality (or perhaps a shift to another *temporal plane,*
in Frank Samarotto's [1999: 129–70] characterization). This shift may involve a
troping of temporalities, very much the way a stream of consciousness may shift
from present to past event or imagined future. By interrupting the unmarked or
expected flow of events, especially in such dramatic or rhetorical fashion, time is
problematized as neither strictly sequential nor smoothly continuous. An example
of this effect is found in the rhetorical interruptions marking the turn to the coda
of the finale of Schubert's Piano Sonata in A Major, D. 959 (example 4.4).

The expressive effects of these interruptions may be reconstructed in the following sequence:

a. measures 328–31 (return, after a rhetorical silence, of the rondo theme in
   A major): This return is a re-experienced present/presence (reflection implied as a consequence of intervening developments and episodes in this
   sonata rondo form).

Example 4.4. Schubert, Piano Sonata in A Major, D. 959, fourth movement, final return of the rondo theme (*Allegretto*) as rhetorical transition to the coda (*Presto*), mm. 328–50

b. measure 332 (breaking off into silence): A sudden thought intervenes, bringing the temporality of the theme to a halt.

c. measures 333–34 (shift to A minor): The thought is plaintive, retrospective, possibly tragic.

d. measures 335 (modulation to V/F major): It shifts prospectively to a more positive state.

e. measure 336 (breaking off into silence, and interrupting a measure short of the four-bar phrase, stopping short on a half-cadence): "Could this be?" (reflecting backward).

f. measures 337–40 (second strain of theme in F): Reassuring and ongoing sense of security in this new, positive frame.

g. measure 341 (breaking off into silence): Again, retrospective: something isn't quite right.

h. measure 342 (F becomes Ger+6 in A in this echo of the last-heard measure from the theme, now up an octave): Rhetorical effect of questioning, poised, as time stands still.

i. measure 343 (breaking off into silence): Reflecting on the portent of this question, which has the seeds of its own answer in its implied modulation, hence also prospective for those aware of the rhetorical use of an enharmonic German augmented-sixth modulation.

j. measure 344 (regaining the theme by restating the turn motive measure and continuing with the last phrase): Reassurance in the correct key, re-engaging the theme *in medias res* but with an initiatory "arrival 6/3" (note the temporal shifts justify this unusual resolution of the German augmented sixth). Regains the present and a sense of ongoing time.[6]

k. measure 348 (breaking off the phrase before its last, cadential measure): All is *still* not well; prospective "what next?"

l. measure 349 (launching a Presto closural treatment of the motive from the last measure [m. 347] of the interrupted theme): Determination to achieve closure at all costs.

This passage involves twelve stages of temporal play, and to call the whole section a trope would be an oversimplification. But clearly, at a higher level, this is an example of dramatic troping with form and meaning. Locally one could specify differences of tropological meaning based on whether there was syntactic or thematic interruption (shift or undercutting of thought) or whether the silence followed a complete syntactic or thematic unit (as a moment to reflect but also to wait in suspense for what will happen next). And one might distinguish the effects of short versus long segments between silences, whether a segment echoes or straightforwardly continues the theme, and whether a segment reaffirms a key or modulates to another.

A related trope involves an interruption that ultimately returns to the music left behind—in other words, parenthetical insertion (Kinderman 1995).[7] An example from the finale of Schubert's Piano Sonata in A Minor, D. 845, involves a texturally marked harmonic shift to III for four bars, before four bars of V restore the expected harmony, leading to a definitive cadence in the next three bars (example 4.5). The temporal effect of the four half-note chords is to freeze time in a momentous, or portentous, shift to a coloristic harmony, and the rift is healed by the four subsequent cadential 6/4 chords—still prolonging a single harmony but one that regains strong syntactic directionality and textural movement (the left-hand arpeggiation).

The first movement of Schubert's Piano Sonata in A, D. 959, provides two contrasting examples of parenthesis, a premature development between versions of the second theme in the exposition (strongly directional) and a more timeless, Ro-

Example 4.5. Schubert, Piano Sonata in A Minor, D. 845, fourth movement (*Allegro vivace*), mm. 177–91

mantic oscillation between harmonies launching the development section proper. The first parenthesis jolts the exposition to a temporal realm more suited to a development section, as a brief fugato and sequential motivic working out proceeds in perhaps self-consciously rhetorical fashion. The second parenthesis tropes upon the expectation of a forward-directed, modulatory development section by oscillating mystically between phrases in C major and B major.

It is also possible, though tricky, to begin a movement with a rhetorically interruptive gesture. The finale of Schubert's Piano Sonata in B♭, D. 960, presents an interesting example (example 4.6).

Here, the octave G "signal" at the opening is interpreted as dominant of C minor, but we soon realize that Schubert is using the same auxiliary cadence, V/ii to ii, V to I, that Mozart used in the finale of his Piano Sonata in B♭, K. 281.[8] Gesturally it is difficult to play this opening G octave with sufficient character to convey its rhetorical role at the very beginning, although it becomes quite obvious in subsequent locations in the sonata.

I close with one last example that demonstrates Schubert's subtle awareness of the effect of temporal shifting, and its tropological potential. The Adagio second movement of the Piano Sonata in C Minor, D. 958, has a striking modulatory shift at measure 23 that takes the second phrase of a theme to a new expressive plane. But shifting from D♭ minor to E major, despite the enharmonic spelling of F♭ major, is merely a move to the relative major (example 4.7a).

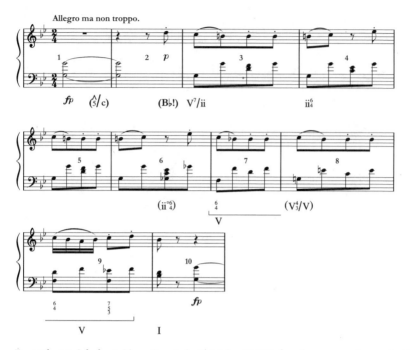

Example 4.6. Schubert, Piano Sonata in B♭ Major, D. 960, fourth movement, mm. 1–10

The same texture is preserved, and only the enharmonic visual element and an extension to six bars mark this second phrase as potentially shifting to another temporality, despite its amelioration from tragic to consoling. But notice what Schubert does when this theme returns climactically in the "development" above triplet octaves (example 4.7b, mm. 70–78, F minor to F major!).

Now, the fourth bar of the first phrase is deleted, and a sudden shift from *fortissimo* to *piano* marks a textural shift to the consoling second phrase. It is an undercutting that tropes the dramatic sense of opposition between the inexorably tragic (the octave triplets) and the miraculously consoling gestures that intervene, with anticipatory urgency, interrupting the tragic lament of the first phrase. Harmonically the shift disrupts V⁶/f with IV⁶/F—an appropriate "retrogression" that supports the retrospective temporal aspect of this consolation. Indeed, the consolation does not last, since F minor returns for one final series of outbursts before subsiding into A♭ major for the closural return of the main theme.

Conclusion

The various means by which composers trope temporality stem from more than play with the ordering of sections in a form. There is an underlying dramatic "story" that is enriched by a nonlinear "discourse" (the terms are from Chatman 1978), as temporal perspectives are mixed and fuse into richer expressive mean-

Example 4.7. Schubert, Piano Sonata in C Minor, D. 958, second movement (*Adagio*)
  a. mm. 18–28
  b. mm. 70–78

ings. A similar strategy is found in the novel *Dungeon,* by Svetlana Velmar-Janković (2002 [1990]), which thematizes even the linguistic elements involved in its compression and juxtaposition of temporalities, with a corresponding enrichment of the expressive meaning of events that may be separated by decades in time.[9] The following passage illustrates the effect, as the narrator poignantly recalls and reimagines her few encounters with the painter of a precious work about to be "requisitioned" for the people, in the shift from Nazi occupation to Communist rule in Yugoslavia:

> No, they could not take that from me, what I was carrying out of Professor Pavlović's former study, that glow taken from the small Sumanović canvas, thrust into my inner being; nor could they take that young Sumanović of 1928, visible only to me, who was waiting for me in the hall, to encourage me. Nor the older one, of 1939, restored after wearing himself out utterly, after the illness which had threatened to destroy him. Nor the non-existent, but nevertheless standing one of 1943, in his white shirt and black waistcoat: he was waiting for me in the part of the flat designated for me to live in, with the children. I did not realise in that *now* that, with the major and the caretaker and *our* Zora behind me and the children beside me, stepping out of Professor Pavlović's former study into the hall, that confused November day in 1944, I was stepping into a crossroads in time, swept clean, in which the distance between little cubes of time that represented epochs was quite immaterial, as was the remoteness of points of time which are usually called years. No, in that hallway, at that crossroads, moments crossed freely, conditioned only by the meaning of their own contents. (2002: 48)

This remarkable passage recounts the intensity of a crisis that provokes the troping of temporality with a shift to pure associationism, a traumatic yet highly significant transition. It is states such as this that Schoenberg and Berg achieve in their hypercharged atonal masterpieces, when the ordered backgrounds of tonal temporality give way to an association based on the contextual times of motives, in the ultimate troping of temporality.

Notes

1. This is not a new distinction, but I will be drawing the boundary somewhat differently from previous work on temporality based on Henri Bergson's distinction between measured and experienced time (see two important surveys by Lewis Rowell [1985; 1996]). Briefly I will be examining the stylistically coded aspects of a play with temporality as "built into" the musical work—hence "measurable" in its boundaries but not as quantitative in its perception.

2. This forthcoming work is based on a paper I presented at the Seventh International Congress on Musical Signification organized by Eero Tarasti in Imatra, Finland, 2001.

3. Obviously a theory of musical meaning is also needed to properly interpret the widely varying expressive effects of such tropes that cross-reference function and location. For such a theory, as well as a more extensive exposition of the concept of musical troping, see Hatten 1994.

4. For topics, see Ratner 1980.

5. The pastiches suggest, in my estimation, toccata, prelude-toccata, and invention-toccata (the latter themselves tropological hybrids). See also Hatten 1994: 199–201.

6. For more on the style type of an "arrival 6/3," see Hatten 2004: 26–28.

7. The *Adagio espressivo* interruption in the first movement of Beethoven's Piano Sonata in E, Op. 109, is a complex example analyzed in Hatten 2004: 169–75.

8. Surprisingly this is also the auxiliary cadence type that Beethoven uses after the interruption in measure 9 of the first movement of Op. 109. Here, applied diminished sevenths are used instead of applied dominants, and Beethoven justifies his interruptive harmonies by yoking them into a progression that leads directly into the key of the dominant for an implied second theme group.

9. I am grateful to Tatjana Marković for sending me a copy of this important novel from her homeland.

5   A Simple Model for Associative Musical Meaning

J. Peter Burkholder

> This whole problem can be stated quite simply by asking, "Is there a meaning to music?" My answer to that would be, "Yes." And "Can you state in so many words what the meaning is?" My answer to that would be, "No." Therein lies the difficulty.
>
> Aaron Copland, *What to Listen for in Music*

For years, the meaning of music was a topic that musical scholars were reluctant to discuss, because it seemed intractable. People obviously find music meaningful. But the meanings people attribute to music often seem idiosyncratic, depending as much on the person as on the music. To a cautious scholar, this makes finding an objective truth about the meaning of a piece or passage of music seem impossible. In addition to the difficulty of deciding what meanings are conveyed, the mechanism by which music conveys meanings has seemed obscure.

In recent years, however, there has been new interest in the question of musical meaning, and it has become one of the hottest topics in music scholarship.[1] Approaches have drawn on philosophy, music theory, musicology, and cultural history, as well as trends in literary criticism such as semiotics, intertextuality, influence studies, deconstruction, and postmodernism. This discussion has brought new and valuable insights, but it has not yet resulted in a clear description of the mechanism by which music conveys meanings.

This chapter proposes a model for one significant contributing element to musical meaning—the principle of association. Using this principle as a foundation, the model is designed to work within certain constraints: (1) the model must be simple; (2) it must be broadly applicable to a significant proportion of musical phenomena; and (3) it must be congruent with existing theories of associative musical meaning. In what follows I first introduce the model and show how it can work in a series of examples. I then discuss its relation to other approaches to musical meaning and address some ramifications of the model.

Language and Music

Many approaches to meaning in music use the metaphor of language.[2] Like language, music involves sound and unfolds in time. In most musical systems, there is something parallel to grammar and syntax in language, in that segments of the music play certain roles and normally take particular positions; for example, one segment provides a good conclusion but sounds out of place as a beginning, while another does the reverse.[3] Several aspects of musical meaning can be understood primarily in syntactic terms, such as the feeling of closure produced by a cadence, the completion of a formal design, or the final descent of an Urlinie to the tonic, or the way the evasion of such closure can evoke feelings of frustration, delay, or desire.[4] But the comparison to language has always foundered on the ability of words to name or mean something specific, the process called denotation, and the lack of such specificity in music.

Despite this problem, language is the right metaphor in my view. Music is widely understood as a form of communication. Nicholas Cook's comparison of music to material artifacts in his recent article, "Theorizing Musical Meaning," is a helpful way to discuss meaning if one accepts his firm statement that "music is not language, at least in more than a partial and analogic sense" (2001: 177–78).[5] But the analogy to language can be rescued and the discussion of musical meaning placed on a firm foundation if we can find a good analogue to denotation in language. I believe we can: there is a mechanism that we intuitively follow, in which music denotes something in particular, which carries connotations, which in turn lead to interpretations, in a pattern similar to the way in which we understand fiction, poetry, drama, or other linguistic artworks. I do not apply the terms "denotation" and "connotation" to musical meaning in their strictest sense, but only insofar as they convey the analogous impression that associations emerge with greater or lesser degrees of probability, variability, and consistency.

Let me begin by noting what I do not mean to say. It has often been asserted that music is the universal language. This suggests that anyone can listen to a piece of music and understand it in the same way as everyone else. The concept comes from the eighteenth and nineteenth centuries, when musicians often traveled throughout Europe and the Americas and had developed an international idiom in music that was recognized across boundaries of nation and language.[6] But this does not mean that a musician could waltz into a court in Japan or Java, where European music was unfamiliar, and immediately be understood. The Japanese, the Javanese, the Chinese, and other peoples had their own music, which was as foreign to Europeans as European music was to them.

To say that music has meaning is incomplete. Any statement that a piece or passage of music means something is actually a claim that it carries that meaning for someone in particular or to members of a certain group.[7] If music is like language, a listener must be knowledgeable in a particular musical language in order to understand it. One has to learn it—either by growing up with it or by learning it as an adult, as one might study a foreign language. Indeed, the central feature of associative meaning in particular is this: *Meaning in music depends upon familiarity.*

Musical meaning is too broad a subject for any one model to encompass: music conveys meaning in many ways. Some of these ways are more perceptually immediate than association. The shocking quality of a loud sound, while potentially evoking similar antecedents, is essentially independent of association. Others are more heavily weighted with an evaluative component. Narrative meaning, for example, requires at least an awareness of semantic oppositions and a tracking of their interactions through a relevant time span. Another typology at least partly partakes of associative principles while remaining at some level distinct; the correlation of musical processes with formal or conventional paradigms, for example, would not be possible without a prior recognition that such paradigms are being invoked. For the sake of simplicity and clarity, I focus in this chapter only on those mechanisms of meaning that to some degree rely on association.

A simple associative model is desirable for several reasons. First, it allows issues of musical meaning to be discussed in a relatively jargon-free manner, rendering it accessible to nonspecialists. Second, for the so-called naïve listener, it provides an accessible way of talking about meaning, of organizing one's impressions, that allows for the possibility of dialogue and shared consensus. Finally, for the music scholar, it indicates that associative principles have a greater reach than that typically ascribed to them.

The Associative Model

When we listen to music, something like the following happens:

1. We recognize and focus on what is *familiar* in the music. This can be any element: the sound of an instrument, a melody or melodic gesture, a rhythmic pattern, a chord, the form, the genre, or any other characteristic. We will likely recognize as familiar a great number of elements in the music.

2. For each element we recognize, we carry certain associations with it, based on other occasions when we encountered it. There are two levels of association. The primary level of association is that we relate this musical element with other music we have heard that uses the same element—a specific passage in the same piece or in a different piece; a broad category of pieces in which the element appears; or a form, genre, or other conceptual paradigm related to music. Hearing a sitar is likely to remind us of other times when we heard a sitar; hearing a fugue begin will remind us of other fugues; hearing a major triad will remind us of other major triads. As we gain experience, we are likely to recognize the instrument as a sitar, the texture as a fugue, and the chord as a major triad *without* necessarily being reminded of any one of hundreds of earlier experiences with that timbre or texture or chord. At an even simpler level, when an event is recognized as belonging to a particular category of reality, an analogy can be drawn to the denotative meaning of a word in language: the sound of a sitar *exemplifies* "sitar" and thus "sitar music." But this is really shorthand for saying that the sound of a sitar reminds us of our previous experiences with sitar music. These associations vary with the listener, depending on his or her familiarity with other music.

3. The secondary level of association casts a wider net than the first. Once we have been reminded of other music or of some musical concept, these associations themselves are likely to carry other associations. For example, a fugue may remind us of fugues by Bach and Handel—the first level of association—and thus of things we associate with Bach and Handel fugues: the circumstances in which they are performed, for example, such as church services or concerts of *Messiah,* and thus of Christian religion; or perhaps we are reminded of the rigor and learning required to compose them, or how complex and difficult they are to perform or follow as a listener. Again, these associations will vary with the listener, but certain associations may be widely shared within a community of listeners. The number of associations evoked is potentially infinite. For a coherent meaning to emerge, the listener will probably select a smaller subset of these associations as significant in the given context. Though the other associations are not ignored, they are filtered out as the listener's perception proceeds to interpretation.

4. Having recognized that which is familiar, and having experienced these two levels of association, the listener then observes how those familiar elements are manipulated or are juxtaposed with new elements in order to say something new. The meaning of the music depends *both* on what is familiar in the music, along with the associations the listener carries with those elements, *and* on how those familiar elements are reworked to create something different. So here the listener notices what is new, how the familiar element is changed in some way or is placed in a new context. Listening to an entire piece entails following the path through the music, encompassing both the familiar and the deviations from it, the novel twists and turns.

5. Finally, the listener interprets all this information, including the associations aroused and the changes or new elements that are introduced. This step encompasses an extremely wide range of cognitive activities and strategies which are outside the primary focus of this chapter. I include this final step here to complete the model, with the understanding that a coherent theoretical or analytical apparatus is required to examine a listener's interpretation of music. Certainly the analyst needs to consider the extent to which the resultant interpretation is either widely shared or is personal or idiosyncratic.

In sum, the listener's sense of what the music means is created through a process of five steps:

1. *Recognizing familiar elements.*
2. *Recalling other music or schema that make use of those elements.*
3. *Perceiving the associations that follow from the primary associations.*
4. *Noticing what is new and how familiar elements are changed.*
5. *Interpreting what all this means.*

These steps are arranged here in logical order, but they may not happen in this sequence as we listen. Steps 1 and 4 are likely to occur simultaneously or nearly so (or, in unfamiliar music, even in opposite order), and the others will follow close in time. These five steps are intended only as a model for how we derive associative meaning from music as we listen, but they also work as an analytical methodology (conceived as a slowed-down listening) and as a way to remember the experience of hearing a piece of music as we become aware of new resemblances, associations, and interpretations. So the steps may occur virtually instantaneously or may follow over a long period. In this, our experience of meaning in music does not differ from our discernment of meaning in literary or visual arts or other life experiences.

It is important to note that this model will not do our interpretive work for us. Rather, my intention in presenting this approach is to break down our consideration of associative meaning into a series of logical, contained steps that will focus our interpretations and clarify the bases upon which we may agree or disagree. Indeed, this may be the most important contribution of this model. You and I may derive different meanings from a piece because we recognize different things in it, hear resemblances to different music, have different associations with that music, notice different changes to the familiar element, or interpret all this information differently, or any combination of these. But conceiving of meaning through this model will at least help us to argue on the same level and will give us concrete issues to argue about at each step, similar to the way we might argue about the meaning of a poem or a story.

Applying the Model

Some examples will demonstrate how this model of associative meaning works. Remember that what we recognize can be any element of the music, anything we are familiar with, and that the meaning conveyed depends partly on the associations we make with the music. For the sake of clarity, the following examples draw on a familiar type of melody (Step 1) with strong and widely shared associations outside music (Step 3); musical material whose associations are less clear would, of course, provoke more dissension about what the meanings of the music might be, but the model would work in the same way. Each example reveals a different way in which music evokes primary associations (Step 2) and explores how this affects the meanings it carries. The examples include reference to other music through performance, quotation, stylistic allusion, topic, and timbre; allusion to a specific piece; reference to generic and formal conventions; reference internal to a piece; and reference to musical syntax. This list is not intended to be exhaustive but rather an illustration of the many ways in which music reminds us of other music.

The pieces examined here include a programmatic work, a texted one, a piece with an evocative title but no ostensible program, a sonata movement with strong topical references, and a sonata with few if any such references. Although not every possible kind of meaning can be considered here, this range of examples should demonstrate that the associative model can accommodate a wide array of meanings, from specific to general, and from avowedly extra-musical to formal, structural, or syntactic.

Arbitrary Encoding

Among the most familiar and widely recognized types of music whose associations are beyond dispute are military calls.[8] These are short melodies that have particular functions within military life. Military calls go back centuries in Europe as well as in America, but the ones probably most familiar to Americans are the bugle calls used in the American military since the nineteenth century. Each call signals a specific message to the troops. Three of the most familiar are shown in example 5.1: *Assembly,* the signal for the company to get into formation; *Reveille,* played early in the morning as the troops fall into formation about twenty minutes after the first wake-up call; and *Taps,* the last bugle call of the day, played when lights are extinguished. *Taps* is also played during military funerals, often when the body is interred, or in memory of the dead, for example, at Memorial Day observances.[9]

All three calls use the same four notes, the third through sixth partials of the harmonic series ($\hat{5}$–$\hat{1}$–$\hat{3}$–$\hat{5}$), because the bugle, like older European trumpets and horns, has no valves and thus can only play notes from the harmonic series. Like most military calls, these share a contour of starting at or near the bottom of the range, rising to the peak through a series of up-and-down motions, and falling back to close on the tonic.

The meanings of individual military calls are almost entirely arbitrary, beyond an observation that *Reveille* and *Assembly* are relatively fast, as befits music intended to induce action, and *Taps* is slow, appropriate to rest and the end of day. Such arbitrarily assigned meanings are in themselves a type of meaning, although they are too specialized to serve as a model for how music conveys meaning in general. Further, military calls are a very specialized instance of associative devices, given their degree of semantic encoding. But they have the advantage of pedagogical clarity and offer a familiar kind of music whose extra-musical associations are widely agreed upon, so that references to specific calls, and to the style of military calls in general, offer a good but still relatively simple test of how the five steps of the model work. The following examples use our familiarity with military calls in various ways.

Performance

Let us first consider a performance of *Taps.* In Step 1 we recognize the music. In Step 2 the music arouses memories of earlier performances of it. In Step 3 memories associated with those earlier occasions come to mind, such as time for lights out (if we were in the army) or a military funeral or a memorial service, memories which then suggest emotional associations. In Step 4, what is new is not the tune but the performance, including the new situation in which we hear it. Fi-

Example 5.1. American military bugle calls
 a. Assembly
 b. Reveille
 c. Taps

nally, in Step 5 we interpret its meanings—a signal of the end of day? a remembrance of the dead?—based on the circumstances, and the emotions these memories evoke will vary with the context of the recollection and one's state of mind at the time.

One reason audiences like to hear music they have heard before is that it is more meaningful to them than unfamiliar music; this is as true of audiences for rock concerts and radio shows as it is of audiences for symphonies and operas. Performance of a piece that is already familiar, and therefore meaningful, to us is the most obvious way in which music conveys meaning, but it is ignored in most theories of meaning, which focus, instead, on how we understand music the first time we hear it. We do not hear music in a vacuum; we hear it having heard music all our lives, and that lifelong experience with music forms the very basis on which we understand music. From this bedrock case of recognizing an entire piece in a new performance context, we can move on to hearing new pieces.

Quotation

Some music uses our familiarity with a certain tune to convey specific meanings. For example, in his orchestral tone poem, *Decoration Day,* Charles Ives depicts the events of that holiday, which, in the late nineteenth and early twentieth centuries, was a day set aside to decorate the graves of soldiers who had died in the Civil War; after World War I, this holiday became Memorial Day, in memory of Americans who had died in every war. At one point in the piece is a scene at the town cemetery, and *Taps* is played by a trumpet, "Off-stage, or muted (as in the distance)," over quiet tremolos in the strings and bells tolling very softly, as shown in example 5.2.

Here Steps 1 and 2 in the model are easy: we recognize both the melody and the sound of the trumpet, and so we associate this moment in the piece with previous occasions when we heard a trumpet or bugle play *Taps.* In Step 3 we know that *Taps* is played at military funerals and memorial services, so it brings with it those associations, especially when we know from the title that the piece is about a celebration to honor dead soldiers. In Step 4, since the familiar tune is played complete and unchanged, what is new is the context: the tremolo strings, the bells, and the framework of a programmatic piece for orchestra. Also, hidden in the upper strings are the opening notes of a hymn tune, *Nearer, My God, to Thee* (A♯–G♯–F♯–F♯–D♯–D♯), played three times; this of course carries its own associations, since it is a hymn often sung at funerals.

Given the information we obtain from Ives's music and the associations it arouses, one interpretation in Step 5 is that the trumpet presents a natural-sounding representation of the way *Taps* might sound played outdoors, while the surrounding context adds depth to the picture, with the bells suggesting the tolling of church bells, the quiet orchestra representing the solemn people gathered at the ceremony, the tremolo in the strings suggesting their quivering emotions, and the hymn tune *Nearer, My God, to Thee* evoking their thoughts of those who lie buried around them.

Stylistic Allusion

What is familiar may be a general melodic shape or style, rather than an actual melody. Many pieces use the general shape of military calls, without quoting a particular tune and without using the timbre of the trumpet or bugle.

For example, George M. Cohan's song *Over There* uses a bugle call figure at the beginning of the refrain. This was a hit song of 1917, written in the first flush of

Example 5.2. Ives, *Decoration Day*, mm. 74–78. Used by permission of Peermusic.

excitement when the United States entered World War I. It was also a recruiting song, designed to mobilize men to volunteer. The verse has these words:

> Johnnie get your gun, get your gun, get your gun,
> Take it on the run, on the run, on the run;
> Hear them calling you and me,
> Ev'ry son of Liberty.
> Hurry right away, no delay, go today,
> Make your daddy glad to have had such a lad,
> Tell your sweetheart not to pine,
> To be glad her boy's in line.

The first half of the refrain appears in example 5.3, and its opening phrase repeats to begin the second half. How does this music fit our model?

Step 1: We hear a familiar melodic shape ($\hat{3}$–$\hat{5}$–$\hat{1}$) and a familiar rhythm (short-short-long), both repeated several times.

Step 2: We associate the melodic shape with military calls we have heard—perhaps not with any particular call but with military calls as a type. Of the three in example 5.1, the short-short-long rhythm most closely resembles that of *Taps*, while the multiple repetitions of these notes ($\hat{3}$–$\hat{5}$–$\hat{1}$) is most like *Reveille*.[10] We may not notice these similarities consciously.

Step 3: Military calls carry strong associations with the military, public ceremonies, and duty to one's country. *Taps* carries its own rather solemn connotations, and *Reveille* connotations of arousal and activity.

Step 4: What is new? First, it is a song, and the military call is being sung, not played on a bugle, as if the singer is speaking for the military or the nation it serves. Second, by not following a particular bugle call, Cohan invokes all military calls and thus military life in general. If we hear a rhythmic resemblance to *Taps*, we will also hear that this is much faster and that the melodic contour is quite different, changing the opening $\hat{5}$–$\hat{5}$–$\hat{1}$, $\hat{5}$–$\hat{1}$–$\hat{3}$ motion to a $\hat{3}$–$\hat{5}$–$\hat{1}$ motive that repeats again and again like *Reveille*.

Step 5: What is our interpretation? The text is another obvious source of meaning that must be consulted, and this will influence the interpretation. We hear a call to arms; the text is strongly reinforced by the music, whose military character is unmistakable. Combining the solemnity of *Taps* with the rousing call to action of *Reveille* is exactly the right touch. This will entail sacrifice, leaving your family and sweetheart, but you *must* go. The melody is even more effective than the words at conveying this meaning.

Topic and Timbre

Besides an actual bugle call like *Taps* or a melody resembling a military call as in *Over There*, we may recognize a combination of elements familiar from military calls. For example, Copland's *Fanfare for the Common Man* uses the sound of trumpets and large intervals of the fourth and fifth, both associated with military

Example 5.3. Cohan, *Over There*, first half of chorus, mm. 40–60

calls, plus drums, linked to military music through drum signals, marches, and fanfares. Fanfares are like military calls, especially in using trumpets or other brass
playing notes from the harmonic series, but can be used in a wider range of situations, including military or state ceremonies. Like most bugle calls, Copland's
melody, shown in example 5.4, begins with a rising gesture, arpeggiates up and
down, and falls at the end to the tonic.

How does this fit the model? In Step 1 we recognize the drums, the trumpets,
and the wide intervals, particularly the rising gesture at the beginning and the falling gestures later on. All these are familiar from military calls and fanfares, so we
are reminded of these types of music (Step 2). At the same time, we recognize a
slow pace; the music keeps stopping, lingering on a note. This reminds us of other
slow, stately music.

In Step 3 military calls are associated with the military, with public ceremonies,
and with duty to flag and country. Fanfares add the connotation of their original

Example 5.4. Copland, *Fanfare for the Common Man*, mm. 1–12. © Copyright 1957 by the Aaron Copland Fund for Music, Inc. Copyright Renewed. Boosey & Hawkes, Inc., Sole Publisher & Licensee. Reprinted by permission.

uses in Europe, in connection with royalty and the aristocracy, creating associations with dignity and nobility.[11] These are reinforced by the slow, stately character of the music, which is associated with ceremonies and processions. The composer recognized these associations; he said about this work that he sought to achieve "a certain nobility of tone, which suggested slow rather than fast music."[12]

Having made these associations, we begin to notice what is new and individual about this fanfare (Step 4). Interestingly, this piece avoids doing much that is stereotypical of military calls. It has all or most of the elements, but unlike *Decoration Day* it does not exactly follow any particular call, and unlike *Over There* it tends to avoid standard bugle patterns, which fall within a particular overtone series. It emphasizes fourths and fifths, gives us full triads, and uses a major sixth, as in *Taps* or *Reveille*, but its repertoire of notes is much wider than a bugle call can be. The range of almost two octaves is too large. Nor does it stay with any one collection of notes that a bugle could play; instead, it alternates notes from the harmonic series on B♭ with that on E♭, juxtaposing the two triads as in measures 9–11.

Presented with these obvious associations and with this new way of treating the elements of a military call or fanfare, the listener then interprets what he or she is hearing (Step 5). Instead of a melody consisting of the notes of a particular harmonic series, we hear notes from two different ones that share a common tone. Instead of four pitches within a single octave, we have nine pitches spread out over almost two octaves. In short, we have what sounds like the raw material for bugle calls, rather than a bugle call itself. We could take this material and put it all into one bugle call, by transposing and rearranging it, but for now it is much more diverse. What can this *mean*?

Here, looking at the title and background of the piece helps us to interpret it. During World War II, in the 1942–43 season, the Cincinnati Symphony Orchestra commissioned several composers to write fanfares for brass and percussion related to the war effort, so that the symphony could start each concert that season with a different fanfare. Other composers wrote *A Fanfare for the Fighting French* (Walter Piston), *A Fanfare for Paratroopers* (Paul Creston), *Fanfare for the Signal Corps* (Howard Hanson), or *Fanfare for the Merchant Marine* (Eugene Goossens).[13] Copland decided that "if the fighting French got a fanfare, so should the common man, since, after all, it was he who was doing the dirty work in the war."[14] In settling on the title *Fanfare for the Common Man*, Copland was inspired by a nationally broadcast and widely reprinted speech in which Vice President Henry Wallace declared that "the century on which we are entering—the century which will come out of this war—can and must be the century of the common man. Perhaps it will be America's opportunity to suggest the freedoms and duties by which the common man must live."[15]

How does this music represent the common man? As noted above, we have the raw material for a military call, rather than a military call itself. This melody spans a wider range than any bugle call and includes a more diverse collection of notes, but each individual gesture could be transposed and transformed into part of a bugle call. This is like the diversity we see among people. A common purpose like the war brings people of diverse backgrounds together, and the military services were famous for molding people from varying social classes and ethnic groups into a unit. If a bugle call has associations with the military, with civic life, and with duty to one's country, then the raw material for a bugle call is like the raw material for the military—that is, the common man. At the same time, once this association is made, the dignity and nobility of the music suggest that the common man has dignity and nobility, that these qualities are present not just in leaders or in soldiers but already in the common people who come forward to do their duty in a time of crisis. This is true whether one interprets Copland's phrase "the common man" to mean males only, since they were the ones going into combat, or—as I prefer—to read "man" here in the sense of humanity as a whole, both men and women.

Note that the previous interpretation would only be possible for one who was familiar to some extent with the historic context in which the Copland work was commissioned, composed, and received. Specialized knowledge engenders associations that are not accessible to all listeners. Such differences point out that associative meaning depends not only on familiarity and context but also on what the listener *knows*. There can be great differences between meanings apprehended by the naïve listener and by the music specialist without either being rendered invalid (although their varying degrees of relevance to particular communicative contexts cannot be ignored).

Allusion to a Specific Piece

Another level of meaning can be found in this work, for it is reminiscent of the famous opening music of Richard Strauss's tone poem *Also sprach Zarathustra*. Both Copland and Strauss begin with rising figures in trumpets, in open fifths and fourths, punctuated with loud drums. No other passage in the orchestral repertoire so nearly resembles the opening of Copland's *Fanfare for the Common Man*, and the resemblance is especially close considering that in both cases it is the very opening of the work. So we can apply our model to the meanings evoked by *Fanfare for the Common Man* for a listener who is reminded of the opening of *Also sprach Zarathustra*.[16]

Example 5.5 shows the opening of Strauss's *Also sprach Zarathustra*. Notice the similarities to Copland's fanfare: the rising figure in the trumpet (mm. 5–6, 9–10, 13–14), comprising a fifth and a fourth (the same open intervals but in opposite order), and punctuated with timpani loudly and repeatedly playing the interval of a fourth (here melodic instead of harmonic). But also notice something different: these rising motives do not have the diversity of Copland's music. We hear the same rising figure three times in a row, all on the same chord, the tonic chord. Later the trombones arpeggiate the tonic chord downward (m. 17). There are changes of chord in the orchestra as a whole (from major to minor and back, and a move to the subdominant before the final cadence), but every time we hear a trumpet or other brass instrument arpeggiating a chord, it is on the tonic. This passage is a powerful affirmation of the tonic chord. And at the end of the opening section, after the orchestra cuts away, an organ continues to sound, giving the music a religious cast.

Is Copland invoking this piece? Or, rather, what meanings might a listener construct if he or she noticed this resemblance? Here we can use our model. We have already taken Steps 1 and 2: we recognize these rising trumpet figures, fifths and fourths, and long, loud, and dramatic drumming in Copland's fanfare, and they remind us of this opening passage of Strauss's *Also sprach Zarathustra*. In Step 3, what associations does this other piece have? Strauss himself said that there was a program of sorts, an attempt to express a certain set of ideas:

> I did not intend to write philosophical music or portray Nietzsche's great work musically. I meant rather to convey in music an idea of the evolution of the human race from its origin, through the various phases of development, religious as well as scientific, up to Nietzsche's idea of the *Übermensch*. The whole symphonic poem is intended as my homage to the genius of Nietzsche, which found its greatest exemplification in his book *Also sprach Zarathustra*.[17]

Nietzsche envisioned a new society led by a superior kind of man, which he called a "superman," whose "will to power" would set him above the general herd of humanity. These ideas were later used by the Nazis as a justification for their doctrines of racial and national superiority, although most scholars agree this was a perversion of Nietzsche's ideas.[18] More specifically, his book *Also sprach Zarathustra* opens

Example 5.5. Richard Strauss, *Also sprach Zarathustra*, mm. 1–21
Continued on the next page

with Zarathustra, after ten years of solitude in a mountain cave, speaking to the
rising sun and telling it, in words Strauss quotes in the score, that he has gathered
much wisdom and, needing "hands outstretched to take it," will descend to share
it with humankind, as the sun goes down in the evenings to light the netherworld
(Nietzsche 1958: 3). Zarathustra is a model of the superman, and the opening
passage of Strauss's piece depicts the sunrise and, by implication, Zarathustra's
wisdom.

If these are the associations this piece carries, what can Copland possibly mean
by invoking them? To answer that, we must move on to Step 4: noticing what is new
in Copland's piece. We have already noted some of what is different in Copland's
fanfare. In Strauss's piece, all the trumpet calls and brass arpeggiations project the
tonic chord, and so do the drums, the powerful timpani. But in Copland's piece we

Example 5.5. Richard Strauss, *Also sprach Zarathustra*, mm. 1–21
Continued on the next page

have diversity, a variety of material that could be molded into a military call but has not been. Even the timpani, instead of affirming the tonic by going back and forth between tonic and dominant, play both at once, so both are affirmed equally (see example 5.4). And there is no orchestra, with its attendant grandiosity, and no organ, with its religious connotations.

How do we interpret this (Step 5)? One way is to see Copland's invocation of Strauss's music as an anti-Nietzsche statement, and thus, in the context of World War II, as an anti-Nazi statement. During the war, Nietzsche was actively portrayed in British and American propaganda as a Nazi philosopher, so the identification is a logical one.[19] In *Also sprach Zarathustra*, there is a celebration of the One—the tonic chord. It reaches a grandiose apotheosis, representing the sunrise but also the superman, in the person of Zarathustra, the one whose wisdom will enlighten the lesser humans. In *Fanfare for the Common Man*, by contrast, there is no such uni-

A Simple Model for Associative Musical Meaning 91

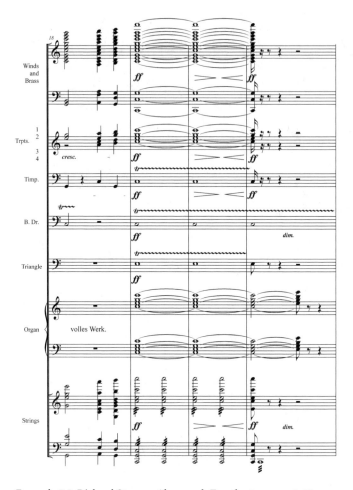

Example 5.5. Richard Strauss, *Also sprach Zarathustra*, mm. 1–21

formity. Instead of a superman, there is "the common man," in his diversity, even his unruliness and unpredictability. Copland ennobles the elements of the fanfare, the raw material of humankind, rather than one primary chord, and he avoids the quasi-religious aspect Strauss introduces with the organ. Against Nietzsche's hero who will lead inferior humankind, Copland asserts the heroism of everyone.

Did Copland intend this meaning? We know that he meant this piece to be an anti-Nazi statement, a celebration of the common man, because it was written in that spirit during World War II; we feel in the music the ennobling of common raw material; and this interpretation gives us an avenue for understanding how Copland achieves this. But I may be overreaching. Perhaps, despite the strong resemblance between the two passages, Copland was not thinking of the opening of *Also sprach Zarathustra* when he wrote his fanfare but only of the generalized repertoire of the trumpet call and drum gestures that Strauss had also drawn on. As a historian, I may wish to be cautious about making the claim that this was Copland's conscious intent. But as a listener, once I make the connection between these two pieces and think through this interpretation, *it has this meaning for me.* I will have more to say about such personal meanings at the end of this chapter.

Interaction with Generic and Formal Conventions

So far we have examined pieces with a text, program, or descriptive title. But what about absolute music? Here our method will not discover a program or message where there is none to be found but instead will lead us to the meanings that may reside in the interaction of musical material with the conventions of genre and form.

Mozart's last piano sonata, K. 576 in D major, begins with a figure that resembles a military call or perhaps a hunting call, as shown in example 5.6. I shall call it a "fanfare," the term Leonard G. Ratner (1980: 18–19, 27–28) uses for military and hunt figures in his discussion of topics in Classic-era music, which I will use here as a guide to interpreting this piece.[20] We recognize the fanfare and follow the associations it brings, of dynamic action in the outdoors. It is answered by an embellished, galant figure that represents an entirely different world: indoors, elegant, refined, perhaps a bow or curtsy rather than a call to action.[21] This juxtaposition introduces the first new element (Step 4), and we may interpret it to suppose that a juxtaposition of opposites, and perhaps of social realms, is occurring and may be a significant issue in the piece.

The fanfare returns, transformed to arpeggiate a minor triad and constitute a harmonic sequence with the opening material (mm. 5–6). No natural trumpet or hunting horn can play a minor triad like this, but the reference is still clear. Here what is new is that the fanfare is being brought into the key system and bent to serve the needs of the harmonic progression. It is answered by a new figure, still galant but representing what Ratner calls brilliant style, with rapid sixteenth-note motion emphasizing accented neighbor tones.

Next the whole first period repeats, with changes. The original melody, alternating fanfare and galant figures, now appears as the bass line in two-voice counterpoint (mm. 9–15). The upper line suggests imitation by answering the fanfare both times with a similar triadic figure, followed by sixteenth-note descending scales in brilliant style. Just before the cadence (m. 15), the arpeggiation of the fanfare is transferred to the sixteenth-note figuration, thus integrating fanfare and brilliant styles in a single gesture, as they have already been joined in succession.[22] As the transition to the dominant key begins (m. 16), the fanfare has been domesticated and subordinated, turned into an arpeggiated accompaniment for a sixteenth-note figure above it. The opening fanfare is adopting a variety of new guises, so that our original interpretation, that opposites and social realms would be juxtaposed, turns

Example 5.6. Mozart, Piano Sonata in D Major, K. 576, mm. 1–17

out to be only partially true: instead of juxtaposition, we are hearing flexibility and change, as the fanfare is integrated into its surroundings.

After the new key is reached, but before the contrasting theme appears, a motive consisting of the fanfare followed by the sixteenth-note descending scales is treated in exact canon at the octave an eighth note apart, in a I–ii–V–I progression confirming the new key, as shown in example 5.7. The imitation invokes the learned style and perhaps, given the 6/8 meter, the imitative gigue.[23] The combination of the fanfare with the brilliant style, harmonic progression, learned canon, and dance shows a mixing of elements that were formerly separate. Our outdoor music is being turned to indoor music making in a variety of styles, as if a huntsman or military man were demonstrating his social graces, including conversation, brilliance,

Example 5.7. Mozart, Piano Sonata in D Major, K. 576, mm. 27–34

Example 5.8. Mozart, Piano Sonata in D Major, K. 576, mm. 56–58

deference to others, intellect, and dancing ability. The arpeggiated figure in the closing tag of the exposition in example 5.8 shows the complete domestication of the opening fanfare, no longer moving but now fixed in place, and no longer reminiscent of the outdoors or of forceful action.

The combination of styles is witty, as is the transformation in character of the forceful fanfare into a deferential accompaniment or learned canon. No other Mozart piano sonata movement begins with a military or hunting call, although several begin with arpeggiated figures. Ultimately this movement is about making the fanfare at home in the elegant, domestic world of the sonata.[24] Our familiarity with the fanfare gesture makes it easy to follow the variations to which Mozart subjects it. Moreover, the fanfare motive helps us to follow the sonata form, for it appears at every major juncture except the second theme. All the formal and expressive elements in the music are made possible because we are familiar with the sonata as a genre and as a form, with military and hunting music, and with the other types referred to here; we know the associations each type carries; we notice what is new in their transformations and combinations; and we interpret what they might mean. If this music has a specific program or message, along the lines of my earlier interpretations of the Copland and Cohan, it escapes me. But the associative meanings the piece does carry are conveyed through the same series of steps.

Example 5.9. Berg, Piano Sonata, Op. 1, mm. 1–3. © 1926 by Schlesinger'sche Buch-u. Musikhdl. Reproduced by permission of Robert Lienau Musikverlag, Frankfurt/Main (Germany). All Rights Reserved.

Reference Internal to a Piece or to a Convention

Like this Mozart sonata, much music engages our attention by creating interesting melodies or other snippets of music and then doing interesting things with them. Here the invocation of the familiar can help us to focus on a musical idea, and then, as that idea repeats, is varied, and is placed in new contexts, we can follow the development of the music. This does not exclude associations with other music, but in some pieces these internal meanings may be more important than external references.

One simple but revealing example is the one-movement Piano Sonata, Op. 1, by Alban Berg.[25] This music is so chromatic and constantly changing that there is little familiar to hold on to. But the opening three-note figure, shown in example 5.9, is like a stylized fanfare; the dotted figuration echoes the rhythm heard in some military calls, and the rising fourth and tritone suggest—but vary—the characteristic rising fourth and fifth (or third) of fanfares. The opening phrase ends with a variant of this figure in the bass (m. 3). In between, falling thirds and chromatically sinking chords create a contrast in character as sharp as in Mozart's sonata (m. 1), and the initial dotted rhythm assumes a new melodic shape, embellishing a semitone descent (m. 2).

In what follows we often hear dotted rhythms, but we do not hear the fanfare-like motive for quite some time. Indeed, Berg uses it remarkably little, given its prominence as the opening motive.[26] When it appears, it signals the most important points of articulation in the form: the closing theme (mm. 49–55), which leads back to the repetition of the exposition; the repetition of the closing theme, now leading to the beginning of the development; the end of the development and beginning of the recapitulation (m. 110); the final climax (mm. 157–61); the recapitulation of the closing theme (mm. 167–75); and the final cadence (mm. 176–79). It works so well as a signal for formal junctures because it is so recognizable, and it is so recognizable because its fanfare-like contour makes it perhaps the most familiar gesture in the music. Also, by being played so prominently at the beginning it gains our attention.

This motive does not have a strong programmatic meaning in this piece, nor does the sonata as a whole. The work is essentially abstract, a play of musical sound. Yet by using a recognizable gesture like a fanfare—or a figure that evokes a fanfare—Berg gives us something familiar to pay attention to, which helps us to follow the music.[27] This can create levels of meaning that arise from the web of interrelationships between musical ideas. In addition, part of the meaning of the Berg sonata lies in its exemplification of the norms of sonata form, a formal archetype the composer invokes with the label "sonata" and makes audible in part by using a fanfare-like motive as a cue. The resultant meanings call forth Berg's reverence for a classical past and his wish to participate in and renew an esteemed tradition in modernist terms.

Reference to Musical Syntax

Meanings related to musical syntax, mentioned briefly near the beginning of this chapter, can also be examined by using our model. A full account of such meanings would require a book-length study,[28] but a brief examination of our last two examples can suggest how the model would work, and how syntactic meanings interact with the semantic ones we have focused on.

In the case of the Mozart sonata, familiarity with the syntax of Classic-era music allows a listener to recognize opening and closing gestures and the relative strength of cadences and thus to understand how the elements relate to one another. The opening fanfare initiates the first phrase but is incomplete in itself: from our knowledge of other music in this style (Step 2), we know that the arpeggiation up to the dominant in measure 2 is a beginning rather than a closing gesture (Step 3); that after rising to the high dominant, fanfares typically fall to the tonic, which has not yet occurred (Step 4); and that therefore the phrase must continue (Step 5). The continuation in measures 3–4 is surprising in style but appropriate in syntax: it is a series of cadential gestures of increasing strength (Steps 2 and 3) and thus could not begin a phrase but serves well to end one. The juxtaposition of styles is all the more striking for the smoothness of the syntax. The phrase structure binds together these two disparate elements into a single unit, creating something new (Step 4). In short, they need each other; each is incomplete without the other, and the galant gesture absorbs the energy of the fanfare and brings it to a conclusion. Even before the fanfare starts to change its guise, it is being integrated into the musical world of the sonata (Step 5). The cadence on the dominant in measure 4, in turn, invites a consequent phrase that will return to the tonic, which can be analyzed in similar terms. Throughout, the semantic meanings of the topics are nested in the syntactic meanings of phrasing, harmony, and form, and the interaction between them creates more complex and interesting meanings than either alone.[29]

In the Berg sonata, our familiarity with tonal syntax is used in another way. There are only three V–I cadences in the entire movement, all on B minor: in measure 3, at the repetition of measure 3 as the exposition repeats, and at the end. The rest of the piece evades cadences and features few triads, floating most of the time in chromatic suspense. As Janet Schmalfeldt (1991: 104–105) notes in her analysis of the work, the tonal cadence in the opening phrase "promises an overall tonal design, and thus it calls our prior experience of tonal music into play; we are encouraged to expect tonal behaviour, and Berg consistently draws upon that expectation, while at the same time withholding its full realization." In other words, the meaning of the piece results from the invocation of the familiar syntax of common-practice tonal music (Steps 1 and 2), with all its associations related to closure, articulation, phrasing, and form (Step 3). Once these expectations are aroused, they are immediately evaded through chromatic and whole-tone harmonies (Step 4), until we come to a half-cadence on the dominant seventh chord just before the closing theme (mm. 45–46, 164) and then to the V–I cadences in the tonic. As Schmalfeldt (1991: 105) points out, the repetition of the tonic cadence serves to close the exposition, simultaneously evoking norms for the sonata (the exposition must close with a cadence) and evading them (the cadence must not be on the tonic). It is as if the basic contrast lies not between the tonic and a contrasting key, as in traditional sonata form, but between tonality as articulated in the opening phrase and the suspended tonality verging on atonality in most of the rest of the piece (Step 5).[30] Our familiarity with the routines of tonal music allows us to follow this process, in which we understand the meaning of the cadence and of the suspended tonality through the same five steps of the model we used earlier in interpreting a programmatic or texted piece.

The meanings we have explored in this sonata largely involve references within the piece and to earlier sonatas. There are other resonances, however, that implicate additional mechanisms of meaning. The very words we use to speak of syntactic elements, such as closure, completion, conclusion, or resolution, remind us of the metaphors with which we understand musical syntax, through analogy to our experiences outside music.

Results of the Model

We have seen music conveying meaning by (1) invoking something familiar, which (2) arouses associations in the listener with other music or concepts related to music, which then (3) may carry certain consequent associations; and then (4) the music we are listening to does something different and fresh, and (5) the combination of these associations with the new twists provokes us to interpret the music and thus derive meaning from it.[31] What is invoked can be anything, from a tune to a melodic type, a rhythm to an instrumental sound color, a genre to a style, a piece of music to an entire musical tradition.

The title of this chapter promised that it would suggest a simple model for associative musical meaning. The model proposed here is simple in that it involves relatively few steps and, perhaps more important, can be explained in terms a nonspecialist can understand.[32] By proposing a simple model, I do not claim that understanding musical meaning is simple. Quite the contrary: we are likely to recognize many familiar elements in each piece or performance, we may be reminded of many other pieces, each of which may carry several associations, and so on.[33]

But the model offers a way of talking about meaning that is concrete and clear-headed.

This approach can account for a wide variety of ways that music carries meaning, from the generally accepted to the idiosyncratic, and a broad range of musical elements that can convey meaning, from quotations to formal conventions. Moreover, it can be combined with numerous other approaches to meaning and can relate them to one another.

Fundamental to the model is reference to other music, or intertextuality in its broadest sense.[34] The model clearly builds on the work of Leonard Ratner (1980), Wendy Allanbrook (1983), V. Kofi Agawu (1991), Raymond Monelle (1992; 2000), and others who have studied the way music can convey meaning by referring to topics, defined as specific musical styles, genres, or dance rhythms associated with particular activities or classes of people. In the Cohan, Copland, Strauss, and Mozart, military calls or fanfares are used in just this way. Robert S. Hatten (1994) has extended the notion of topics to encompass what he calls "expressive genres" and has argued that the expressive aspects of music are as inherent in music as the structural ones; throughout his analyses, he relies on a listener's familiarity with other music in a way that conforms well to the model presented here. Agawu, Monelle, and Hatten approach musical meaning from a semiotic perspective, which is clearly relevant to the model.[35]

Similarly relevant to the model is the social construction of musical meaning through its associations, discussed by Theodor W. Adorno (1976), Peter J. Martin (1995), and others. Studies of music and politics in twentieth-century France by Jane F. Fulcher (1995; 1999a; 1999b) show how particular musical styles became associated not merely with topics, as in Ratner's approach, but with political factions. Such intensive examinations of the associations carried by musical styles in a particular place and time help us to discover the meanings listeners received, which may otherwise remain closed to us.

Reference to other music is also central to studies of musical borrowing, as in the Ives, and to recent attempts to apply to music the theory of influence of Harold Bloom (1973), from work by Jeremy Yudkin (1992) on Beethoven to that of Kevin Korsyn (1991) and Mark Evan Bonds (1996) on the nineteenth century and Joseph Straus (1990) and David Michael Hertz (1993) on the twentieth; the Copland may be seen as a "misreading," in Bloom's use of the term, of the Strauss.[36] Studies along these lines recognize that the acts of finding references and identifying associations—actions the analyst, or listener, takes, rather than something intrinsic in the music—are not enough to account for the meaning of a piece. One must also consider what is new, including how these musical elements are placed in new contexts, juxtaposed with one another or changed from our previous experience of them. The particular meanings of the examples explored here depend not only on their references to military calls and fanfares but also on what they do that departs from our expectations.

Another branch in the study of musical meaning focuses on the way that elements within the music relate to one another, suggesting that these internal relations create meaning by conveying or mimicking psychological effects. Peter Kivy

(1980) has proposed that certain musical shapes or types of motion represent emotion by their resemblance to the way humans move or speak when feeling or expressing a certain emotion; thus we might hear a rapid, angular melody as angry and a slow, drooping line as sad. Leonard Meyer (1973) and Eugene Narmour (1977) have argued that, within the common practice of the eighteenth and nineteenth centuries, the motion of a melody creates implications for where and how it will move next and where its final point of arrival will be; a composer can then play with our expectations, delaying the goal or swerving in new directions, and so evoke a certain psychological state. Similarly Susan McClary (1991) has shown how composers suggest sexual desire, resistance, and ultimate fulfillment by creating in the listener the desire for a particular goal, frustrating that desire, and finally granting its fulfillment. There are processes in music that resemble dramatic action, as Fred Maus (1988), among others, has pointed out. It is part of our normal discourse about music to speak of tension and resolution, building to a climax, dramatic surprises, and so on, and Eero Tarasti's (1994) book on musical semiotics tries to place this kind of talk about music on a firm foundation. Recently Arnie Cox (1999) has explored the cognitive and historical foundations for describing music in terms of motion and space, perhaps the most basic metaphors we use about music, which are fundamental to many discussions about meaning.

These approaches to meaning may seem to be free of references to other music and thus lie outside our model. But each depends on expectations we have for music based on our experience with a particular musical repertoire or tradition, and typically in these models it is the interplay between the conventional and the unexpected that creates meaning—that is, the interplay between the familiar and the new.[37] For example, Copland's comment that he sought to achieve "a certain nobility of tone, which suggested slow rather than fast music" can be related both to Kivy's idea that music represents emotion through its resemblance to the way humans move or speak when expressing emotions and to the model described here, in that the emotion expressed depends in part on invoking our previous experiences with music that was slow and associated with nobility. The very notion that music represents movement comes from our previous experiences with music. Similarly the approaches of Meyer, McClary, Maus, and Tarasti all depend on the evocation of musical conventions, and thus on our familiarity with other music.

Even musical gestures that seem to gain their meaning from direct imitation of emotional gestures, an idea central to Kivy's theory, find a place in our model. For example, the dramatic pauses in the middle of words and phrases at the opening of Ottavia's lament in the third act of Monteverdi's *L'incoronazione di Poppea* convey her grief by making it sound as if she cannot speak through her sobs. Such music conveys its meaning by playing against the expectation that singers will not breathe or pause in the middle of a phrase; we seek an explanation for the new element in the music (Step 4), find it in the dramatic situation, and hear the direct imitation of emotional speech.[38] When this technique became a convention, listeners already familiar with it could also understand its meaning through association with other music that used it.

The model proposed here can also encompass approaches that are entirely formal, focused on meanings created through internal relationships within the music, like those of Edward Hanslick (1986) or Wilson Coker (1972).[39] The same model applies: we become familiar with a musical element because of its use in the work we are listening to; if we hear a musical idea we have heard earlier in the same piece of music, we associate it with its earlier appearance; something may be new (at the very least, the fact that we are hearing this musical idea for a second or third or fourth time changes our perspective on it, relative to the first time we hear it); and we may interpret the combination of the familiar, the associations it brings, and the new context, and attribute meanings to it.

Reflections on the Model

This chapter has suggested that the problem of associative meaning in music can be solved by looking at the way music manipulates the familiar. Music conveys associative meaning by taking us through a series of steps parallel to but different from the way language has meaning. In closing, I will review those parallels and suggest some general ramifications of this model.

When someone says something to us, we hear familiar sounds that we recognize as words. These words have denotative meanings, but they also may carry additional connotations, associations that the words do not exactly denote. Paying attention to the words, their dictionary meanings, their connotations, and the way they are arranged, we interpret all of that as we try to figure out what has been said. Ultimately the meaning that is communicated depends on our own understanding of all these elements and on our own interpretation.

Meaning Depends on What the Listener Knows

Music follows a similar path. We recognize elements in the music, and these evoke associations with other music or concepts related to music. This parallels but of course differs from denotative meaning in language. When these associations are widely shared within a community of listeners, they are as objective and referential as denotation in language.[40] Just a few notes on the sitar can remind us of whole evenings of sitar music. But not everyone in the world has heard sitar music; just as in language, *meaning depends on what the listener knows*. We will not all recognize the same familiar elements, and the "other music" we are reminded of is likely to vary among listeners according to previous familiarity with the music and the musical traditions from which it springs. We cannot argue about the *intended* meaning of a piece of music until we know what other music its creators and intended audience knew and would have associated with it, just as we cannot know the meaning of a sentence or literary work until we know the language it is written in. This does not mean, of course, that the music is meaningless but rather that the meaning of the music is based on the listener's knowledge.

Music Acquires Meanings through Use

This other music or musical concept may then have associations outside music. *Music acquires associations, and thus meanings, through use.*[41] These associations can be as specific as denotation in language; for example, the military calls *Taps* and *Reveille* have specific meanings because of their use and function in military life. But most of the time this process of association is like connotation in language, as a musical element suggests something without denoting it exactly.

Motives that resemble military calls have become associated with the military, and hence with heroism and adventure. These undoubtedly are associations that led Alexander Courage to use horns and trumpets playing a fanfare-like motive, featuring successive rising fourths in a dotted motive, in his theme music for the *Star Trek* television series in 1966. Through this theme, and also through Stanley Kubrick's appropriation of *Also sprach Zarathustra* for the main title of *2001: A Space Odyssey* in 1968, the combination of trumpets and other brass playing large intervals, especially fourths and fifths, acquired a new association with space, exploited in the title music for all the subsequent *Star Trek* series (before the most recent, *Enterprise*) and in John Williams's score for *Star Wars* in 1977, which opens with a brass fanfare. But none of these reaches the level of denotation—except, of course, that this very familiar music now denotes *Star Trek* or *Star Wars* to those who know the connection. Once again, reconstructing the associations a composer might have intended to arouse requires studying how music in that time and place was used and the associations it had acquired.

We Find Meaningful That Music Which Is Familiar

We are not only interested in what a *composer* may have meant, of course; we also want to know what meanings others have found in this music, and especially what meanings we ourselves find in it. Like connotation in language, the associations music carries vary from public and widely shared meanings to personal ones. *Among the music we find most meaningful is that which is most familiar,* whether it is a widely shared and public familiarity, like *The Star-Spangled Banner* or Beethoven's Fifth Symphony, or a private one, such as the warm memories aroused for me by hearing the slow Bulgarian song *Polegnala E Todora*, often used for the last dance at the Friday-evening folk dances I attended almost every week in college. This model fully accounts for this kind of personal meaning, which is very important in most people's lives but is rarely addressed in theories of musical meaning.[42] But for composers, of course, the more useful connotations are those shared by a large number of people, like the associations aroused by the military call figures in the music examined here.

Meaning Depends on Context

The fourth step in the model is a critical one, since *the meaning of a reference to other music depends on its context* and on how it is changed within that new context. For example, Copland invokes *Also sprach Zarathustra* and its associations not to affirm them but rather to subvert them. Parallels to language are obvious; we all reuse words and whole phrases constantly but invest them with meanings appropriate to the new and unique circumstances in which we find ourselves, by changing or combining them in new ways, and those around us follow our meanings by attending both to what is familiar and to what is new.

Meaning Often Depends on Interpretation

Finally, and most significant, comes the fifth step: the interpretation of the musical and extra-musical associations an element arouses together with the new contexts and variations in the music we are hearing. Although some meanings are more immediate, *much meaning depends on interpretation.* It is no secret that we often interpret the same event, the same evidence, even the same sentence differently. The meanings we derive from music are also variable. And yet, if there were no common thread, it would be impossible for film composers to achieve what they do. They are able to convey meanings through music because they know we will recognize certain elements, associate these with other music we know, understand the associations the culture has with that other music, and notice how each element and its associations are being manipulated in the music; finally, they trust we will then interpret the music within a certain range of possible meanings.

Our Understanding Changes as We Learn

Although, in theory, interpretation may allow for an infinite range of meanings, in practice we judge interpretations to be more or less convincing by the degree to which they conform to the facts as we understand them. For example, if we seek to understand a piece or type of music from the past as its creators and first hearers might have understood it, we look to historical evidence at each step, trying to reconstruct the other music they may have known and what associations it carried for them. Through the study of individual works, of music's history, of the music of various regions, traditions, periods, and composers, we can hear more and more of the associations the music carried for those who made and heard it. *As we learn more about music from any time and place, and become more familiar with the music those who lived at that time and place would have known, we increase our capacity to understand what the music meant to them,* and thus might mean to us.

The Model Facilitates Communication

This model for associative musical meaning has one final advantage: it provides a framework for examining the meaning of music that interests us, and explaining that meaning to others, without requiring an elaborate apparatus or specialized jargon. Our explanations can be as general or as sophisticated as we wish, as all-encompassing or as partial and tentative as we deem appropriate. The model promises that some meaning can be found for any piece of music, given the knowledge of the traditions from which it springs. Without suggesting that we could ever fix a final and ultimate meaning to the music, the model provides a basis for considering different interpretations and then deciding which explain more about the music or fit better than others. At the same time it accounts for entirely personal or idiosyncratic meanings, while allowing us to focus scholarly debate at the level of widely shared associations. By doing all this in relatively non-technical language focused on how pieces resemble other music and on the associations the other music evokes, we may be able to share what we find most valuable and significant in the music we study with a wide public, with performing musicians, and with those who are creating new music through improvisation and composition, and their experience of music, their performances, and their creative process may be enriched as a result.

Notes

Earlier versions of this paper were presented at Converse College, Williams College, the University of Texas at Austin, and University of Cincinnati College–Conservatory of Music. Thanks especially to Robin Wallace, Edward Nowacki, Robert Hatten, Lewis Rowell, and Byron Almén for their helpful comments.

1. Just since 1990 the following major studies or collections addressing issues of meaning from various perspectives have appeared in English, among others: Cook 1990; Kivy 1990; Kramer 1990, 1995, 2002; Nattiez 1990b; Agawu 1991; Higgins 1991; Kassler 1991; McClary 1991, 2000; Budd 1992; Jones and Holleran 1992; Monelle 1992, 2000; Davies 1994; Hatten 1994; Krausz 1994; Rosen 1994; Tarasti 1994, 1995; Goswami 1995; Martin 1995; Pople 1995; Levinson 1997; Robinson 1997; Scruton 1997; Swain 1997; Bowman 1998; Campbell 1998; Stefani, Tarasti, and Marconi 1998; Chua 1999; Cumming 2000; and Juslin and Sloboda 2001.

2. For a useful summary and consideration of such theories, see Swain 1997. For a considered rejection of the analogy, see Davies 1994: 1–49.

3. See, for example, Riemann 1877; Ratner 1980; Lerdahl and Jackendoff 1983; Agawu 1991; and Caplin 1998.

4. Meyer (1956; 1973) includes classic discussions of the emotional effects of evading syntactic expectations, and McClary (1991: 125–27) relates desire to delayed resolution.

5. This valuable article clarifies many philosophical issues regarding musical meaning, and Cook's conclusions dovetail well with my own approach.

6. In 1785 Michel-Paul-Gui de Chabanon called music the "universal language of our continent" which "at the most undergoes some differences in pronunciation from one people to another" and, finding melodies from Asia, Africa, and America that "absolutely resemble our own," concluded that music is "a universal language whose principles and effects are not based on any particular conventions but emanate directly from human nature" (translation in Lyall 1975: 155–56, 183, 181). The best-known assertion of music as a universal language is Schopenhauer's in *Die Welt als Wille und Vorstellung* (1818, trans. in Schopenhauer 1883:

330–46). For an American parallel, see Longfellow's *Outre-Mer* of 1834: "Music is the universal language of mankind" (1904: 181).

7. See the discussion of "musical communities" in Swain 1997: 81–83; 1994.

8. Nota bene: I am not claiming that the model accounts for the specific meanings carried by military calls. As noted below, those meanings are assigned arbitrarily. Rather, because military calls carry a wide range of associations from the specific to the general, pieces that incorporate them or include passages reminiscent of them provide a good test of the model.

9. For a discussion of the specific roles and associations of these bugle calls, see Colby 1942: 14, 175–76, 208–11. See also Sousa 1886: 67–68, 14; and Canty 1916: 2–3, 5, 10, 14, 16, which present the calls in the context of a guide to their use.

10. The particular pattern of repetition here also resembles the "street beat" drum pattern, which in its simple 2/4 form consists of half note, half note, quarter, quarter, half.

11. See Monelle 2000: 38.

12. Interview with Phillip Ramey; quoted in Ramey 1988: 5.

13. See Crist 2000: 123.

14. Quoted in Ramey 1988: 5.

15. Henry A. Wallace, "The Price of Free World Victory: The Century of the Common Man"; as quoted in Crist 2000: 126–27. It appears that the title may have been written after the piece itself, since Copland tried out many titles before settling on this one (see Crist 2000: 125–26). But it is the perfect title for this music. This is the only fanfare from the Cincinnati Orchestra's commissioning project that has become popular; indeed, it is among Copland's best-known and most widely played pieces. No doubt that is owing in part both to the nobility of the title and the perfect fit of the music with its subject.

16. The following does not purport to analyze the meaning of the Strauss but seeks to explore another aspect of the meaning of Copland's *Fanfare for the Common Man,* in addition to its references to military calls.

17. Notes written for the first Berlin performance, translated in Del Mar 1962: 134.

18. See, for example, Kuenzli 1983; Whitlock 1990: esp. 11–16; and Santaniello 1994.

19. See Kuenzli 1983: 429.

20. See Ratner 1980: 18–19, 27–28. Ratner compares this movement to a wind serenade (135) but does not discuss its use of topics. The key of D major and the relatively low register may suggest horns and therefore hunting rather than trumpets issuing a military call, but the styles overlap. For a fuller and more historically sensitive exploration of military and hunting topics than Ratner supplies, see Monelle 2000: 33–40.

21. The extent to which an "academic" understanding of topical associations from an earlier era, such as that laid out by Ratner, is associative when compared to the meanings that a person living in that era would have understood is an issue in this interpretation but is more a matter of degree than of kind.

22. Although they have triadic features in common, fanfare and arpeggiation figures have their own distinct associations that do not necessarily interpenetrate. In this piece, however, the listener brings these two figures closer together semantically because the context suggests it.

23. See Ratner 1980: 23–24, 15.

24. Compare the mixture of military and salon topics in Mozart's Piano Concerto in B♭, K. 595, as described by Monelle (2000: 35–36). The movement might also be interpreted psychologically rather than socially; this would, of course, lead to very different conclusions.

25. See Robert Hatten's discussion of the same movement in chapter 4 of this volume.

26. It is, however, part of the initial basic idea, or *Grundgestalt*, from which the entire sonata derives through developing variation, as Janet Schmalfeldt has demonstrated; see Schmalfeldt 1991. Although its elements are pervasive, as Schmalfeldt shows, the motive itself, in original or altered form, is reserved for special occasions.

27. For a general discussion of Berg's use of the familiar in this manner, see Burkholder 1991: esp. 29–39.

28. See the sources cited in note 3 above.

29. On the interaction of syntax and semantics, see Swain 1997. Of course, the interplay between syntax and denotation is not a simple question either in language or in music; the example given here is meant only to illustrate how the model might work in elucidating such interactions in specific cases.

30. See Schmalfeldt 1991: 109.

31. It should be noted, however, that it would be possible for associative meaning to emerge in a way that did not result from a new twist on something already familiar; that is, the familiar association alone accounts for the emergent meaning.

32. Indeed, I have had a good response from general college-level audiences when I presented this model in the context of lectures, and nonmusicians also tend to react positively, as if immediately taken with it. My model, although simple, allows for complexity in music, as it may lead to multiple interpretations under different applications.

33. Nicholas Cook's (2001: esp. 178–80, 185–88) excellent point that music has many potential meanings which may be actualized in a particular interpretation is relevant here.

34. Early studies of intertextuality in music include Karbusicky (1983) and Hatten (1985). The concept has been applied in numerous studies of individual works and composers; see Burkholder 2001: bibliography.

35. See, for example, Monelle's discussion of the "indexicality of the object" (2000: 16–19), in which a musical topic refers to a type of music, which in turn carries a particular set of associations; this corresponds exactly to Steps 2 and 3 of the model.

36. On borrowing in Ives, see Burkholder 1995a.

37. See McClary 2000.

38. See Burkholder 1995b: esp. 376–77.

39. See also Cook 2001: 174–76, for a nuanced discussion of Hanslick's views which argues that he does not deny music's ability to be expressive.

40. The community of listeners in this case constitutes what Stanley Fish (1980: 171) refers to as an "interpretive community."

41. This view parallels that of Jean-Jacques Nattiez (1990b: 9), who defines meaning in this way: "An object of any kind takes on meaning for an individual apprehending that object, as soon as that individual places the object in relation to areas of his lived experience— that is, in relation to a collection of other objects that belong to his or her experience of the world."

42. See Higgins 1997, for a defense of idiosyncratic meanings as important.

6 Uncanny Moments: Juxtaposition and the Collage Principle in Music

Nicholas Cook

Analysis and Bedtime Stories

The opening of Beethoven's Fourth Piano Concerto in G Major: the orchestra remains silent while the piano plays a five-measure phrase outlining the clearest possible tonic to dominant in G major, undercut however by the lack of a clear phrase structure; a half-measure's silence, and then the orchestra enters inconsequentially on the mediant major. The change in tonality combines with that in timbre to give the impression that the sound is coming from far away. Even the invariant element, the melodic B, is relocated, now wedged up by its own leading note, A♯, where before it had initiated the descent to A♮ with which the first phrase ended (a descent which any experienced listener would expect to be completed, in due course, through a further descent to G). And now begins the unwinding of the force held within the B major, which acts rather like the twisted rubber band that powers an old-fashioned model airplane: the harmonies move in a succession of flattening fifths (B⁶–E–A⁶–D–G⁶) supporting a chromatic descent in the melody, with the first-inversion tonic—the point where the rubber band becomes untwisted—providing the stepping stone for the big root-position subdominant that initiates the tonally and metrically unambiguous cadence. You have a sense that the real beginning of the piece occurs when the orchestra re-enters—in the right key—with everything prior to that a kind of dream.

In my account of these measures, which I relate as a kind of story allowing myself one or two idiosyncratic metaphors, I do not believe I have said anything original: there seems to be little scope for disagreement or misunderstanding. So it comes as a surprise to discover how problematic Heinrich Schenker (1954: 253–54) found this passage when writing about it in his *Harmonielehre* (originally published in 1906): "How many doubts does he [Beethoven] conjure up with this B major! Will it develop into a real B major . . . ? The major triad on *E* . . . is it a IV step in B major? Obviously not, as it is followed by a major triad on *A*, which has no place in the diatonic system of B major." And Schenker continues in this manner for an entire page: at each stage in the unwinding process, he suggests, we think we have reached the tonic, only to abandon the supposition as the flatward motion continues to unwind. "Our feeling gets confused," he says, "because we feel tempted, step by step, to impute to each one of them the rank of a tonic. Until we understand, at the end, that the B major was nothing but a III step in G major . . . so that we kept moving throughout within the same key."

What are we to make of this? Is Schenker giving us a rare glimpse into the vivid tonal imagination of listeners a century ago, whose ears had not been stretched out of shape by atonality and serialism, and whose tonal disorientation in musical situations like this must have been matched at the regaining of the tonic by cathartic relief of an intensity that we, in the twenty-first century, can at best imagine? Or is Schenker constructing a kind of perceptual straw man, an exaggeratedly disorientated and wrongheaded way of hearing the music, with the purpose of lending credibility to the solution when it emerges: that we were in G major the whole time, that "the B major was nothing but a III step in G major?" The telling phrase, of course, is "nothing but," which has the rhetorical force of dismissing everything that has come before. Indeed, this is underlined by a characteristic footnote added by Oswald Jonas, editor of the version of *Harmonielehre* from which the English translation is taken, at the end of Schenker's discussion of the passage: "In a later phase of his development, Schenker would have placed the main emphasis on the motion (*Zug*) which creates the unity of this whole" (Schenker 1954: 254 n. 2).

It is all too easy to imagine what Schenker might have said had he chosen to graph this passage in *Der freie Satz*. Actually the graph would have said it all: the opening $\hat{3}$, falling at a subsidiary level to $\hat{2}$ in measure 5, is prolonged through the B major section, being picked up in the second half of measure 11 (note the registral identity of the outer parts with the opening) and thence falling through $\hat{2}$ (m. 12) to $\hat{1}$ (m. 14). Extracting the motion that creates "the unity of the whole," to borrow Jonas's words, a graph like this precisely represents the B major episode as "nothing but a III step in G major": the characteristic quality of the music—the quality that led Schenker to write about it in *Harmonielehre*—is explained but only in the sense of being explained away. Put another way, what appears at first to be a striking discontinuity in the music is revealed as continuity at a deeper level: if, as Schenker (1979: i, 6) claimed in *Der freie Satz*, "every relationship represents a path which is as real as any which we 'traverse' with our feet," then we can tread securely from the G major of measure 5 to the B major of measure 6—it is just that we have to take a step or two down, making a detour from the surface to the middleground level at which the B major is "nothing but a III step in G major" (the staircase metaphor is built into Schenker's language). Making sense of discontinuity, then, requires the positing of an underlying continuity; in Beethoven's music, Schenker is saying, there is no such thing as discontinuity, only continuity badly understood. In this way the moment-to-moment unfolding of the music is to be understood as precisely that, the unfolding of a structure that exists at a certain remove from moment-to-moment time (that is what it means to speak of it being unfolded). The analysis prioritizes what Xenakis would call the outside-time structure, and so the moment-to-moment experience is explained away.

And the suspicion is that engrained thinking of this kind brings about the apparently self-evident, but, in fact, profoundly deproblematized, experience of the music outlined in my opening paragraph. A century of Schenkerian analysis has, perhaps, made music like this too easy to hear. It has turned it into a refined form of easy listening.

It needn't be like this, of course. In *Harmonielehre,* after showing how the B major is "nothing but a III step in G major," Schenker (1954: 254) concludes:

> Thus Beethoven exploits our doubts in order to render his G major key richer and more chromatic than would have been possible otherwise. These doubts, however, never would have been aroused in us, had not each scale-step a tendency to appear as a tonic, if possible, or, to put it anthropocentrically, were we not ourselves inclined to ascribe to each scale-step its highest value, i.e., the value of a tonic.

So whereas at one level the B major passage is "nothing but a III step in G major," at another level it is the moment-to-moment experience of the passage as a disorienting succession of tonics no sooner achieved than revealed as illusory that makes the music what it is. Or perhaps what is crucial is the tension between these two different levels. Yet I am inclined to agree with Jonas that, had Schenker talked about this passage in *Der freie Satz,* he probably would have outlined its larger motion and left it at that.

Maybe that is because he would have taken the rest for granted, particularly in a book like *Der freie Satz,* designed to explain the overarching theory and written against the clock; maybe we have the same problem in reading Schenker as in reading historical treatises on performance, that the most important points are never mentioned because, if everybody knows them, why mention them? But whether historically justified or not, the result is that the experience of music from one moment to the next seems to elude analysis in the Schenkerian tradition; juxtapositions like the shift of tonal, timbral, and rhetorical register between measures 5 and 6 of the G major Concerto go either unexplained or, if explained, unexperienced. In short, discontinuity becomes a null category (there is no discontinuous music, only bad analysis). It is as if explanation and experience were at odds with each other, and yet what is the point of analysis if not to explain experience?

Actually that, too, is a historical matter. It has often been said, which makes it no less true, that analysis as we understand it came into being as a way to defend Beethoven's works against conservative critics. For contemporary listeners, the most striking feature of Beethoven's music—the most obvious, the most taken for granted—was its discontinuity, its juxtaposition of incongruous tonal, dynamic, or emotional registers, in a word, its incoherence. (If Schenker's initial account of the opening of the G major Concerto sounds like an echo of that kind of listening, bear in mind that Schenker's *Harmonielehre* is half as old as the G major Concerto.) The purpose of analyzing Beethoven's music, then, was precisely to emphasize what was *not* obvious: the underlying coherence of the music, those more profound—deeper—levels of musical continuity in relation to which the discontinuity at the surface could be seen as apparent rather than real.

From the beginning, then, analysis had a complex relationship with experience: it aimed less to reflect a prevailing way of hearing Beethoven's music than to change how it was heard, to argue that it could and moreover *should* be heard in a particular manner. But the point is a more general one: there is a plausible argument that analysis should not reflect what is obvious in the music—what could be more redundant than that?—but rather aim to bring to light, to emphasize, things about the music that are *not* obvious, that might never be heard without the analysis. It follows, then, that what is good analysis at one time may not be good at another, because what is obvious changes. If anything is shown by my opening analysis of the G major Concerto (which surely falls into Richard Taruskin's [1995: 24] category of comforting bedtime stories), it is this: what is obvious now, at least to a certain category of listener, is precisely what was *not* obvious to most of Beethoven's contemporary listeners, or even perhaps to the young Schenker. Conversely, what *was* obvious to contemporary listeners of Beethoven's music—its progression from one moment to the next through a series of shocks that might be violent, expressive, ironic, whimsical, or surreal but were always unpredictable—may no longer be obvious today, indeed may be hard to hear at all in a world in which Beethoven's music has been heard so many times. If the aim of analysis is to challenge rather than comfort, to interrogate sedimented responses and thus revive jaded perceptions, then we might expect its emphasis today to be on the experience of music from one moment to the next and, above all, on the juxtapositions between contrasted events of which that experience so largely consists.

Structure, Narrative, and "Concatenationism"

Yet it is not easy to identify analytical approaches that directly confront the experience of musical juxtaposition. Even phenomenologically oriented writers have generally worked to an agenda parallel to that of Schenkerian and other structural theorists, in that their emphasis has been on the manner in which momentary percepts are integrated to create meaningful wholes. Thomas Clifton (1983: 106–107), for example, distinguishes "contrast" from "interruption" on the basis that contrasted elements may be assimilated at an adjacent level of organization (C and D, distinct at one level, merge at the next within "the unified experience of an ascending line"), whereas an interruption implies the need to skip to a third level before integration is possible, rather in the manner of Schenker's staircase: it is simply taken for granted that the analytical task is to demonstrate how coherence arises. Indeed, the Husserlian model of internal time-consciousness that has traditionally formed the foundation for writing in this area might be defined as precisely concerned with the construction, through retention and protention, of a coherent experience of time; experienced time, in short, is defined as coherent time. (Just as in the case of structural analysis, there are good historical reasons for this agenda, the history in question being as much of phenomenology as of music.) And I would argue—but this is an argument that needs to be made at greater length—that the same applies, perhaps surprisingly, to the narratological approaches which have enjoyed at least sporadic currency among musicologists and theorists during the last two decades.

If this is surprising, it is because issues of time are so central to the narratological approach as to define it. As is well known, at the foundation of narratology lies the distinction between what are now generally known as "story" and "discourse" (corresponding to Victor Shklovsky's "fabula" and "syuzhet"), each implying a different temporality: narration is a time-based activity that references a second time within which the narrated events are located, and other narratological principles— for example, the meaningfully variable relationships between narrator and reader— follow from this primary one. Anthony Newcomb (1987), perhaps the most influential musicologist to draw on narratology in the 1980s, applied this approach to music by distinguishing between what he called a "paradigmatic plot,"[1] which he defined as "a standard series of functional events in a prescribed order" (165), and the manner of its presentation within the experienced time of the music. Seen in this way, the analytical question becomes, as Newcomb put it, "how does the composer handle this narrative, what is the nature of the interaction between paradigmatic plot and succession of events in the individual movement or piece?" (167). The purpose of the article from which I am quoting is to argue that, in compositions like *Carnaval*, Schumann employed narrative devices based on "what the Romantic novelists called *Witz*—the faculty by which subtle underlying connections are discovered (or revealed) in a surface of apparent incoherence and extreme discontinuity" (169): a narratological approach may allow us to "make the best possible argument for a piece" like *Carnaval*, which traditional structuralist approaches with their organicist and teleological assumptions will represent as "uninteresting and even clumsy." ("If one section must 'lead imperceptibly' to the next across 'concealed seams,'" says Newcomb, "then we shall have to reject much Schumann out of hand.") In this way narratology is set up as a complement to structural analysis: to reference a long-defunct but not forgotten Heineken ad, it reaches those parts that traditional approaches fail to reach.

Newcomb's discussion of *Carnaval* stimulated much commentary,[2] but I do not intend to summarize that debate here. Instead, I focus on two related aspects of his approach: its relationship to conventional structuralist analysis, and its treatment of discontinuity. Taking these in the opposite order, it is almost as if Newcomb were recapitulating the Beethovenian origins of structural analysis: he reveals the larger narrative continuity underlying Schumann's "surface discontinuity," writing that Schumann's "truly original idea . . . was to interconnect these seemingly disparate fragments by almost subliminal pitch connections, the musical equivalent of *Witz*. Thus a single little cell of pitches was used to build up melodies that were superficially different in rhythm, overall melodic contour, character, tempo, and so on" (Newcomb 1987: 169–70). Terms like "surface" and "superficially" reveal the linkage between Newcomb's approach and both the embedded metaphors and the agenda of structural analysis. If Newcomb's narratology complements traditional analysis, it is not by offering a different agenda but rather by broadening its application: essentially he is showing that there is a wider range of "paradigmatic plots" than approaches like Schenker's allow.

It follows from that, of course, that Schenkerian analysis is itself a kind (but just one kind) of narrative analysis. This is not simply a matter of the type of narrative vocabulary Fred Maus (1991: 4), for example, identified in Schenker's writings: it has to do with the relationship between Schenkerian structure and design, which is precisely parallel to that between story and discourse. For Schenker, structure embodies musical causality, a pattern of relationships with its own intrinsic logic expressed through the strategies of musical design (and performance, but that is another issue): he makes sense of the moment-to-moment continuity of the music, and of its dynamic relationships, orchestration, and so forth, by interpreting these in terms of structure, just as the narrative theorist interprets the discourse in terms of the story. (Seymour Chatman makes the link unmistakable when he unwittingly uses two Schenkerian keywords in his definition of "discourse" as "the *expression,* the means by which the *content* is communicated.")[3] This explains the strong resonances between Newcomb's narratology and Schenkerian theory: when Newcomb describes the paradigmatic plot as "a series of functions, not necessarily defined by patterns of sectional recurrences or by the specific characters fulfilling the functions," he could be talking about Schenkerian structure,[4] and when, in a passage I have already quoted, he describes the basic analytical question as how the composer handles the narrative ("what is the nature of the interaction between paradigmatic plot and succession of events . . . ?") he might as well be describing Schenkerian design (Newcomb 1987: 165, 167).

Schenker's concept of musical causality was not only exclusive (in the sense of being based on certain admissible prolongations of the "chord of nature") but was also epistemologically distant from the assumptions of contemporary writers on narratology, for whom causality is an interpretive construct: Nattiez (1990a: 245) argues that narrative is not inherent in historical facts but only in the relations of causality between them which we establish through interpretation, while Almén (2003: 7) concludes that, whether in history or music, "it is the observer who ultimately makes connections between events." And Newcomb sees his "paradigmatic plots" being based not in nature but in history, as he makes clear when he refers to them as "codes or conventions" (Newcomb 1987: 167). This, then, is the source of the broadening to which I referred, the greater inclusiveness of narratological approaches as compared to structural analysis, but it comes with its own dangers. One is that narratology relies upon traditional formulations of structure and is therefore a new way of saying old things. The potential, at least, for this is evident in Newcomb's reference (with regard to the finale from Schumann's Quartet, Op. 43, No. 3) to "the paradigmatic plot of the rondo type" (174), and underlies such critical judgments as Lawrence Kramer's (1991: 142): "Narratology has acted as a kind of methodological halfway house in which musical meaning can be entertained without leaving the safe haven of form" (again, bedtime stories). The other danger is simply dilution, as when, in the final sentence of his article, Newcomb refers to the "fundamental narrative activity" of "matching successions of musical events against known configurations"—which, after all, is how cognitive psychologists describe *all* perception.

It is such considerations that led Carolyn Abbate (1991: xi) to ask: "What is the value of a critical methodology that generates such uniformity and becomes a mere machine for naming any and all music?" Between them, Nattiez and Abbate helped to bring about a more skeptical and discriminating view of narrativity, now seen not as the normal condition of music but as something anomalous (Abbate's position) or, more generally, as a characteristic of some but not other music. For Vera Micznik (2001) there are "degrees of narrativity," so that Mahler's music has more narrative characteristics (and requires more narrative analysis) than Beethoven's,[5] whereas for Kramer (1991: 144) "narratography can be understood as a principled means of resistance to continuity and closure"; it is a way we can understand how composers themselves have sometimes chosen to resist or subvert structure. (Kramer illustrates this in terms of the finale from Beethoven's Quartet Op 135.) This may dispose of the suspicion that narrativity is a new way of saying old things, yet—despite Kramer's reference to it as a "principled" means of resistance—narrative seems to be represented more as structures other than as an independent principle. A little later, Kramer spells out the implied hierarchy: "music becomes *narratographically* disruptive when it seeks to jeopardize (or unwittingly jeopardizes) the dominant regimes (or what it fictitiously represents as the dominant regimes) of musical composition and reception" (145). And his account of narrativity in Op. 135 focuses on a mismatch between the demands of structure, on the one hand, and, on the other, the process by which the *Es muss sein!* motive takes on the questioning character of *Muss es sein?*—a process that culminates in the passage preceding the coda: "From the standpoint of musical structure," Kramer writes, this passage is "an interpolation, a patch of detail applied to the foreground. From the standpoint of narrativity, the same passage is a passage of the highest importance" (153). (He then goes on to read this mismatch in terms of gender ideology.) The focus, then, is on the relationship between two competing models of continuity; effects of juxtaposition and discontinuity are treated as epiphenomena rather than as embodying any kind of musical principle in their own right.

There is, however, a further approach which is specifically oriented to the consideration of juxtapositional relationships in music: the outcome of a productive reading of the late-nineteenth-century author Edmund Gurney's *The Power of Sound,* it is what Jerrold Levinson (1997) calls "concatenationism." This, as Levinson defines it, is the doctrine that everything that matters aesthetically about the experience of music can be expressed in terms of the individual events in a piece of music and their successive relationships (in Levinson's words, "the individual bits and the transitions between them" [27]), without any need to invoke conceptions of the whole, large-scale formal prototypes, and so forth: where traditional aestheticians, critics, or analysts speak of the relationship between part and whole, everything they say can be expressed without loss of meaning in terms of relationships between one part and the next. The claim is that the successive, edge-related kind of listening this implies—what Levinson calls an "attentive absorption in the musical present" (23)—is perfectly sufficient for the "basic musical understanding" (27) required for the appreciation and enjoyment of music in the Western "art" tradition. (Levinson neatly sidelines the Schenkerian version of musical narrativity when he draws a firm line between "the issue of the causal relevance of musical relationships and that of their *appreciative* relevance for a listener" [36].) This does not mean that musicians, theorists, and others may not think intellectually about remote musical relationships, but that such intellectualizing is meaningless if it is not built on the foundation of a moment-to-moment listening perhaps too obvious for aestheticians, critics, or analysts to have taken it seriously: as Levinson (1997: 175) says, on the final page of his book,

> Music for listening appreciation, of whatever scale or ambition, lives and dies in the moment—as no one has emphasized more effectively than Gurney—and it is there that it must be fundamentally understood, there that its fundamental value lies, whatever more rarefied excellences supervene on that foundation.

While the general thrust of Levinson's argument is well taken, and despite the promising foregrounding of "transitions," the issue of how we experience juxtaposition and discontinuity once more slips through the net. This is partly because it is not Levinson's primary aim to offer such an account (his project is an aesthetic rather than analytical one), but it is also because of a basic approach that derives from Gurney. For Gurney, any passage "which is to be musically valuable must satisfy the test that each bit shall necessitate, as it were, and so enter into organic union with the one next to it. . . . The cardinal idea of organic form in any musical sentence or paragraph is . . . cogency of sequence at each point."[6] As Levinson (1997: 17 n. 7) himself notes, this conception is surprisingly close to Husserl's phenomenology of internal time-consciousness—surprisingly because Gurney was writing a quarter of a century earlier and within a different tradition—and the result is that Levinson works to the same kind of integrationist agenda that I spoke of with reference to musical phenomenologists like Clifton. Nowhere is this more evident than in his account of Tchaikovsky's Fantasy Overture *Romeo and Juliet,* which Levinson discusses for the specific reason that it is "a composition rich in, among other things, transitions" (1997: 111). He lists the twenty-seven main transitions of the piece and goes through a selection of them to see if there are any "whose aural cogency unmistakably depends on or is even plausibly aided by awareness of formal relations" (120). Predictably there are none.

Gurney's agenda is evident in the very way that Levinson formulates his question round "cogency," as well as in the kind of interpretation of the music that results. Of the passage from measures 97–115, for example, Levinson writes that "grasp of its particular cogency depends on close attention to the way the b minor triad emerges out of the slow counterpoint of measures 97–104, with the violin sliding prominently from A♯ to B, the alternation and quickening of the chord thus arrived at in measures 105–111, and the subsequent assimilable, if unexpectedly assertive, proclamation of measures 112–115" (1997: 119). But that seems as erratic a way of listening to this music as Schenker's distracted experience of the opening of the G major Concerto, because cogency is surely not what this music is about, beyond the fact that there is first something (or rather nothing much, since the whole passage has an introductory quality) and then something else. What I find striking about this music is not the kind of linkages that Levinson enumerates but rather the long, false calm, with a dominant pedal that is not so much prolonged as unraveled (from m. 96): the bass descents to $\hat{3}$ (mm. 100, 104), supporting tonic harmony, mean that the power of the anticipated V–I resolution has dissipated before anything happens—rather as if the curtain were lifted only to reveal an empty stage. This is followed by a rhetorical but syntactically unmotivated *stringendo* on repeated first-inversion triads that alternate meaninglessly between strings and winds, with the *stringendo* creating a sense of hurtling with increasing speed toward something that remains entirely undefined: the music bears all the signs of agitation and expectation, and yet the first-inversion tonic harmony denies any prospect of coherent progression. And then, suddenly, for no better reason than that *something* has to happen, the *Allegro giusto* theme crashes in, or we crash into it. The entire episode has all the cogency of a road accident—I am thinking of the *Allegro giusto* as a kind of musical wall—and that is what makes the moment of impact (m. 112) what it is.

In short, Levinson has taken one of the most studiedly non-cogent moments in the repertoire and contrived to show how despite appearances, despite the way it actually sounds, it really is cogent after all. He argues compellingly for the importance of juxtapositional relationships in music but provides no model of how they might be analyzed for their own sake rather than for their contribution to a putative whole (even if, in Levinson's case, the whole is a concatenationist one). At a basic level he works to the same agenda that has dominated music analysis from Beethoven's apologists to at least the early narratologists. Whereas the emphasis on cogency is taken for granted, however, Levinson's focus on the moment-to-moment nature of musical experience leads him to approach the comparison between music and narrative with some caution: "Narrative is clearly less central to the import of music," he says, "than it is to the import of literature and film" (Levinson 1997: 169), because to keep track of a novel you need a sense of the overall story that you do not need in music. And so, he concludes, "the degree of analogy between literature or film on the one hand and music on the other is easily overstated" (168). I would go further and suggest that, if we really want to address the issue of moment-to-moment relationships in music, it might be better to stop looking for parallels with literature altogether—which only reinforce the historical tendency to think of music as a kind of text related at best problematically to its real-time experience—and start looking instead for parallels with material culture.

The Collage Principle in Material Culture

I do not wish to suggest that there is an either/or relationship between material culture and narrative construction. Quite the reverse: the museum might be described as a site for the creation of narratives out of material objects (by contrast with the seventeenth-century cabinet of curiosities, in which objects were displayed as intriguing individuals).[7] As in the case of the narrative archetypes adopted by music narratologists such as Newcomb and Almén, museums have traditionally structured their collections around a small number of "master narratives," such as "Art, Nature, Man [*sic*], and Nation."[8] Represented at their most explicit by collections of ethnographic artifacts so arranged as to construct a developmental sequence from the simple to the complex, such displays clearly invoke the two distinct times definitive of narrative: on the one hand, that of evolutionary history, and, on the other, its reproduction in miniature by the visitors as they walk around the exhibition. As Tony Bennett (1995: 186) puts it, "the museum, rather than annihilating time, compresses it so as to make it both visible and performable."

An immediate parallel can be made here with music: in fact, Nadia Boulanger made it, comparing program planning with the hanging of pictures in an art gallery. As Jeanice Brooks (2004) explains, Boulanger's views emerge from an exchange of letters with the BBC in 1936 concerning a proposed series of broadcast concerts. The BBC wanted each program to be ordered chronologically around a distinct historical period: apart from any pedagogical function, this kind of planning can be seen as an act of teleological appropriation of the past similar to that of the ethnographic displays I referred to. Boulanger's ideas were quite different: as she explained in her idiosyncratic English, "my intention was to have in each ancient moderne as groups of tendancies rather than chronological. . . . I should like: XVI very modern XIII very modern XVI—or something in this direction. . . . I truly believe that parentages or contrasts through history are more useful for education & pleasure, than going century by century."[9] Her aim, however, was not—or at least not simply—to create a series of striking, memorable, bizarre, or aesthetically interesting juxtapositions. She made this clear in the introductory talk she wrote when the concerts were finally broadcast: "In building these programmes," she said, in rather more standard English, "we were intending to illustrate the way in which a certain character or human type continually appears throughout the ages different in clothing, different in manner, different in language, but expressing a same thought, a same aspiration, a same emotion": thus Poulenc's *Litanies à la Vierge noire de Rocamadour* (of which she was giving the first performance) was "obviously related with the 13th century music technique not as a revival of an old form, but as a new form of an old spirit."

The BBC planned to create one kind of meaning from the juxtaposition of different pieces within the program; in the event, Boulanger created a very different one. This illustrates the fundamental museological principle, as described by Peter Vergo (1989: 54): "The same material can be made to tell quite different stories not just by means of captions or information panels or explanatory texts but by the sequence in which works are displayed." Put another way, meaning is created through a succession of juxtapositional relationships: any object by itself has an indefinite range of potentially meaningful properties, but the juxtaposition with a second object brings certain of those attributes into play and de-emphasizes others. For instance, the juxtaposition of a vase with other artifacts might variously foreground its shape, its material, a manufacturing technique, an ornamental motive or painted representation, its use, or its social connotations. Meaning created through juxtaposition is comparable with textual meaning only to a limited degree, for, as Eilean Hooper-Greenhill (2000: 114) explains,

> The categories of meaning are less clear with objects than with texts. Although it could be argued that words necessarily have a material character (they may be expressed in book form, or written round a piece of pottery), the material form rarely comprises part of the meaning of the text. . . . To treat an artefact as a text is to expand the concept of textual meaning too far. It is also to focus primarily on the discur-

sive character of meaning, with the material meaning being allocated a secondary, less significant role.[10]

The result, she continues, is a neglect of the propensity of material objects to produce "powerful 'gut reactions,' mobilizing feeling and emotions, but in a non-examined way" (116). And Daniel Miller (1987: 100) gives the same thought a more psychoanalytical turn when he speaks of "the power of an unconscious oriented towards objects rather than language. . . . Rather as with other areas fundamental to the operation of the unconscious, artefacts may resist conscious articulation and in a sense be embarrassed by language." This is presumably why museological narratives have a quality of apparent self-evidence, of simply representing things as they are rather than participating in discourse—which is, of course, what gives museums their particular ideological force.

Any number of similarities with music may be drawn here, beginning with the striking likeness between *The New Museology*, as Vergo entitled his 1989 collection, and its musicological equivalent. (The problem with the old museology, Vergo explained in his introduction, was its emphasis on method at the expense of meaning, its unconcern with social function and ideology, its lack of critical awareness.) Miller (1987: 100) complains about "our difficulty in dealing with objects through academic studies dominated by language," and that is equally the musicologist's dilemma: too often the text-oriented discourses of analysis substitute themselves for a musical meaning that seems to be unconscious or at least intangible, rather than helping to bring it to light. Indeed Hooper-Greenhill's (2000: 115) characterization of the particular quality of material (as opposed to textual) culture could be applied to music with minimal change:

> It is an openness to re-meaning; a capacity to carry preferred meaning; a potential for polysemia; and the material potentials and constraints, that lie at the heart of the appeal of artefacts. The dialogic relationship between what can be said and thought, and what cannot, offers opportunities for both domination *and* for empowerment.

If anything, however, the role of juxtaposition in the creation of musical meaning is even more resistant to identification than in the case of material culture, because of the pervasive influence of the notation-based metalanguage through which we represent music not as a concrete experience but as a symbolic construction always already abstracted from experience. The textualist paradigm is so deeply embedded in music-analytical thinking that it is hard for us even to be aware of it, and that, perhaps, is the strongest argument in favor of the comparison with material culture that I am advancing.

If what might be termed the semiotics of juxtaposition forms the foundation of museological meaning, it is central to collage. The idea of collage is not unfamiliar in musicology but has generally been slanted toward ideas of intertextuality that stem primarily from literary studies: Björn Heile (2001) and David Metzer (2003), for example, invoke it when discussing the destabilization or erasure that results from the combination of materials with different generic or cultural associations—erasure not only of those associations but also of authorial identity. Closer to the visual arts is the idea of collage which Glenn Watkins (1994) sets up as a leading motive in *Pyramids at the Louvre: Music, Culture, and Collage from Stravinsky to the Postmodernists.* On page 1 Watkins quotes Kim Levin's description of collage as "the all-purpose twentieth-century device," but in practice the term weaves confusingly in and out of the book: on the following page he claims that collage must be discussed across the arts, and that "eschewing loose analogy wherever possible, I have sought to conjure up the methods, the effects, and the contexts of artistic theory, social inference and technological progress"—and then on the page after that he adds, "It should be understood from the outset . . . that the term *collage* is used here as a metaphor [which] typically refers less to thematic recall of familiar tunes than to the assemblage and rearrangement of a rich parade of cultural loans" (2–3). Thus characterized as a metaphor but not an analogy, collage seems to be turning into a floating signifier, an effect without a cause. There is a way, however, to ground the idea of collage, and that is in terms of a specific model for the generation of meaning.

According to the art historian Franz Mon,

> The formula "collage principle" indicates that collage does not mean simply one artistic technique among many, but reveals a basic attitude to artistic activity which pervades the whole of modern art. . . . The principles and techniques of composition in collage—such as the selection of seemingly incompatible materials, assembly and destruction, integration and disintegration, juxtaposition and confrontation—also govern the experimental work which takes place in other artistic disciplines, in literature, in the theatre, in the film and in music.[11]

But we can take this further. The clearest explanation of the core concept of collage comes from the most influential of its surrealist practitioners, Max Ernst, according to whom collage is "the systematic exploitation of the fortuitous or engineered encounter of two or more intrinsically incompatible realities on a surface which is manifestly inappropriate for the purpose—and the spark of poetry which leaps across the gap as these two realities are brought together."[12] Ernst's formulation itself embodies a fortuitous or engineered reference to the celebrated phrase— much taken up by the surrealists—from Lautréamont's (1970: 177) *Les chants de Maldoror:* beautiful "as the chance meeting on a dissecting-table of a sewing machine and an umbrella,"[13] of which Yves Bonnefoy writes that

> When Surrealist thought took pleasure in reuniting, after the *Songs of Maldoror,* the sewing machine and the umbrella on the dissection table, those three objects remained specifically the instruments that we know by the integrity of their structure, which was at once abstract and rigorously defined. This structure, however, because of the obliteration of the rational perspective caused by the bizarre combination, henceforth appeared opaque, irreducible to its own meaning or any other, and the reunited objects became mysterious, carrying us by their purposeless existence to a new form of astonishment.[14]

And this, in turn, resonates with Ernst's description of making a collage:

> I see advertisements of all kinds of models, mathematical, geometrical, anthropological, zoological, botanical, anatomical, mineralogical, palaeontological and so forth, elements so diverse in nature that the absurdity of bringing them together has a disorien-

tating effect on the eye and the mind and generates hallucinations which give new and rapidly changing meanings to the objects represented. I felt my "sense of sight" suddenly so intensified that I saw the newly emerged objects appearing against a changed background. In order to hold them fast, all that was needed was a little colour or a few lines, a horizon, a desert, a sky, wooden floorboards and suchlike. And so my hallucination had been fixed.[15]

Each element of a collage, in other words, works on the others so as to release previously hidden or overlooked meanings within each element (the surrealist painter and writer Paul Nougé referred to everyday objects as "practically invisible")[16] and, in combination, to generate new, emergent meaning: each element transforms others and is itself transformed, while at the same time (as Bonnefoy says) retaining its original, mundane identity. In Elsa Adamowicz's (2000: 91) words, in reference to a collage by André Breton entitled "Chapeaux de gaze,"

> In the disruptive juxtaposition of a landscape and ladies' hats, the viewer moves between the image as a literal collection of disparate elements and as a figurative space, where metaphorical associations are generated. Collage parts both retain their original identity and are transformed by their new context. . . . They suggest a metaphorical transcendence without accomplishing it, obstinately declaring themselves hats, yet no longer hats.

True to Breton's Freudian definition of surrealism as expressed in the first (1924) *Manifeste du Surréalisme* ("Thought dictated in the absence of all control exerted by reason, and outside all aesthetic or moral preoccupation"),[17] the intention of surrealist juxtaposition—the creation of the surrealist object—was to elude or unravel narrative or other forms of rational interpretation. As J. H. Matthews (1977: 88) puts it, "Collage shares with other modes of surrealist expression in rescuing thought from the reductive effect of reasonable postulation"; so, for example, he says of Ernst's "*roman-collage*" of 1929 (which consists only of captioned images fastidiously assembled from late-nineteenth-century book engravings) that "in *La femme 100 têtes* we can detect no evidence of any effort to compensate through tonal unity for the bewildering diversity of pictorial material, turned to subversive account" (96). And he offers a description of a specific image (figure 6.1) that makes the point better than any amount of theoretical discussion (95):

> Ernst's *roman-collage* treats the novel form with as little respect as it does visible reality by blending its forms in inhabitual ways. On the extreme right, by a bed in which lies a human figure, head completely bandaged, stands a priest, his features apparently grotesquely masked. Close to us, to the left, an Amazon, her face concealed but her breasts visible, stands in a pose reminiscent of that of a Flamenco dancer. Discreetly crouching far left is a monkey, the only figure seemingly borrowed without modification from the natural world. Diverting reason from its prime task—establishing what is going on here—the caption asks: "Would this monkey be Catholic, by any chance?"[18]

That such thinking might be applicable to music is suggested by a comparison Breton invoked in order to explain the surrealist idea of emergent meaning: the quality of a melody, he said, "is totally different from the sum of its component qualities."[19] And an obvious musical equivalent (although from a very different

Figure 6.1. Max Ernst, engraving from *La femme 100 têtes*. Used by permission of Dorothea Tanning.

cultural milieu) might be John Zorn's *Snagglepuss*, track 7 from the *Naked City* album (played by Zorn's group of the same name).[20] Like much of Zorn's music from the late 1980s, this is a hard-driven amalgam of riotously different genres and styles, organized as a series of sound blocks. The moment I want to focus on is the beginning of the seventh of these blocks, which comes at twenty-eight seconds into the track. In Zorn's chart of the piece (reproduced in Service 2004: figure 1.4) this block is identified as "C BOOGIE BLUES BAND (sax solo)"; it follows a block marked "PNO SOLO," the genre of which might be described as moderately modernist but at the same time slightly jazzy. The established musicological approaches to collage to which I referred could find much to engage with here. The combination of highly contrasted generic types serves to problematize each of them, their meanings unraveling one another, in the same way that (in Adamowicz's [2000: 93] words) collage undoes meaning "from within, by dismantling oppositions, challenging discursive hierarchies and parodying pictorial conventions"; Ernst's collages bring to light the bourgeois worldview embedded in the nineteenth-century images they are made of (as Uwe Schneede [1972: 140] says, "The least intervention inverts or clarifies the banal pictorial situation, makes it speak, reveals it"), and in the same way Zorn's juxtapositions highlight through de-familiarization the humdrum, stereotypical qualities of his sound materials. At the same time they problematize the nature of the creative act and consequently the authorial identity of "the composer John Zorn" (Service 2004). But what concerns me here is the immediate experience of what happens at twenty-eight seconds into the track, what sticks in the ears.

At this point, however, I become mired in the concrete, unable to meet the challenge of generalization that words present, because—as always in the performing arts—*everything* counts in creating the effect.[21] The raucous, saxophone-dominated sound of the boogie band instantaneously blows away the piano, overwriting the auditory space it inhabited: the band sound erupts so suddenly and so cleanly that you almost have the impression that the band was playing all the time and has just been spliced in. (This effect must be particularly striking in live performance.) Yet the after-image of the piano sound persists and undercuts the presence of the boogie band: the music is loud and all-encompassing, and yet it takes on an unreal, even surreal, quality of metaphorical transcendence through the juxtaposition of incompatible sound worlds, of elements so diverse in nature that the absurdity of bringing them together has a disorientating effect on the ear and the mind. The reunited objects become mysterious, carrying us by their purposeless existence to a new form of astonishment: the sound image is uncanny, haunting, obsessive, a moment that plays itself over and over in your memory. Nor is there evidence of any effort on Zorn's part to compensate through tonal unity for the bewildering diversity of sound material. If we wanted at all costs to demonstrate the cogency of the transition, we could observe the neighbor-note linkage between the alternating D and E with which the piano block ends and the E♭ with which the boogie band begins, but this is the kind of analysis that knows all the answers before it has discovered the questions. It might be about as productive to ask if the saxophone could, by any chance, be Catholic.

Music as Montage

It is my intention, of course, to suggest that such effects are not restricted to overtly collage-based pieces like *Snagglepuss* but are in some sense ubiquitous in music (which is why I started with Beethoven). But first it will be helpful to develop the semiotics of juxtaposition through consideration of montage, which is essentially the application of the idea of collage to film. Whereas in French and Russian, "montage" is the standard term for film editing, in English it has specific connotations relating to the approach of the Russian Formalists and, in particular, Sergei Eisenstein (1898–1948), who was himself in touch with such Formalists as Victor Shklovsky, Boris Eikhenbaum, and Yuri Tynyanov (Eagle 1981: 30); Eisenstein extended the concept of montage to encompass relationships within a single frame and even picture-sound relationships (what he called "vertical montage"), but what I am concerned with here is its basic, horizontal sense of shot-to-shot editing. Montage, in a nutshell, is collage transferred to a temporal medium, and that is why it is the most direct model for the collage principle in music.

As I intended to suggest by my previous reference to "de-familiarization," there is an evident (if not well-documented) affinity between, on the one hand, the surrealist practice of re-contextualizing familiar objects or images and so rendering them (in Nougé's word) visible, and, on the other, the Russian Formalist idea that art subverts established patterns of perception and so brings about a new awareness of reality. There is a crucial difference, however: whereas the surrealist project of rescuing thought from the hegemony of reason resulted in a highly distinctive artistic movement, the Formalists aimed to develop a general aesthetic theory, applicable to all artistic productions. So did Eisenstein, who illustrated his theory of montage through reference to sources ranging from Japanese *haikai* to Dickens to Pushkin (Eisenstein 1949; 1991: chap. 6); as Trevor Whittock (1990: 73) puts it, he believed that his principles would "reveal the fundamental laws of all aesthetic construction and would scientifically illuminate the creative processes of the human mind itself." Given the importance of Eisenstein in the history not only of the narrative film but also of narrative film theory, it may seem strange to draw a comparison between his theory of montage and the principles adopted by the surrealists precisely to undercut narrativity—but less so if narrative and non-narrative film are seen not as mutually exclusive genres but rather as points on a continuum. For another Formalist, Adrian Piotrovsky, Eisenstein's films represented a hybrid combining "fictional narrative with purely poetic linkages and digressions" (Eagle 1981: 27), and this is an approach entirely compatible with Micznik's idea of "degrees of narrativity."[22] My concern in what follows, however, is not with narrative construction but with the basic semiotics of juxtaposition, the element I argued was missing from present-day narrative theory, and to which I see the theory of montage making an indispensable contribution.

Formalist film theory was distinctive in its attempt to construe film as an autonomous art; Tynyanov wrote, "To describe cinema in terms of contiguous art forms makes as much sense as it would to describe these art forms in terms of cinema: to call painting 'static cinema'; music as 'the cinema of sounds'; literature as 'the cinema of words.'"[23] For the Formalists, the essential nature of film lies in the activity of the viewer who makes sense of the film by understanding each shot in terms of the one preceding it. The basic principle, as Tynyanov explained, is that of "differential replacement"—the principle that "each shot should be related in some way to the preceding shots (either in terms of 'plot' or 'stylistically'), but in other respects should be contrastive and differential" (8). In Herbert Eagle's (1981: 15) words, each new shot acquires its meaning through "the presence of new objects or actions or of altered stylistic elements—which must be correlated (semantically) by the viewer with the corresponding elements of the previous shot." And this has a number of important consequences. First, meaning is not primarily inherent in the individual shot, but in the relationships with adjacent shots established through montage: as Eikhenbaum stated, "the basic semantic role belongs

to montage, since it is precisely montage which colors the shots with definite semantic nuances in addition to their general sense. There are well-known examples
of film editing where the very same shots, placed in a new montage 'context,' take
on a completely new meaning."[24] (That, of course, is the same point Vergo was
making in a museological context.) And, second, film is a time-based medium in
the most radical sense: a few sentences later Eikhenbaum says that "cinema is a
successive art, through and through," while Eisenstein (1949: 239) described it as
an "art of juxtaposition." It is precisely, in Levinson's term, "concatenationist."

A third consequence has to do with the relationship between shots. In Tynyanov's formulation, shots "deform" or "infect" one another, or, as he explained
more fully,

> Shots in cinema do not "unfold" in a successive formation, a gradual order—they
> *replace one another*. This is the basis of montage. They replace one another as a single
> verse, a single metrical unit, is replaced by another—at a precise boundary. Cinema
> *jumps* from shot to shot, just as verse does from line to line.[25]

This was basically Eisenstein's point when invoking *haikai*, Dickens, or Pushkin:
in each case he shows that the writing is constructed as a shot list, a series of elements that replace one another, and Eisenstein (1998: 96) further developed Tynyanov's idea of replacement when he wrote that, in film, "each sequential element
is arrayed, not *next* to the one it follows, but on *top* of it." But his most famous
contribution is the idea that "montage DERIVES from the collision of two shots that
are independent of one another" (95), and this provides the context for Eisenstein's
controversy with the contemporary Russian film director Vsevolod Pudovkin,
which Eisenstein described in a passage itself illustrative of his "shot list" approach. He begins by asking how montage is to be characterized, and answers:

> By collision. By the conflict of two pieces in opposition to one another. By conflict. By
> collision.
>   In front of me lies a crumpled yellow sheet of paper. On it is a mysterious note:
> "Linkage—P" and "Collision—E."
>   This is a substantial trace of a heated bout on the subject of montage between
> P (Pudovkin) and E (myself).
>   This has become a habit. At regular intervals he visits me late at night and behind
> closed doors we wrangle over matters of principle. A graduate of the Kuleshov
> school,[26] he loudly defends an understanding of montage as a *linkage* of pieces. Into a
> chain. Again, "bricks." Bricks, arranged in a series to *expound* an idea.
>   I confronted him with my viewpoint on montage as a *collision*. A view that from
> the collision of two given factors *arises* a concept.
>   From my point of view, linkage is merely a possible *special* case. . . .
>   Not long ago we had another talk. Today he agrees with my point of view. (Eisen-
> stein 1949: 37–38)

As my previous references to linkage in relation to Levinson and *Snagglepuss*
may suggest, this controversy is more than a matter of sophistry (like—to follow
Eisenstein's cue—the chestnut about whether the purpose of mortar is to stick
bricks together or keep them apart). This is because the idea of linkage implies a

preexisting meaning, inherent in the individual shot, whereas the basis of Eisenstein's approach is that juxtaposition creates emergent meaning: "*the result of juxtaposition,*" he wrote, "always differs *qualitatively* . . . from each constituent element taken separately" (1991: 297). Or as Eagle (1981: 34) expresses it, "Because the still frame as photograph contains potentially infinite properties, it is only in collision with other frames that signs can emerge as distinct by opposition."

Here we can begin tying together a number of loose ends. Eagle is effectively saying that the relationship between successive stills selects certain of their potentially infinite properties, makes them available for signification, while suppressing other properties—which is exactly the point I was making about the juxtaposition of a vase with other artifacts: different juxtapositions construct different meanings (and there is Vergo's point yet again). This kind of interaction between juxtaposed elements was also at issue in the discussion of collage, for instance, when Adamowicz talked in relation to Breton's "Chapeaux de gaze" of the disparate elements giving rise to a figurative space "where metaphorical associations are generated." Indeed, Breton himself saw metaphor as intrinsic to collage, describing the *Exquisite Corpse* (the surrealists' version of "Consequences," allegedly so termed because the first sentence they obtained from it was "The exquisite corpse will drink new wine") as "an infallible way of holding the critical intellect in abeyance, and fully liberating the mind's metaphorical activity."[27] Nougé, too, affirmed its centrality when he looked forward "to the day when metaphor will not be considered a mere artifice of language, a means of expression 'without reverberation in the mind using it or in the world to which it is addressed.'"[28] And if for the surrealists metaphor was the foundation of collage, then for Eisenstein (1949: 248), who saw metaphor as lying "at the very dawn of language," it was the foundation of montage; indeed, Whittock (1990: 70) claims bluntly that "Eisenstein's theory of montage is . . . a theory of metaphor."

In his 1944 essay, "Dickens, Griffith and the Film Today," Eisenstein introduces the idea of metaphor in relation to the effect, much used in his early films, that he called "intellectual montage," such as when, in *October,* he cut between Menshevik speeches and balalaikas ("The balalaikas were not shown as balalaikas, but as an image of the tiresome strumming of these empty speeches" [1949: 245]) or between Kerensky and a peacock. Tynyanov had previously discussed a similar montage of a man and a pig, concluding that "the result of such a sequence will not be the spatial and temporal continuity of man and pig, but rather a semantic figure: the man *is* a pig."[29] The figure in question is, of course, the metaphor, and the conjunction of Kerensky and a peacock—or a pig and a man—can be precisely analyzed in terms of Eisenstein's (1991: 33) description of metaphor as "an exchange of qualities between a pair, to one of which a certain quality properly belongs and to the other of which that quality, normally not associated with it, is unexpectedly transferred from somewhere else": such qualities as vanity, stupidity, noisiness, and decorative uselessness are transferred from the peacock to Kerensky (the man *is* a peacock). We could, moreover, bring the story up to date, for Nougé's wish came true. It is a basic principle, for many present-day cognitive linguists, that metaphor is not simply a literary figure but "a salient and pervasive cognitive process that links conceptualization and language," as Gilles Fauconnier (1997: 168) describes it, and the conjunction of Kerensky and the peacock could easily be represented in terms of the "conceptual integration networks" used by linguists like Fauconnier and Mark Turner: we would have two input spaces (a "Kerensky space" and a "peacock space") in which matched qualities are paired, and a "blended space" in which the resulting meaning emerges—that Kerensky is vain, stupid, noisy, in short, a peacock.

If the succession from the sixth to the seventh block of *Snagglepuss* is an example of sound collage, it is even more an example of sound montage. The juxtaposed blocks do not "unfold" in a successive formation, a gradual order—they *replace one another*, which is why I said that the sound of the boogie band overwrites the auditory space inhabited by the piano (although, as we saw, the piano's afterimage persists, so to speak, bleeding through and infecting the sound of the boogie band). And because each block in itself contains potentially infinite properties, it is only in collision with other blocks that signs can emerge as distinct by opposition; the result is a blended space in which the exchange of qualities gives rise to the uncanny, haunting, obsessive sound image to which I referred. But as I said, what I want to claim is that the principles of collage and montage apply not just to explicitly juxtapositional, intertextual music like *Snagglepuss* but to a much broader range of music, or even to music in general. And Queen's "Bohemian Rhapsody" (from the 1975 album *A Night at the Opera*) conveniently makes the point, because its famous and familiar video—generally seen as the first-ever music video—allows us to set visual and musical montage alongside each other.[30]

I begin with the lyrics, however, which—as with much British progressive rock seeking to expand beyond the constraints of the three-minute single—suggest but do not sustain a narrative. Following a reflective introduction (actually taken from a song written by Freddie Mercury before he joined Queen), the first two verses, in an expressive ballad-like style, set out a rudimentary story in the past tense and outline a present situation. This is expressed in the first-person singular and with an explicit addressee: "Mama, I just killed a man, / . . . If I'm not back . . . / Carry on, carry on as if nothing really matters." The final section, in heavy-rock style, also has an addressee, now unspecified ("So you think you can stone me and spit in my eye"), while the conclusion represents a reversion to the confessional mood of the introduction and even to its lyrics ("Nothing really matters to me. / Any way the wind blows" reflects the earlier line "Any way the wind blows doesn't really matter to me"). The central, operatic section also mirrors the words of the introduction ("I'm just a poor boy" and "Easy come, easy go"), but here the context is completely different: an invocation apparently addressed to a strikingly multicultural assembly of demons ("Bismillah . . . Mama mia . . . Beelzebub") and involving a number of interlocutors—the "I" of the outer sections, the anonymous supplicants, and the equally anonymous devils, the latter two groups represented as a chorus created by multi-tracking. Mercury said, in 1976, that "it's one of those songs which has such a fantasy feel about it. . . . I think that people should just listen to it, think about it and then make up their minds as to what it says to them."[31] Certainly the idea of trying to extract a specific, concealed meaning from the exotic references in the operatic section is unappealing: I imagine that not only "Bismillah," "Mama mia," and "Beelzebub" but also "silhouette," "Scaramouche," "Fandango," "Galileo," "Figaro" and "Magnifico" were chosen primarily for their sonorities and connotations, that is, for the immediate semantic effect they create. Moreover, to retain some kind of interpretive balance it is important to remember the band members' accounts of killing themselves with laughter during the recording session as they increasingly camped up this section, which, as a result, became far longer than originally intended.

But the farcical register of the entire central section is built right into the musical style. Both Mercury and contemporary commentators have described the central section as "operatic," but it is possible to be more specific: to my ears, the couplet "I'm just a poor boy and nobody loves me [first-person solo] / He's just a poor boy from a poor family [third-person chorus]" is straight out of Gilbert and Sullivan, where such effects were perhaps intended to parody the conventions of the chorus in Greek drama, while the inappropriate scansion (fa-mi-lý) heightens the ironic or farcical quality through its evocation of the world of amateur musicals. The shift from first to third person (the first appearance in the song of the third person, other than the retrospective "now he's dead" of the first verse) is realized musically not only by the contrast of solo and chorus but also by that of minor and major modes, while the video—cut by musical phrase throughout this section—alternates between Mercury's face and a symmetrical composition of the faces of all four band members that re-creates the cover image from the album *Queen 2* (animating that album was, of course, one of the starting points for the video). The whole of the operatic section essentially consists of a permutation of still images and thus can be seen as classic montage, classic differential replacement, so illustrating the affinity between the music video and the techniques and principles of the Russian filmmaking tradition:[32] rather than "unfolding," the video *jumps* from shot to shot, just as verse does from line to line, so that each sequential element is arrayed, not *next* to the one it follows, but on *top* of it. And that is precisely what the music does, too: if we are not accustomed to thinking of music in this way, it is because of the effect of sedimented notational and analytical representations that translate temporal succession into spatialized form and thereby domesticate the series of temporal shocks of which music, as a *successive* art, consists. (Maybe Wagner should be the patron saint of analysts: "Here time turns to space," as he famously wrote in *Parsifal*.)

But for my money the most uncanny registral shift of "Bohemian Rhapsody," both visually and musically, comes at the point where the operatic section gives way to the hard rock with which the final section begins. The transition between these two sections is as highly engineered as anything in *Romeo and Juliet*, with a characteristically overblown dominant cadence piled up stage-by-falsetto-stage over the repetitions of "for me" at the return to the tonic: Brian May's guitar riff, the most unambiguous possible arpeggiation of the tonic triad, somehow combines the qualities of ternary and quadruple meter, and thereby functions as a bridge between the duple or quadruple meter of the operatic section and the simple or compound ternary meter of "So you think you can stone me and spit in my eye." But, as before, this kind of cogency-oriented analysis seems to miss the point, which is located precisely at the moment of resolution. Visually and musically, it is again as if the constricted space and role-playing artifice of the operatic section are instantaneously blown away, with what sounds like the bang when a pantomime villain appears in a puff of smoke, though it is actually just a backbeat (both music and picture have been edited so that the final section starts on the fourth beat of the bar). Ocular and aural space open up to reveal a live heavy-rock performance with all the signifiers of authenticity fully in evidence—although one of the effects of the juxtaposition is to call this authenticity, and perhaps the whole idea of authenticity, into question: the rock vocal style retroactively infects the operatic vocal style, and vice versa, the collision of two incompatible constructions of vocal style transforming each into a "marked" term, revealing each not as a natural expression of passion but as a construction of artifice. (Why read Derrida on Rousseau when you could be watching "Bohemian Rhapsody"?)

The traditional approach to analyzing this uncanny moment would be to understand it in terms of the transition between two distinct structural entities or narrative registers: this would mean deriving the experience of the moment from the larger structure it expresses, in the way that I described at the beginning of this chapter in relation to the G major Concerto. But that, of course, is just the kind of side-by-side view, turning time to space, that I have been trying to avoid. The radical—but, for the reader, by now surely predictable—alternative is to say that music is a *successive* art, through and through, and that the focal point of the experience is the moment of disjunction, the differential replacement of one section by another eliciting certain qualities from the indefinite number available within them and so grounding the identification of them as sections in the first place. Understood from a strictly concatenationist point of view, any structural identification beyond this—even something as basic as seeing the final section as in some sense a return of the first—would fall into Levinson's category of "rarefied excellences," something built on but not necessary for basic music understanding. Although I have been consistently arguing this second point of view as a means of resisting the grip on music-theoretical thinking of the first, however, I would not describe the choice between two such bald positions as an appealing one. And here another parallel may be drawn with montage.

When Shklovsky's concept of story (fabula) was first applied to the cinema, it was by seeing film as the representation of an external reality, with the events of the story functioning not just as raw material but as "a kind of pre-existing schema or core structure" (Stam, Burgoyne, and Flitterman-Lewis 1992: 72). Tynyanov opposed this, arguing what might be called a "constructivist position":[33] he "insisted on the role of the shot in *defining* the significant semantic elements themselves, in differentiating objects and people in terms of their meaningful oppositions to one another" (Eagle 1981: 8). In short, Tynyanov argued that film is an agent in the construction of the reality it purports to represent, in the same way that Nattiez and Almén see musical narrative as being constructed through musical processes of signification. (The same argument could be applied to the Schenkerian variety of narrative, seeing background structures as constituted by the "expressions" which are said to be their results,[34] but I shall not pursue that idea here.) Still, film is obviously not the *only* source of that reality. Just as this approach to musical narrative gives rise to Micznik's idea of "degrees of narrativity," implying a continuum between narrative and non-narrative (or more and less narrative) genres, so Tynyanov's principle necessarily coexists with the principle of representation: it involves a correlation on the part of viewers between film elements and a reality that lies beyond the film—a reality whose perception is crucially mediated but not exclusively determined by the film. In short, the film narrative is codetermined by what is represented and the means of its representation.

Similarly we can think of a relationship of codetermination in music between the moment of juxtaposition and the structural formations or narrative registers that are juxtaposed, that is, between the part and the whole, the temporal and the spatial. Juxtapositional principles such as differential replacement not only elicit properties from what is juxtaposed and so create meaning, but also initiate chains of association (Tynyanov's "infection"): associations that run not only backward, through retention, as when you identify the final section of "Bohemian Rhapsody" as in some sense a return of the first, but also forward, through protention—as in the opening of the G major Concerto, where the juxtaposition of G major and B major sparks a search for, or at least an interpretive sensitivity to, the possibly significant recurrences of the G/B relationship throughout the rest of the concerto. The point, then, is not to reduce music to the semiotics of juxtaposition, to insist that it consists of nothing but differential replacement—we have suffered enough from "nothing but" theories of music—but rather to recognize the partial but creative and underestimated contribution that the collage principle plays in music.

Afterword: Music and the Great Wall of China

A start, at least, has been made on the task of reconstructing the historical links between the concepts of collage and montage, on the one hand, and, on the other, the music of twentieth-century composers for whom principles derived from the visual arts and—particularly—from film served as direct or indirect models for the shaping of music: examples include the work of Rebecca Leydon (2001) on Debussy,[35] Richard Burke (1999) on Shostakovich, and Ian Pace's ongoing study of Michael Finnissy's *History of Photography in Sound*. I have attempted a perhaps easier task in this chapter, drawing broad conclusions without trying to demonstrate direct influence, but the reader may reasonably ask: What has the grandly named "semiotics of juxtaposition" actually delivered in analytical terms? For example, what might "differential replacement" really mean as applied to music, over and above the Ruwet/Nattiez style of "paradigmatic" analysis, with its segmentation of music into shots, so to speak, on the basis of repetition (with each segment "replacing" the last), and with its identification of the "differential" relationships between segments? My answer to this revolves around the abstraction which any such analytical approach involves (another version of the "nothing but" syndrome) and can be expressed in terms of the G major Concerto: it is easy to define the relationship between G major and B major in technical terms (for instance, as keys removed by four notches on both the semitone and fifth cycles, the latter more relevant in this particular context), but the meta-language of musical notation—which becomes further abstracted through the transformational relationships between levels in hierarchical analysis—captures only a very restricted range of the qualities possessed by musical sounds. (It is this, perhaps, as much as an obsessive urge toward unity, that explains why the transition between measures 5 and 6 slips through Schenker's fingers.) The juxtapositional relationships I have focused on, by contrast, bring into play the full range of their semantic potential in the specific context of their occurrence—the characteristic quality, as I put it, that led Schenker to discuss the G major Concerto in the first place. There is something very concrete about juxtapositional relationships in music, as indeed there is about the collage principle in general: both resist generalization.

This focus comes at a cost, however: in this chapter I have consistently found myself running out of things to say—out of words or other determinate symbols—just when I should have had the most to say, that is, at the point where emergent meaning arises. I can see there is new meaning, an uncanny effect; I can even point to it and encourage you to think the same. But my efforts to specify exactly *what* is uncanny or emergent fall far short of the customary criteria for academic discourse. That is why I use the word *uncanny*, with its Freudian connotations: moments such as those I identified in *Snagglepuss* and "Bohemian Rhapsody" seem imbued with meaning, but the meaning remains stubbornly unconscious, cut off just as it reaches the tip of the tongue. Arguably this is a predictable consequence of the basic metaphorical process I have described: the emergent meaning that results from the transfer of attributes subsists precisely in a unique *blend* of attributes—a blend that is contrafactual, that does not exist in the real world, that we have not experienced before, and that, accordingly, is intrinsically hard to put into words.[36] (A comparison might be drawn with recipe books: the words give out just when the "semantically compositional" work [Dempster 1998], that is, the cooking, begins.) Seen from an analytical point of view, we consequently end up with the familiar structural or narrative constructs still in place, the only difference being two health warnings: first, that we should not see these constructs as autonomous entities from which moment-to-moment experience can be derived, but should instead view that experience as codetermined by the effects of juxtaposition; and, second, as if we didn't already know it, that notation-based analysis cannot capture more than a limited subset of what there is to hear in music. If the aim is something that looks, feels, and smells like traditional analysis—the sort of thing that can earn you a Ph.D. in theory—then this project must be judged a failure.

But instead of apologizing for the way we run out of words just when we want to say something new about music, I would prefer to present this in a positive light. In doing so, I want to distance myself from the negative critique of musical ineffability which the "New" musicologists of the 1990s put forward on the grounds of its association with discredited aesthetic ideologies of musical autonomy, and which Kramer (2002: 5), at least, has maintained into the new millennium: "I am always suspicious of claims to ineffability," he writes, "because people who invoke the unspeakable may use it to justify unspeakable things." One might object that this is little more than a pun on two distinct senses of "unspeakable," but at a deeper level I wonder whether his critique may not reflect a confusion between ineffability and the more dubious concept of transcendence—the point being that the ineffable may perfectly well be banal, it just can't be put into words.[37] Miller (1987: 98) makes the point in this way:

> Imagine for a moment attempting to describe in detail the difference in shape between a milk bottle and a sherry bottle, or the taste of cod as against haddock, or the design of some wallpaper. Clearly, compared with our ability to make fine discriminations of perceptual qualities and immediately to recognize and discriminate amidst a profusion of ordinary objects, linguistic description may appear slow and clumsy.

This does not mean, of course, that one *can't* use words to describe haddock, or music for that matter; as Kramer (2002: 14) says, "Addressing the nonverbal . . . is one of the most traditional functions of language." But the simple fact is that words do not work equally well for everything. Sticking—and not without reason—to the culinary theme, Adrienne Lehrer's book *Wine and Conversation* (1983) is a particularly clear demonstration, both eloquent and empirical, of the different ways that words may be applied to something inherently resistant to words, and the severe constraints on effective communication that result: even wine buffs, Lehrer found, were hard-pressed to formulate descriptions that would enable other wine buffs to identify the wine they were discussing. Her most telling observation was that, although her subjects believed they were learning to be far more discriminating through talking about wine, their actual performance at wine tastings did not improve.

And here I can invoke a final parallel with Russian film theory. Eisenstein (1988: 155–56) recognized, but at the same time deprecated, the incommensurability of rational language and what he called the "language of images": "It is the task of the coming age in our art," he wrote, "to tear down the Great Wall of China that separates the primary antithesis of the 'language of logic' and the 'language of images.'" Barthes echoed this recognition, but not the deprecation, in his essays on photographic images, which were strongly influenced by Eisenstein—most obviously in the case of "The Third Meaning," first published in 1970, which is subtitled "Research Notes on Some Eisenstein Stills." (Barthes's references throughout to "SME" establish a tangible intellectual intimacy.) An obvious difference between the views of Barthes and Eisenstein is that Barthes locates the core of filmic meaning in the still, whereas the basic principle of montage is that meaning arises from the conjunction of frames. Yet in "The Third Meaning" Barthes (1977: 67) invokes Eisenstein's concept of vertical montage to justify his position, and, in any case, the difference may be more apparent than real: for anyone who knows the film, the stills derive meaning from the juxtapositional relationships of which they are a trace (Barthes implies as much when he refers to the still as a "quotation" [67]). The difference, then, more than anything else, may be one of tense: whereas moving pictures represent actions as they unfold, stills, by definition, reference the past.

By the "third meaning," Barthes intends a distinction between primary and secondary signification (what he calls "denotation" and "connotation"), but given the density of references in these essays it is hard to overlook the echo of a similar term used by Eisenstein, as for example when he said he was "obsessed by the fact that unrelated sequences, when juxtaposed by the will of the film editor—and often *despite* being unrelated—gave rise to a 'third something' and became related" (1991: 298). Barthes (1977: 54) calls his third meaning "the one 'too many,' the supplement that my intellection cannot succeed in absorbing, at once persistent and fleeting, smooth and elusive," and adds: "I propose to call it *the obtuse meaning*." Prompted by the detail of a headdress, the angle of an eyelid, a fish (Barthes selects his images from *Battleship Potemkin*), the obtuse meaning "appears to extend outside culture, knowledge, information," and is "indifferent to moral or aesthetic categories" (55, perhaps echoing Breton's 1924 definition of surrealism). Inherently carnivalesque, it is "theoretically locatable but not describable" (65), "a signifier without a signified, hence the difficulty in naming it" (61), "outside (articulated) language while nevertheless within interlocution. For if you look at the images I am discussing, you can see this meaning, we can agree on it 'over the shoulder' or 'on the back' of articulated language" (61). Probably unintended by the director, Barthes adds, the obtuse meaning operates independent of the overt meaning that forms the focus of film criticism: it is "the epitome of the counter-narrative; disseminated, reversible, set to its own temporality, it inevitably determines (if one follows it) a quite different analytical segmentation to that in shots, sequences and syntagms (technical or narrative)—an extraordinary segmentation: counter-logical and yet 'true'" (63). Put another way, it is the locus of the uncanny, which, for Freud (1953), was distinguished by three factors, all characteristic of Barthes's obtuse meaning: its linkage to repressed mental contents (repressed, in this case, by the overt meaning that forms the focus of film criticism); its de-familiarization of the everyday; and its ineffability. The resonances with Breton and Miller on surrealist and material objects are palpable.

For Barthes, "it is at the level of the third meaning, and at that level alone, that the 'filmic' finally emerges. The filmic is that in the film which cannot be described, the representation which cannot be represented" (64). But to anyone who thinks that music analysis works on the back of language rather than through it, that music flows below the level of and often in opposition to official, administered culture, that musical meaning is theoretically locatable but not describable, Barthes's obtuse meaning must sound as much musical as filmic. And the connection in Barthes's own mind becomes evident when "The Third Meaning" is read alongside "The Grain of the Voice" (1972), for although Barthes refers in the later essay to neither a "third" nor an "obtuse" meaning, his comparison between the singing of Panzera and Fischer-Dieskau can hardly be read as anything other than a case study in precisely that. (The giveaway, if proof is needed, is the reference in "The Grain of the Voice" to Kristeva's concept of *signifiance* [Barthes 1977: 182], which links to the statement in the earlier essay that "this third level . . . is that of *signifiance*" [54].) While Fischer-Dieskau's singing is the perfect expression of everything that can be said about music, Panzera's represents "the materiality of the body speaking its mother tongue" (182): it expresses everything about music that *cannot* be said. And so the 1972 essay, which ends with a speculation about how different the history of music would be if written around the grain of the voice (which is almost to say if written around performance rather than composition), returns to its opening gambit: if language "is the only semiotic system capable of *interpreting* another semiotic system," Barthes asks, "how, then, does language manage when it has to interpret music?" And he answers, "Alas, it seems, very badly" (179).

But perhaps we shouldn't be surprised at this linkage between Barthes's "third meaning," Eisenstein's "third something," and music, for music plays a foundational role in Eisenstein's thinking—or at least (and this comes to much the same thing) he saw it as having a foundational role in film. This is not just a matter of his definition of "vertical montage" in terms of an orchestral score (Eisenstein 1991: 330), or his ubiquitous use of terms like "counterpoint," "polyphony," "the tonal dominant," or "overtonal montage"; even more telling is Eisenstein's contention that music "is not something totally new which only came into cinema along with sound films, and that in the preceding stages of cinema we are right in discerning a kind of 'pre-music'" (239). In saying this he is referring to the examples of "intellectual montage" in *October*, such as the juxtaposition of the Mensheviks with balalaikas and of Kerensky with a peacock—juxtapositions that modern viewers find rather forced and that Eisenstein (1949: 245) himself refers to as "slightly naive." These, he explains, represented attempts "to anticipate that which is now done with such ease by the music track in the sound film" (245), and so "the 'future' of montage lies in musical composition" (1991: 4). It is evident that for Eisenstein, then, montage is as inherently musical as it is filmic.

And at this point I am reminded of one of my earlier quotations from Tynyanov, which I now present in a modified form: "To describe music in terms of contiguous art forms makes as much sense as it would to describe these art forms in terms of music: to call painting 'visual music'; film as 'the music of moving pictures'; literature as 'the music of words.'" Maybe we should resist the constant urge to borrow models from literature, from material culture, even from film, and instead understand music as the paradigm case of the uncanny, the third meaning, the meaning that can be heard but not spoken.

Notes

A much abbreviated version of this chapter was presented at the Symposium of the International Musicological Society in Melbourne, July 11–16, 2004. My thanks to Nick Reyland and Carol Vernallis for their comments on a draft of it.

1. This term was perhaps unfortunately chosen, as the established narratological terminology drawn from the Russian Formalists uses the word "plot" as equivalent to "discourse" or "syuzhet": Newcomb's "paradigmatic plot" corresponds, then, to "story" (fabula), *not* "plot."
2. See, for instance, Kramer 1991; Maus 1991; Nattiez 1990a.
3. Quoted in Micznik 2001: 219; my emphasis.

4. The Schenkerian resonances become even stronger when Newcomb (1987: 167) seeks to distinguish these functional relationships from "the formal diagrams in music appreciation text books," the nearest American equivalent to the "false theory" against which Schenker inveighed.

5. Stam, Burgoyne, and Flitterman-Lewis (1992: 74) make a similar suggestion in relation to literature, paraphrasing Mieke Bal: "one can use narrative theory to analyze poetic or verse texts which possess a narrative component, such as T. S. Eliot's *The Waste Land;* but the narrative dimension is of secondary importance in such works, so that narrative analysis is perhaps not the most salient approach."

6. Cited in Levinson 1997: 6–7.

7. See Bennett 1995: 213, citing Carol Breckenridge. The following is a delayed follow-up to n. 57 of Cook 2001.

8. Hooper-Greenhill 2000: 25; the "[*sic*]" is Hooper-Greenhill's.

9. Letter to Anthony Lewis; quoted in Brooks 2004.

10. Daniel Miller (1987: 95–96) makes a similar point: the danger of the semiotic approach to material culture, he says, is "subordinating the object qualities of things to their word-like properties. . . . [A]rtefacts need to be explicitly distinguished from language. There have been very few attempts systematically to contrast their different properties."

11. Translated in Schneede 1972: 122.

12. Ibid., 29.

13. (Le Comte de) Lautréamont was the pseudonym of Isadore Ducasse (1846–1870).

14. Translated in Waldberg 1965: 29.

15. Translated in Schneede 1972: 30.

16. Matthews 1977: 219.

17. Translated in Waldberg 1965: 72.

18. "Ce singe, serait-il catholique, par hasard?" is the twenty-first image from chapter 2 of Ernst's *La femme 100 têtes* (1956). The book's title is based on the identical pronunciation of "100" (*cent*) and "without" (*sans*): the woman with 100 heads is at the same time headless (Matthews 1977: 98). Figure 6.1 is reproduced by kind permission of Dorothea Tanning.

19. From André Breton, *Le Surréalisme et la peinture,* translated in Waldberg 1965: 84.

20. Nonesuch 79238 (1989).

21. In Baz Kershaw's (1992: 22) words, it is "a fundamental tenet of performance theory . . . that no item in the environment of performance can be discounted as irrelevant to its impact."

22. Eagle (1981: 8–9) writes that by "defining cinematic narrative in terms of *differential succession* of shots (and not necessarily a succession based on 'development'), Tynyanov opened the possibility of considering the established story-oriented narrative and the new 'poetic' devices and genres as differing realizations of the same conceptual model."

23. Translated in Eagle 1981: 85.

24. Ibid., 78.

25. Ibid., 93.

26. Lev V. Kuleshov was a director and early theorist of montage, known, among other things, for experiments demonstrating the influence of context on the meaning of individual shots. See, for example, Burke 1999: 419–20.

27. From "Le cadavre exquis: son exaltation" (1948), translated in Waldberg 1965: 95 (the claim about the origin of its name is on the previous page).

28. Translated in Matthews 1997: 195. The quotation is from a section of Nougé's essay "Les images défendues," entitled "Le métaphore transfigure."

29. Translated in Eagle 1981: 89.

30. The following is based on the remastered version of the "Bohemian Rhapsody" video on *Queen: Greatest Video Hits 1* (DTS Parlophone 7243 4 92944 9 3 [PAL]). The video was made in November 1975 for a "Top of the Pops" appearance at which the band was unable to be present; it was shot at Elstree Studios in two days and cost about £4,000. The full lyrics may be found on the web.

31. See http://www.queencollector.com/Monthly/blueborap.htm; accessed 7 July 2004.

32. For further discussion, see Vernallis 2004: 29–30.

33. My use of this term is in reference to Hodge 1993.

34. Here I am echoing Judith Butler's (1990: 25) claim that "gender identity . . . is performatively constituted by the very 'expressions' that are said to be its results."

35. Leydon's account of early audiences' experiences of the cinema, before the development of established narrative conventions and the competence to read them, offers a striking parallel to the experiences of incoherence in Beethoven's music with which I began this chapter—just as, arguably, the complacent experience of present-day narrative cinema parallels that of so-called structural listening to classical music.

36. Raffman (1993: 4) defines "nuance ineffability" in terms of "the absence of certain categorical structures at early ('shallow') levels in the listener's series of representations of the musical signal. It turns out that certain features of the music, often called 'nuances,' are likely to be recovered so early in the representational process that they fail to be mentally categorized or type-identified in the manner thought necessary for a verbal report." Although the juxtapositions with which I am concerned do not specifically involve nuance in Raffman's sense, nevertheless a general affinity exists with the model she proposes.

37. I owe this formulation to Peter Franklin.

7 The Sacrificed Hero:
Creative Mythopoesis in Mahler's *Wunderhorn* Symphonies

Byron Almén

There is something undeniably grand about the symphonies of Gustav Mahler. Their popularity with modern concert audiences, their pride of place in the orchestral repertoire, and their continuing presence on the best-seller lists of classical music recordings lend credence to the view that Mahler's music has acquired a sort of mythic resonance within Western society. The appeal of these symphonies can probably be traced to multiple factors, among them an epic scale, an unabashed emotionality in combination with formal complexity, a willingness to explore the heights and depths of human experience, brilliant orchestration, an expressive palette ranging from delicate simplicity to overwhelming power—and a profoundly intuitive appropriation of symbolic associations and patterns.

Mahler's symbolic landscape has been extensively mapped, most influentially by Constantin Floros in his three-volume German-language study, *Gustav Mahler.*[1] What is striking about Mahler's particular employment of cultural symbols is not only their relative abundance and variety but also the primary role they play in shaping and maintaining the musical discourse. If narrative procedures indeed govern these works, such procedures are inseparable from the symbolic network in a manner exceeded by no other symphonist's output. Given the centrality of symbol and metaphysical confession in Mahler's music, and given the resonance these works have engendered in our culture, it would not be inappropriate to propose that this music has become for us the embodiment of a contemporary myth, a vision of profound importance. This process is made possible by Mahler's encoding of a historically rich symbolic corpus within a frame that endows it with new and vital meaning, enlivened and informed by technical virtuosity and keen compositional instinct. In other words, Mahler's music has become attached to conventional or traditional symbols that are configured in unique and innovative ways, thereby effecting a change in the way these symbols are understood. I will argue in the following pages that Mahler—and those of us who encounter his music—are engaging in what myth scholars call *creative mythopoesis,* forming new myths from old to introduce different ways of confronting reality.

Although Mahler's symbolic artifacts have increasingly become available to us for observation and analysis, a fuller understanding of the identification of Mahler's symphonies as myth is required. Approaches to analyzing programmatic symbols in a musical work typically fix symbolic meanings from the standpoint of the composer's intentions or the composer's historical and cultural milieu. This approach can reveal certain primary connotations that a listener would carry into an interpretive appraisal of the work. Although a necessary starting point, this method is also limiting, since it creates a closed semantic space from which the listener is at least partially excluded, culturally and temporally separated from the composer's constructed world. Furthermore, the composer, in making use of certain symbolic elements, cannot exclude the listener from apprehending a wider range of historical meanings that had attached to these symbols over time, meanings that both enrich and expand the boundaries of specific interpretations intended by the composer. Finally, the symbolic network, however intricate, loses its interpretive specificity if it is not correlated with details of the temporal unfolding of the work. Thus, to bridge the gap between composer and listener, to account for the way that the larger history of the constituent symbols plays against an orthodox interpretation, and to ground the hermeneutic process through the constraints of the score, an act of creative mythopoesis is also required of the analyst. The danger of putting cerebration in the way of direct experience is offset by the awareness such an approach provides of the multifaceted components of a living myth.

As an illustration of this approach, the chapter features an analysis of symbols in Mahler's *Wunderhorn* symphonies from a variety of interrelated perspectives. First, the semantic space of Mahler's symbols is opened out to include historically antecedent meanings. This adds a greater specificity and richness to the interpretation. The *Wunderhorn* symphonies have been singled out both for the richness of their semantic and metaphysical elements and for their cyclic narrative structure (see below). I do not dwell on the specific contexts of these symbols in late-nineteenth-century Western Europe, as this has been studied at great length.[2] Rather, I expand the interpretive reach of the analysis to search for the historical antecedents to those of the nineteenth century, associations derived from the biblical, classical, and medieval Romance traditions. Although these symbols accrued more culture- and time-specific associations in the late-Romantic period, the addition of more comprehensive associations better illuminates the "bundle of semiotic potential" through which meaning emerges (Melrose 1994: 221–22; quoted in Cook 2001: 179). I also indicate how the specific configuration of these venerable symbols in Mahler's music leads to the discovery of new dimensions in traditional materials. My analysis takes as its object the living body of symbols that have become sufficiently attached to the *Wunderhorn* symphonies through contributions from *any* relevant source—the composer, biographers, acquaintances, analysts, historians, and critics. This body of symbols is then posited to possess a semantic unity, which can be subjected to exegesis, interpretive amplification, and narrative coding. My intention is both serious and tongue-in-cheek: although there is something arbitrary about joining together symbolic resonances from multiple sources—along with their historical antecedents—to form a discrete cultural object, it is precisely this object which is posited and constructed by scholars speaking to a culturally aware audience. Further, it calls attention to the even greater degree of arbitrariness that results from focusing exclusively on Mahler's apparent intentions or the symbolic language of his cultural zone.

Second, the symbolic meanings are coordinated with respect to a clearly observable cyclic organizational scheme in the *Wunderhorn* symphonies, illustrated via a critically influential treatment of cyclic imagery by the literary critic Northrop Frye. Frye's (1957) cycle of four mythic archetypes, or *mythoi*, are distinguished by the use of certain constellations of imagery and by particular dramatic trajectories, which are summarized in the subsequent analysis.[3] These cyclic interpretations of the symbolic material echo Mahler's own cosmological perspectives and are meant to clarify the large-scale mythic and formal design, not to universalize a particular analytical or methodological paradigm.

Third, a sociological analysis of Mahler's hero as a scapegoat for cultural transgression using the formulation of René Girard is put forward. Finally, a partial narrative analysis coordinates symbolic material with formal and thematic process in individual movements. Each of these four perspectives reveals a different facet through which creative mythopoesis is enacted within the *Wunderhorn* symphonies, and can serve to enrich the interpretation of Mahler's "program" by developing it in depth.

Since myths are often considered to be primitive explanations of the world, or ancient stories about the gods, it would be useful first to clarify just what is meant by myth. William Doty (2000: 33–34), a mythographic authority, suggests the following comprehensive definition:

> A mythological corpus consists of a usually complex network of myths that are culturally important, imaginal stories, conveying by means of metaphoric and symbolic diction, graphic imagery, and emotional conviction and participation the primal, foundational accounts of aspects of the real, experienced world, and humankind's roles and relative statuses within it.
>
> Mythologies may convey the political and moral values of a culture and provide systems of interpreting individual experience within a universal perspective, which may include the intervention of suprahuman entities as well as aspects of the natural and cultural orders. Myths may be enacted or reflected in rituals, ceremonies, and dramas, and they may provide materials for secondary elaboration, the constituent mythemes (mythic units) having become merely images or reference points for a subsequent story, such as a folktale, historical legend, novella, or prophecy.

The exhaustiveness of this definition reveals that myth can function in multiple ways, appear in multiple forms, and be understood via multiple perspectives. In the case of Mahler's music, issues such as cultural significance, symbolic diction, imagery, the role of humanity in society and the world, the values of a culture, the natural versus the cultural order, and the secondary elaboration of material can all be elaborated.

In the process of exploring the *Wunderhorn* symphonies, I develop the thesis that their symbolic landscape presents the listener with both a powerful critique of the relationship between the individual and society, and a worldview that attempts to rethink that relationship. To use Nicholas Cook's (2001: 184) formulation, I illustrate how mythic symbols and organizing structures engage specific musical features to support a "blended space" that communicates a synergistic meaning not found in any component alone. In the interest of employing a shared terminological consensus, I appeal to the thematic, motivic, and formal labels established by Floros in the volumes indicated above.[4]

Romance Mythos (First Symphony)

The first stage in Frye's narrative cycle that appears in the *Wunderhorn* symphonies is the romance. Frye's conception of romance is that of a sociopersonal wish fulfillment, a dramatic valorization and reconfirmation of the value hierarchy of a society (1957: 186). There is generally a clear separation of "good" (that which is acceptable to, or idealized by, society) and "evil" (that which is unacceptable to, or demonized by, society), with the protagonist representing a heroic embodiment of the former and a bulwark against the latter. The romance is the successful quest, the dangerous journey leading to a struggle against that which would threaten social existence or coherence (187). In the Western world, the primary models are classical, biblical, or Christian/mythological: the rescue of the Athenian youths from the Minotaur in the labyrinth by Theseus, the apocalyptic victory of Christ over Satan, the slaying of the dragon by St. George. The emphasis of the romance, according to Frye, is on adventure and the overcoming of insuperable difficulties (195). In essence, the romance derives from a particular combination of the protagonist's place in society (largely reflecting the social order) and the narrative outcome (the reconfirmation of that hierarchy), in conjunction with the particular symbolic constellations described above.[5]

In the First Symphony's "myth," romance is both affirmed and denied. I argue that Mahler's hero takes up the struggle on society's behalf, despite his problematic relation to society. This leads to a conflicted sense of resolution: within the frame of the symphony, a conventional romance anchored on the opposition of paradise and inferno unfolds successfully; within the *Wunderhorn* symphonies as a whole, however, the hero is both unsuited to the task and expendable, motivating a reevaluation of the individual and society in the remaining *mythoi*.

The title listed for the First Symphony in the concert notes of the Hamburg performance on October 27, 1893, was "Titan."[6] There has been considerable discussion about the extent to which this title reflected a kinship between the symphony and Jean Paul's novel of the same name. Whether the connection is extensive or merely analogical, the term itself has an obvious historical symbolic existence that would also be familiar to audiences in Mahler's time. In keeping with the mythographic framework expressed above—that the literary and philosophical foundations of the tetralogy's symbols have been extensively treated and that a wide-ranging, if general, approach to symbolic association would be a useful analytical supplement—I examine these symbols in their mythic and folkloric contexts.

The Titans, according to Greek mythology, were the sons of Heaven (Uranus) and Earth (Gaia), who, led by Cronos, castrated their father in an attempt to seize power over creation but were then themselves defeated by their Olympian children. Insofar as the rule of Zeus coincides with the establishment of social order, we can understand the Titans as *pre-cultural* manifestations of natural power. They thus embody a physical, earthy potency arising from the lack of boundaries associated with a point of beginning. The Titans are ambivalent figures, possessing vitality, youth, and elemental force, yet lacking restraint or the benefits of spirit and consciousness (Diel 1966: 117–19). Accordingly, they would seem to be identified with the nature-hero before the attainment of consciousness: such a hero is illustrated in the first movement of the First Symphony (144). Yet the Titans have also come to represent the tyrannical impulses of society that are justified in the name of universal progress, in that they sought dominion over the nascent consciousness of the spirit represented by the Olympians (144). Here, too, is a contrast with the humane, conscious individual but from the other pole, from society. Hence the Titans inhabit the extremes against and through which the individual becomes realized: on the one hand, the unruly potency and chaos of "nature" and, on the other, the arbitrary exercise of power by "culture." If the hero of the Titan symphony is a Titan in the sense of "a strong, heroic person, living and suffering, struggling with and succumbing to destiny" (Bauer-Lechner 1984: 173), he is also a being set apart from the Titans of chaotic, undifferentiated nature and arbitrary, overdifferentiated society. The role of the individual, the creative artist, in the world and in society is the theme suggested by the symbol of the Titan.

The first two movements of the First Symphony (along with the excised *Blumine* movement) are grouped together in the Hamburg concert notes under the heading "From the Days of Youth: Music of Flowers, Fruit, and Thorn."[7] The First Symphony illustrates the second of Frye's types, or phases, of romance, which Robert D. Denham (1978: 81) calls the "pastoral innocence phase."[8] This phase emphasizes the youthful hero, living within "a pastoral and Arcadian world" and "longing to enter a world of action" (Frye 1957: 200). One of the critical features of this phase is the tenuousness of the hero's strength, which has not yet been tempered by experience. As a result, this phase is closer to the threshold of tragedy, since the hero's relative innocence makes him vulnerable.

The subtitle "Music of Flowers, Fruit, and Thorn" (which also alludes to the writer Jean Paul [Floros 1977a: 54]) contains three images that reinforce the governing symbols of youth and nature. Flowers, which without effort receive rainwater from the sky and nutrients from the earth, are symbols of passive growth and manifestation. The German writer Novalis equates the flower with the innocence of childhood and of primeval nature (Chevalier and Gheerbrant 1994: 395).

Fruit, of course, suggests abundance and plenty; but several myths suggest a further meaning, the acquisition of knowledge and power which is both divine and forbidden (the Garden of Eden narrative, the Golden Apples of immortality from the Garden of the Hesperides, and Paris's Apple of Discord all illustrate this trope [Chevalier and Gheerbrant 1994: 55]). The combination childhood/abundant food appears both at the beginning and at the end of the *Wunderhorn* symphonic cycle but in very different guises. In the first movement of the First Symphony, it is the hero *in potentia* who possesses riches yet undiscovered, while in the final movement of the Fourth, the cornucopia of the heavenly feast is the prize, the result of the hero's transvaluation of society and the world.

The thorn's most obvious feature is its ability to deliver pain, suggesting the notion of obstacles to be overcome. Thorn bushes, however, are also associated biblically with the wild, untamed soil, and therefore with virginity and unrealized potential. For example, Goethe's little poem, "Heidenroslein," set by Schubert, suggests this equation of thorns with virginity. In conjunction, flowers, fruit, and thorns constellate a series of impressions that reinforce the textual and musical elements.

The programmatic explanation for the first movement, "Spring and No End," requires little elaboration.[9] The "awakening of nature from a long winter's sleep" indicated by the Hamburg program is the first overt linkage between *Wunderhorn* cycle and seasonal cycle.[10] The cultural semantic complex of *spring–youth–primeval nature–nascent creativity* is clearly indicated here. The phrase "No End" suggests overabundance and exuberance, although the implied notion of eternity is interesting in a larger sense: the slumber of Nature depicted at the beginning of the movement seems to take place "out of time," as though the action had not yet leaped across the gap from the divine, the unformed, the timeless, into the human, the social/individual, and the temporal cycle(s). Indeed, as David Birchler suggests (1991: 134–36, 249–50), the opening octave As' delineation of a vast registral space is suggestive of simple, undifferentiated nature; the use of harmonics in this passage gives it an expectant, non-conditioned character. The emergence of the individual and the social *together* in this movement is required before anything meaningful can happen.

The process of emergence is presented to us through the device of the musical topos, particularly (and not surprisingly) those connected with nature and with simple, rustic society. The cuckoo, the fanfare, the folk melody are all familiar, even *clichéd*, musical-semantic devices, but of course they have a wider context in Western culture, from which this particular network of symbols is drawn. The interval of the fourth spawns almost every important motive in the first movement, bringing all the relevant symbols into a subtle unity that is also the unity of the beginning times. The initial descending "Theme of Fourths" (Floros 1994: 33) lacks any obvious semantic connotation, but since it contains the germinal motive, it can stand for the undifferentiated source from which the hero, the society, the world emerge. Eric Gould, in his *Mythic Intentions in Modern Literature* (1981), speaks of myth as striving to span the ontological gap between event and meaning, a process that mirrors the listener's attempts to construct a meaningful network of relationships in music. Although this process occurs at every moment in a myth, we have at the beginning of the *Wunderhorn* symphonies a stylized crystallization of the creative urge to give meaning to reality. Birchler (1991: 250, 257) argues that the "Theme of Fourths" is the first constructive element of culture, partitioning the empty octaves into their most fundamental components, the fourth and fifth. Of the multivalent ways to interpret this passage, we can see not only the emergence of "reality" from an inchoate nature but also the emergence of the creativity of the artist out of pure potential.

a) Ob.

pp

b) Tpt. 1-2

Schnell

c) 1. 2.

Hn.

4.

molto espress.

pp sehr weich gesungen

pp espress.

d) Cl. 1

sf > *sf* > *sf* > *sf* >

Example 7.1. Mahler, Symphony no. 1, first movement
  a. "Theme of Fourths," mm. 18–21
  b. Fanfare, mm. 36–38
  c. Horn call, mm. 32–36
  d. Cuckoo, mm. 30–32
Continued on the next page

   The "Theme of Fourths" (example 7.1a), as mentioned above, spawns the significant material for the remainder of the movement: the fanfare (example 7.1b), the horn call (example 7.1c), the cuckoo (example 7.1d), the folklike melody from the song "Ging heut Morgen über's Feld" (example 7.1e), and even the *cantabile* cello theme introduced 4 measures before rehearsal 16, with its series of wide intervals culminating in a perfect fourth (example 7.1f).[11] "Ging heut Morgen über's Feld" is the second of four songs from Mahler's earlier song cycle, *Songs of a Wayfarer,* and the *Wunderhorn* symphonies contain a number of other significant musical borrowings from this cycle. The cuckoo, in the Western musical tradition, is an icon of Nature and of the pastoral. In classical mythology, the cuckoo figures most prominently as a symbol of Hera, who resisted any advance from Zeus until

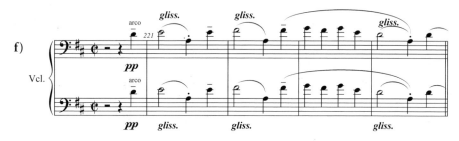

Example 7.1. Mahler, Symphony no. 1, first movement
  e. Melody (from "Ging heut Morgen über's Feld"), mm. 63–71
  f. First phrase of *cantabile* cello theme, mm. 221–24

he took the form of a "bedraggled cuckoo," whereupon she tenderly embraced him and was taken advantage of by the re-transformed god and shamed into marrying him (Graves 1992: 50). This legend contributes two layers of meaning to the Mahler symphonies. The first of these relates to Hera's role as goddess of fertility. The cuckoo is a particularly apt symbol for this, as it is traditionally the harbinger of spring. Second, the association of this bird with the seduction of Hera by Zeus has given rise to a secondary association of the cuckoo as the manifestation of the divine Spirit in the rain cloud (which also stands for Hera [Lanoé-Villène, quoted in Chevalier and Gheerbrant 1994: 268]). It is also worth noting that in nineteenth-century Germany the cuckoo was considered a sign of good fortune and future abundance (Leach 1984: 267). All these aspects reinforce the central themes of the first movement of the First: fecundity, spiritual awakening, beginnings.

The bird is also a universal symbol of the soul, particularly in its capacity as the instrument of rebirth or transformation.[12] Avian symbolism pervades the *Wunderhorn* symphonies from this moment on; note the "Bird of the Night" in the dramatically critical finale of the Second, the return of the cuckoo in the forest movement of the Third, and the magic flight through Paradise in the third movement of the Fourth (Floros 1977b: 205; 1994: 102, 127). Although each of these images has its specific connotations, the concept of the hero's journey is reinforced by the cultural significance given to the bird-as-spirit.

The horn call, unlike the cuckoo, has a distinctly social orientation. It first appears in the clarinets in measure 9, with a *pianissimo* dynamic as though located far off. The key of the call is a half-step higher than the prevailing key of A major as though being in, but not of, nature (Birchler 1991: 137). Here the horn call clearly represents the appearance of the human, of culture, in the natural landscape.

The military fanfares that first appear in measure 36 have a similar character. In conjunction with the network of images already discussed, the fanfare is simultaneously a call to action, a manifestation of "culture" out of the natural, and the sonorous display of divine power and authority. The most obvious function of the fanfare and the horn call in Western music, as writers like Ratner (1980: 3–27) and Hatten (1994: 74–75) have pointed out, is as an icon of the military or hunting worlds. Apart from the participation of nature in the hunt, however, this connotation seems out of place here. Instead, the ceremonial role of the fanfare appears to initiate or proclaim the arrival of an event of great cultural or cosmic importance—represented musically 6 measures before rehearsal 26, when the call recurs in trumpets and horns. The sound of the fanfare ushers in the biblical Apocalypse, and in many cultures trumpets are blown to summon the gods (Lavedan 1931: 980, quoted in Chevalier and Gheerbrant 1994: 1039–40). The fanfare is also ubiquitous in Mahler's music: most important, it figures in the Judgment music in the Second Symphony. In the First, however, the fanfare suggests what Campbell (1968: 49–58) terms the "Call to Adventure," the first stage of the hero's journey. The hero emerges out of the purely mythical world of "nature" (itself a cultural construction) and into the human world, with its codes, its hierarchies, and its dramatic field of competition. In a sense, the fanfare is the presence of the construction of culture even amid the manifestation of the primordial. Mahler's evocation of slumbering nature itself gives rise to the communal, in that the hero cannot exist except in relationship with (and against) the society he belongs to. The fanfare is potent not merely because it speaks with the voice of society, however. The power of the brass instruments to carry over large distances gives fanfares an awe-inspiring quality, a power through which the divine can speak. Even the wind fanfares create the fiction of horns heard at a distance. Fanfares in this symphony are essentially ambiguous: we do not know the source of the call (social? personal? divine?), so it acquires the character of mystery in keeping with the atmosphere of potential and anticipation.

If the introduction does not exclude either the natural or the social, neither does it appear as entirely positive in value. The foreboding, chromatic line introduced by the cellos and basses after rehearsal 3 (mm. 47–50) is not simply a foreshadowing of the finale but illuminates the amorality (the sense of being "beyond good and evil") of the germinal material. This passage, with its triplets and chromatic melodic construction, is akin to the Infernal music of the finale,[13] but it does not yet act in opposition to the hero; in fact, this music prepares for the emergence of culture and the hero as represented by the "Ging heut morgen" melody. Thus the hero is "premodalized" by divine, neutral, and infernal features.[14] The introduction effaces the good-versus-evil dichotomy, such that the hero is not aligned with one pole or another and can potentially act outside this distinction. The opposition "good versus evil" can only arise with the emergence of societal consensus.

The particular culture hero that emerges after rehearsal 4 (the "Ging heut morgen" melody) seems to represent a mediation of previously unresolved oppositions.

Example 7.2. Mahler, Symphony no. 1, first movement, first phrase of "Tirili" motive, mm. 136–39

The semantic world being evoked here is that of an idealized *Volk* that both participates in society and is close to nature. This is, of course, a common nineteenth-century reaction to the dehumanization of urban society: the call to "return" to a social structure centered on the naïve yet spiritually attuned rural peasant. The *Gesellen* song alluded to by this theme is a celebration, a joyful communion between a countryside wanderer and the (overly) benign natural landscape he wanders through. Note also the "Tirili" motive (example 7.2; see Floros 1994: 34) that first appears in the closing section beginning seven measures before rehearsal 10: its hybridized semantic character, evoking both the natural world via birdcall and a simple, "folklike" stylization of the former, precisely expresses the role of the hero of the First as an idealized link between nature and culture.

In the development section (rehs. 12–25), the relatively undifferentiated material of the introduction is separated into distinct "worlds"; the movement from a timeless world into the cyclical world of human existence necessarily results in the classification and separation of semantic elements into a cultural matrix. Through this matrix, we see how society views the world and the relation of its members to it. The "worlds" mentioned above are temporally separated and sequentially presented. First there is the natural world in both its benign, folk aspect (rehs. 12–13; fourths, Tirili, cuckoo) and its unsettling, dangerous aspect (reh. 14; chromatic line with triplets). This is followed by the social world, still idealized, replete with hunting topics (reh. 15 ff.). The hunt can be understood in one sense as a ritual circumscribing of nature, in that it enacts human mastery over the animal world with a minimum of danger. It has the effect of separating man as knowledgeable tool-maker from the beast as instinctual and ignorant. On the other hand, the hunt is a microcosmic version of the quest (Chevalier and Gheerbrant 1994: 532).

Running parallel to the gradual emergence of the cultural matrix in the early stages of the development (rehs. 12–16) is the equally gradual emergence of a new *cantabile* theme that first appears in fragments in the cello after rehearsal 12, and becomes more coherent until fourteen measures after rehearsal 15, when it is stated fully for the first time (see example 7.1f, above). The hesitancy with which this theme first manifests itself is appropriate to the preliminary character of the cultural identity being established in this movement. Mahler's unusual employment of a kind of "cumulative setting" (Burkholder 1995: 195–96) for this theme acts as an inner icon of the process of construction itself. As the theme emerges, so does the hero.

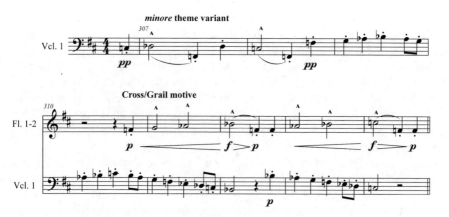

Example 7.3. Mahler, Symphony no. 1, first movement, *minore* version of *cantabile* cello theme and Cross/Grail motive, mm. 307–14

The third world, appearing musically beginning seven measures after rehearsal 21, has an apparently negative character: the *cantabile* theme introduced as early as rehearsal 12 is now presented in a *minore* version, along with a motive whose rhythm and contour are akin to the Cross/Grail motive from Wagner's *Parsifal* (example 7.3).[15] This passage, like the motivically similar passage at rehearsal 47 of the finale, precedes what Adorno (1992a: 5–6) calls a "breakthrough" moment, the point at which the semantic element pushes its way most strongly out of the formal element. In the first movement, only the dysphoric aspects of the Cross and the Grail are emphasized—note the minor mode and the excessive motivic repetition. Although the symbolic-musical connections are not clear to the listener until rehearsal 26 of the finale, when it appears in a form similar to that of *Parsifal*, the appearance of this motive in the first movement seems to signal the emergence of the sinister aspects of society. The Cross and the Grail are both ambivalent symbols, and they are ambivalent in similar respects: both embody the convergence of suffering and redemption. These symbols also engage two of the three most important symbolic constellations for Western society: the biblical tradition and the medieval Romances (the third being Greco-Roman mythology). In the context of the first movement, the necessity of suffering for the divine (read, culturally sanctioned and valorized) hero is indicated.

The fanfare passage six measures before rehearsal 26, Adorno's "breakthrough" passage (1992a: 4), is the expressive climax of the movement: the sudden increase in dynamics, the euphoric shift of key and mode, the Lisztian cadential 6/4 mark the point at which the hero takes the quest as his own. The introduction, exposition, and development bring the hero into consciousness and power, but the adventure begins with the "breakthrough." (In this light, the preceding Cross/Grail motive, seemingly out of place in this early movement, takes on the character of an initiation rite.) The fanfares had been distant and muted earlier in the movement, but these give way to the expressive "here and now." The placement of the fanfare at this moment is significant both for its heraldic, annunciatory character and as a point of convergence for the hero and culture which he affirms. As if to confirm this, the nature music from the introduction and the first part of the development is absent from the remainder of the movement. Furthermore, the fanfare itself prepares a recapitulation from rehearsal 26 replete with the themes and symbols most tied to the world of culture. The hunting music at the tonic arrival (reh. 26) is also presented *fortissimo,* sounding the initiation of the quest. Rehearsal 27 combines the now fully formed *cantabile* melody—the hero in full possession of his powers—with the stylized "Tirili" motive—nature harnessed by culture. The remaining thematic material, from rehearsals 29 to 33, is the "Ging heut morgen" melody, the text of which precisely fits the character of a wanderer setting confidently off on a journey. By the end of the first movement, the social frame has emerged, established a network of values, and selected a figure charged with these values as its savior/victim. The youthfulness, the lack of seriousness, of this figure is nicely suggested by the eight-measure coda. Note also the Haydnesque beginning-become-ending in the lower voices in the final measure. The discursive freedom of the hero's "Ging heut morgen" melody is constrained to the extent that only the initial fourth is present.

If the first movement of the First reveals the emergence of the culture hero, the second and third movements feature his journey across the divide from the everyday world of appearances to the eternal world of the mythic and (potentially) universal.[16] Mahler's programmatic titles, "In Full Sail" and "Aground,"[17] are notable for their allusion to a journey by sea.[18] For Carl Jung, the sea represents the deep well of the unconscious, the unknown that must be traversed in order to achieve individuation (see, for example, 1990: 210). The ship is the vessel, the collection of "safe" ideals, that makes the journey possible and that embodies motion toward a goal. But the ship, of course, can founder on hidden obstacles, on realities not encompassed by one's ideals. Chevalier and Gheerbrant (1994: 876) note the parallel with Wagner's *Flying Dutchman:* "The old Scandinavian legend of the ghost-ship . . . symbolizes the quest for fidelity in love and the shipwreck of that ideal, exposed as nothing more than a phantom." Likewise, the hero of the First is the bearer of society's ideals, apparently embodied musically by the various folk dances that comprise the second movement (Ländler, and waltzes of both the moderately fast and moderately slow variety).

There are several interlocking mythical and symbolic elements to be untangled in the third movement: the programmatic title, the often-discussed ironic character of the piece, with its peculiar use of "popular" music topics, and the woodcut that served as Mahler's inspiration. The title, "Aground," suggests that the previously uneventful journey has temporarily led to an obstacle. Conflict within a cultural network is inevitable, since choices about what to affirm and reject are made within that culture, raising up some elements (in the case of Mahler's culture, Christianity, Germanic peoples, the separation of "art" music and popular music, etc.) and denigrating others (Judaism, Slavic peoples, the intermingling of "art" music and popular music, etc.). Conflict will eventually be necessary because culture casts a shadow, and the repressed elements demand to be heard.

It appears that Mahler understood the third movement as providing the external stimulus for the hero's outburst of despair at the beginning of the fourth movement (Floros 1994: 50). With the funeral-march material as background, the minor-mode *Bruder Martin* variant (reh. 2), the jaunty street band music (reh. 6), and its subsequent parody (reh. 16) portray the everyday world as banal and pointless in the face of tragedy. Given the hero's role as champion of societal values, the impact of this movement becomes even clearer. Romance requires for its effectiveness a wholehearted approval of the social system, but the third movement undermines this message. It is, in fact, an ironic intrusion into an otherwise romantic (in the sense of *mythos*) symphony. This would appear to be the reason why the third movement strikes some listeners as inappropriate. It is not simply that the dysphoric character of the movement is too contrasting after the pastorale-like previous movements (after all, Beethoven's storm in his Sixth Symphony does not provoke a similar reaction). Rather, it is that the movement's corrosive character emanates from *within* the hero's worldview, rather than from without (as with an external threat). Existential doubt threatens the whole edifice of the symphony; if we do not believe in the ideals of the society, then the eventual victory will not be a satisfying one.

In the Moritz von Schwind woodcut that served as inspiration for this movement ("The Hunter's Funeral Procession"), a woodsman's coffin is escorted to its grave[19] by a comical group of fairy-tale animals and village musicians (Mitchell 1995: 237). Alexander Ringer (1988: 589–602) has pointed out that the theme occurring in the middle section of the movement, a theme borrowed from the final song of the "Lieder eines fahrenden Gesellen," is itself a quotation from Donizetti's opera *Don Sebastian,* taken from a point where one of the characters is observing his own funeral. Although, according to Mahler, the hero is merely an observer of this scene, the animal procession accompanying the dead man seems to function like a *psychopomp,* a spiritual intermediary between the everyday world and the mythical world. They are thus *liminal* figures, figures of the threshold, allowing the hero to partake of the power that exists at the margins of society, the same power that was available to the hero before the emergence of society (in the introduction). This is a dangerous power, however, since it does not draw on the normative patterns of society.[20] The hero must step outside society in order to defend it, and the third movement presents the resulting threshold crossing in musical terms.

The finale of the First Symphony bears the programmatic title "From Inferno to Paradise" (Floros 1994: 26). This title suggests a relationship to another famous hero-quest—the Divine Comedy of Dante Alighieri. Mahler seems to confirm this relationship with two finale motives that echo the *Dante Symphony* of Franz Liszt: the previously mentioned Cross/Grail motive (which shares the same rhythm with the "Magnificat" setting in the Liszt symphony) and the descending chromatic triplets, which can also be found in the first movement, "Inferno," of the same (44).

By appropriating Liszt, Wagner, Dante, and the Christian/Arthurian traditions, Mahler is situating his hero's "identity" in the Western (and specifically Germanic Western) spiritual tradition.[21]

The symbolic conflict in the finale is intended to be entirely in line with Western tradition and convention: the hero is the defender and representative of the forces of good, life, and orthodox spirituality, with few indications to the contrary. On the other side are the conventionally established forces of death, evil, and the profane. The introduction to the finale (mm. 1–54) gives initial priority to the dysphoric elements, which appear in quick succession and define the character of the rejected elements to be faced: the dissonant "outcry of a heart deeply wounded" (Martner 1979: 178) (example 7.4a, mm. 1–5), the *minore* version of the Cross/Grail motive (example 7.4a, mm. 6–8, 39–54), the Lisztian "Infernal" triplet motive (example 7.4a, mm. 8–18, 21–24, 32–39), and music borrowed from *Das Klagende Lied,* rehearsal 81 and originally set to the text "Weh!" (example 7.4b, mm. 25–30).[22] The *minore* Cross/Grail motive and the triplet figure suggest the negative aspects of this motive: death without the balance of rebirth (Cross), perhaps even damnation (Infernal triplets), the unhealed wound of the Fisher King, and the resultant Waste Land (Grail). The "outcry" and "Weh" motives suggest the impact of this moment on the hero, who is not yet able to fend off the onslaught.

The exposition themes that follow narrativize the conflict. The primary theme group is predominantly dysphoric: the first primary theme (reh. 6) has as its initial half the *minore* Cross/Grail motive, while the second primary theme (reh. 8) is a *minore* version of the *cantabile* cello theme from the opening movement. Recall that this theme mirrored the emergence of the hero's social persona in the opening movement. Its appearance here is the only ambivalent semiotic element in the finale, in that it now seems that the socially constructed identity of the hero has itself become one of the obstacles to be overcome. The hero's origin appears, not for the only time, to be of a mixed or *a*moral character. (A third primary theme, four measures after rehearsal 9, is derived from the first theme, particularly from the contrasting idea that follows the Cross/Grail motive.) The dysphoric material, having dominated the finale, reaches a sort of climactic apotheosis at rehearsal 12, with its brass outbursts and expressive pauses.

In rehearsal 16, the lyrical major-mode theme, emerging from the Infernal triplets that die away after rehearsal 14, introduces the first euphoric, redemptive topical element into the narrative. This passage seems finally to lift the conflict out of the infernal world, but the shift is only temporary: at rehearsal 21, both the *minore* Cross/Grail motive and the Infernal triplets eventually undermine the sense of repose established by the secondary theme. More striking, rehearsal 21 also recalls the music of the introduction to the first movement (descending fourths, chromatic cello line); we are reminded that *even the dysphoric elements presented as Infernal are, in fact, to be found in the initial undifferentiated, pre-social condition.* This position does greater justice to the first appearance of this material than would an interpretation of the passage as "foreshadowing," as if that explained anything. At the end of the exposition, there is a strong indication that the strength of the dysphoric elements far outweighs that of the euphoric. The culture-hero is young

Outcry

Example 7.4. Mahler, Symphony no. 1, fourth movement
  a. "Outcry" music, Cross/Grail motive, and Infernal triplets, mm. 1–11
Continued on the next page

Example 7.4. Mahler, Symphony no. 1, fourth movement
   a. "Outcry" music, Cross/Grail motive, and Infernal triplets, mm. 1–11
Continued on the next page

Example 7.4. Mahler, Symphony no. 1, fourth movement
   b. Wailing motive (from *Das Klagende Lied*), mm. 25–30

Example 7.5. Mahler, Symphony no. 1, fourth movement, "Victorious" theme, mm. 297–304

and inexperienced, and cannot gain the upper hand. Mahler comments that "my intention was simply to represent a battle in which victory is always farthest away at the exact moment when the warrior believes himself to be closest to it. This is the character of every spiritual battle, since it is not so easy to become or to be a hero."[23]

Cutting across the development (rehs. 22–40), recapitulation (rehs. 41–58), and coda (rehs. 59–61) is a dramatic portrayal of the ascendant culture-hero pitting himself against the declining dysphoric forces rejected by the culture. The working out of this conflict occurs in several stages, each representing an advance by the culture-hero:

Stage 1 (rehs. 22–27): The return of the initial "outcry" material in rehearsal 21 and the subsequent chromatic interplay of motives is answered by the first appearance of motives that suggest redemption and conquest images. Floros has untangled the complex symbolic identity of the theme that appears in rehearsal 26 (example 7.5): the Cross motive, derived from Liszt and previously employed in the minor mode, now appears in the major mode, combined with a variant of the *Dresden* Amen. The entire theme is itself a variant of Wagner's Grail theme from *Parsifal* (Floros 1994: 47; Brown 2003: 568–69). These references have been employed above to define more precisely earlier manifestations of this material, but the full range of associations only becomes unlocked at this moment, which firmly establishes the hero's stature in the drama and provides a key to understanding what has come before. Mahler calls this theme the "victorious" motive (Bauer-Lechner 1984: 174–75), although it does not achieve final victory here: the *minore* version of the *cantabile* cello theme from the first movement interrupts its progress in rehearsal 27.

Stage 2 (rehs. 28–44): The return of the minor mode at the end of the previous stage and the chromatic motives after rehearsal 28 signal a resurgence of the dysphoric elements. A climax is reached at rehearsal 30, after which material from the introduction to the finale is heard, particularly the "outcry" and the Infernal triplets (reh. 31 ff.). Another climax seems to be approaching at rehearsal 33, and this is indeed the case, but the thematic material at the climax is the "victorious" motive: the hero has subverted the goals of the infernal material and come into his own. As if to signal this, a surprising modulation from C major to D major is effected at rehearsal 34. This is perhaps the dramatic turning point of the symphony. The key shift indicates that the hero has brought about a real change in the musical-cultural environment, after which victory seems likely. A formally unexpected new theme—a chorale-like passage—emerges at rehearsal 35 following the key change. This theme combines both cultural associations (allusion to religious worship) and natural associations (fourths derived from the introduction to the opening movement). The hero is now a powerful amalgamation of these two spheres. The necessary influence of the natural sphere and the initial primal condition is affirmed by the subsequent return of the "Theme of Fourths" (reh. 38), the fanfare motive (six measures before rehearsal 39), the cuckoo (four measures after rehearsal 39), and the "Tirili" motive (four measures before rehearsal 41). The fanfare motive, in particular, acquires a further layer of meaning here: it not only mirrors the mutual influence of culture and nature but it also signals the triumphant victory of Paradise over Inferno. The instances of foreshadowing in the first movement and of recall in the finale become clearer when seen in the light of the symbolic network constructed above. Also clearer is the reason for the omission of the primary theme group at the beginning of the recapitulation at rehearsal 41: the secondary theme is free of the dysphoric elements characteristic of the primary theme group, so it is better suited to reinforce the ascendancy of the culture-hero at the end of the development. The notion of recapitulation as resolving the conflict of the first two sections of the sonata is put into practice here not through the reconciliation of home key and subordinate key but through the realignment of themes based on their placement on the euphoric/dysphoric axis.

Stage 3 (rehs. 45–61): The Cross/Grail motive returns in the minor mode (reh. 45), as does the *minore* version of the *cantabile* cello theme (reh. 47). These themes are both bi-functional, that is, they have both a euphoric and a dysphoric manifestation. Their appearance here in the latter guise suggests a battle *within* the hero, against the equivocal elements that both give power to, and work against, the hero. Again, a dysphoric climax is approached and then subverted to become a euphoric climax at rehearsal 52, signaled by another abrupt key change up a step, and by the appearance of the fanfare motive, the "victorious" motive (reh. 53 ff.), and the chorale theme (reh. 56). The coda (rehs. 59–61), with its affirmation of the "breakthrough" harmony of D major and frequent fanfares, confirms the victory of the culture-hero.

The specific employment of the primary symbols in this movement indicates that we are to understand this movement as following the pattern of Christ or the narrator of the Divine Comedy: a descent into the underworld, an encounter with the powers of this realm (and with one's own weaknesses), and a subsequent ascent to Paradise. The title "Dall' Inferno al Paradiso" clearly suggests this interpretation.

It is noteworthy that, amid the numerous setbacks and changes of fortune in this movement, the gradual improvement in the hero's status is in direct proportion to the assimilation of these "natural," pre-cultural elements from the introduction. The sudden recovery of the key of the first movement (D major) at rehearsal 34, the elaboration of the descending-fourths motive into a longer melody at rehearsal 35, the further reminiscence of the introduction at rehearsals 38 and 52, and the most forceful appearance of the fanfare motive at rehearsal 52 are cyclical devices in purely musical terms. But they are also semantic markers indicating the nature of the battle being waged in the finale. The hero is successful not only because of the power he inherits from society but also because that power is *supplemented* by the primeval forces that gave rise to it.

Tragic Mythos (Second Symphony, First Movement)

The victory of the hero at the end of the First Symphony creates a dilemma for society as a whole. It requires the hero to preserve its orthodoxy of values, but that hero must step outside orthodoxy to succeed. As a result, the difficulty arises as to *what to do with the hero when the external threat is removed,* since the hero himself has become an internal threat to social cohesiveness. Some who encounter Mahler's statement that it is the hero of the First that goes to the grave in the Second (for example, Martner 1979: 180) will find the change of circumstance to be arbitrary. But the sacrifice of the hero as a scapegoat for society is an extremely common ritual practice and makes complete sense in light of the hero's uneasy position both inside and outside society.

Tragedy is the second stage in Frye's narrative cycle that is found in the *Wunderhorn* symphonies. In opposition to the idealized, somewhat two-dimensional characters of the romance, tragedy presents the authentic human being against the backdrop of the world of reality, with its social norms and taboos (Frye 1957: 207). The hero, which in romance is the embodiment of cultural values, is now in violation of moral law, which requires that the hero be sacrificed (208). Tragedy is inconceivable unless the protagonist is both strong enough to confront the social order and sufficiently independent to be culpable for failure. In the Western world, the primary models are classical, biblical, Christian/mythological, and Shakespearean: the social rejection of Oedipus, the fall of Adam, the death of Moses in sight of the promised land, Christ crucified by a culture answering to the religious code of God the Father, the death and defeat of Arthur, Lancelot, and the Knights of the Round Table, the fate of Macbeth, Hamlet, Othello, Lear. Tragedy, according to Frye, confronts us with the "theme of narrowing a comparatively free life into a process of causation" (212). It is the narrative of decline, sacrifice, and fall. Consequently we expect to find symbols expressing these elements and their antitheses.

The specific character of the tragedy derives from a particular combination of the protagonist's place in society (supported by, then in conflict with, the social hierarchy) and the narrative outcome (the re-imposition of that hierarchy at the expense of the hero), in conjunction with the particular symbolic constellations described above. At the beginning of the Second Symphony, Mahler's hero has confronted and defeated the threat to cultural stability but has therefore become a dangerous figure. René Girard (1977), one of the most influential modern theorists on the function of ritual, has argued that social division is frequently exorcized by the use of purgative violence, sacrificing a scapegoat who will paradoxically restore the collective spirit by being forced to bear the blame for the previous disunity. Job is the clearest example of such a figure. Doty (2000: 380) summarizes Girard's argument:

> Job's "friends" become the Mob of God, seeking to preserve justice by finishing off Job. Great calamity in the land is now attributed to Job's unholy actions. For Girard, what is so unique about Job is that the mimetic mechanism—rather than being suppressed, as elsewhere in literature—has been lifted to the surface and openly criticized. Job is the failed scapegoat, the victim who will not cease proclaiming his innocence. His bleating on the gallows only increases the anger of his enemies. As Girard understands the text, Job was not restored to his wealthy state (as the fairy tale at the canonical book's present ending reports, in contrast to the much older folktale version), but met a certain death, sacrificed to the god of retribution.

This scenario of ritual violence is the link between the hero's victory in the First Symphony and the hero's inexplicable death in the Second. It is unlikely that the hero must die merely so that Mahler can enact a personal resurrection drama. From the standpoint of the *Wunderhorn* cycle as a whole, the hero's death is senseless except insofar as it is required to restore the wholeness of the culture for which the hero served as defender, to put aside the memory of a time when division was present and necessary. The tragedy of Mahler's hero is that he transgresses against society simply by being a reminder of social division and must therefore be sacrificed, and we sympathize with the hero because his actions had secured the survival of the culture. At the moment of sacrifice, Mahler's hero is the archetypal victim, but that sacrifice ultimately elevates the mythical stature of the hero, allowing him to demand a reconfiguration of the mechanism of death, judgment, and rebirth.

The Second Symphony takes us to the other side of the mythical divide, to the world of death, dreams, and transformation. The first movement highlights images of death and sleep that link it back to the finale of the First Symphony, but in a new functional configuration. The rhythmic fluidity and melodic emphasis on the low strings at the opening of the Second contribute to the subterranean, recitative-like effect of the passage, which gives the impression of a decree or a death sentence. The funereal theme that first appears seven measures before rehearsal 1 has an ascending incipit reminiscent of the Cross/Grail motive from the First Symphony (Floros 1994: 58). This motive has now passed through three incarnations with respect to the hero. The first (example 7.3 above) presents the Cross (death, dissolution) as the enemy of culture, against which the hero strives. The second (example 7.5 above) portrays the Cross as symbol of victory over death, with the hero as champion. The third (example 7.6), found in the *Todtenfeier* movement,

Example 7.6. Mahler, Symphony no. 2, first movement, Cross/Grail variant, mm. 18–25

reestablishes the connection of the Cross with death, this time referring to the hero's own death.[24]

This motive continues to play a pivotal role in the remainder of the movement, appearing in different guises, and serving to centralize the ambivalent character of the Cross and the Grail in dramatic form. It is as if, having engaged these forces on behalf of society, the hero must now face them directly, and the various metamorphoses of the Cross/Grail motive in the first movement reflect this struggle. On the side of dissolution, there is the inverted version at rehearsal 2, a variant isolating the Cross rhythm above the Infernal triplets at rehearsal 6, a chromatically inflected variant with tam-tam at rehearsal 11, and so on.

Also significant are the natural breaks resulting from rests or distinct changes of dynamics and texture at rehearsals 4, 7, (13), 15, 16, and six measures after rehearsal 20. Within each of the six resultant musical spans (which correspond partly to sonata form divisions), a conflict is played out between funeral/lament topics and pastoral/heroic topics, and, in most cases, the former arrests the development or musical completion of the latter, playing out the struggle between the society responsible for the death warrant and the hero-victim that resists this verdict in favor of society. This interpretation is summarized below in Table 7.1.[25]

Several symbols and topics in this movement (Cross/Grail, Infernal triplets, nature music, fanfares) are employed much as in the First Symphony, with the hero's powers still represented by the pastorale and the fanfare: see rehearsal 3 (pastorale), rehearsal 5 (triumphant major-mode fanfare using the Cross/Grail motive), rehearsals 7 (pastorale) and 8 (descending fourths), rehearsals 13 (pastorale) and 14 (fanfare), 4 measures after rehearsal 17 (major-mode Cross/Grail + anticipation of finale motives), 9 measures after rehearsal 22 (pastorale). On the other hand, the music of judgment and society largely employs the funeral march, sigh motives indicative of collective lament (see, for example, 4 mm. after rehearsal 16), and the Infernal triplets from the First Symphony. The Cross/Grail motive, thanks to its dual symbolic role, is found in both semantic constellations.

One key to interpreting narrative meaning is the following generalization: *the transitions between different semantic elements determine the character of their interaction.* Abrupt transitions generally signal a repressive response, more subtle modulatory and transitional techniques suggest a more reasoned and natural response, and music that dies away implies a lack of strength or willpower.

The effect of this distribution of symbols is to oppose collective expressions of

Table 7.1. Narrative Summary of Mahler, Symphony No. 2, First Movement

Stage 1 (beginning–reh. 3): Individual overruled by society
  a. Recitative-like "decree" (beginning) + Cross/Grail variant theme (reh. 1; example 7.6 above) + Cross/Grail retrograde (reh. 2) in C minor answered by
  b. Pastorale theme in E major (bass line before reh. 3 yields to new key via chromatic descent); this theme is interrupted (via direct modulation) by Stage 2

Stage 2 (rehs. 4–6): Individual yields to society
  a. Return of Cross/Grail variant theme in C minor (reh. 4); modulates via longer chromatic descent to
  b. Heroic theme in E♭ major (reh. 5) with incipit also derive from Cross/Grail motive; modulates quickly away, leads to
  c. Descending chromatic line in G minor akin to Infernal triplets (reh. 6) with tam-tam providing funereal associations; dies away

Stage 3 (rehs. 7–12): Dominant society giving some ground to individual in Stage 4
  a. Pastorale theme developed in C major (reh. 7); bass descends to "calm of the sea" music in E major; dies away, leading to subtle reentry of
  b. March music in E minor associated with Stage 1a above (4 mm. after reh. 9), followed by development of Cross motive (4 mm. before reh. 11) and quotation from Gesellen song "Ich hab' ein glühend Messer" (4 mm. after reh. 12); answered by

Stage 4 (rehs. 13–14): Possible reconciliation
  a. Subdued variant of heroic theme in F major (reh. 13), quickly giving way to
  b. March music heard at a distance interspersed with rustic music (reh. 14); suggests possible reconciliation, but strongly interrupted by

Stage 5 (reh. 15): Repudiation of reconciliation
  a. Return of opening "decree" (reh. 15) with *fff* dynamic in E♭ minor; dies away

Stage 6 (reh. 16; 5 mm. after reh. 20): seemingly definitive victory over hero
  a. March music in E♭ minor (reh. 16) with "sigh" motive, Dies Irae quotation (8 mm. before reh. 17), motives from Stage 1a
  b. Anticipation of finale (Cross motive + Resurrection motive + Eternity motive [Floros 1994: 60]) suggesting redemption in spite of current crisis (4 mm. after reh. 17); negated by
  c. Dies Irae quotation (3 mm. before reh. 18), then climactic dissonant passage with Infernal triplets (reh. 18), ending with cadential finality in C minor

Stage 7 (6 mm. after rehs. 20–end): Social elements converge to execute hero
  a. "Decree," themes from Stage 1a restated in C minor; bass descends to
  b. Final appearance of pastorale theme in E major (10 mm. before reh. 23); dies away
  c. Chromatic descent with Infernal triplets combined with tam-tams, themes from Stage 1a (reh. 24); synthesis of motives; dies away
  d. Major triad followed by minor triad followed by strongly descending triplets–death of hero (2 mm. before reh. 27)

death (funeral march, lament, requiem chant) with symbols of vitality, life, and power (nature music/pastorale, fanfares), with the Cross/Grail once again as the linchpin. Just as in the First Symphony, society is preserved, but in the first movement of the Second this preservation is at the expense of the hero, who forces a change in the symbolic equations. *The hero's powers derived from nature and folk vitality are no longer available to society, while the previously defeated infernal elements reappear in the social realm.* This is the price of the hero's sacrifice.

A striking symbolic configuration unfolds after rehearsal 17. Previous to this (reh. 16), a slow funeral march is heard, accompanying a song of lament and, surprisingly, the incipit to the requiem chant *Dies Irae*. As if drawing strength from the public display of mourning, a major-mode variant of the Cross/Grail motive appears (4 mm. after reh. 17) at the head of a phrase that sweeps upward to the local tonic pitch via a fanfare-like arpeggio, then falls by step to the fifth. This phrase is answered by another that begins with an octave leap on $\hat{5}$, then a leap back down to the tonic. These two motives (Floros's "resurrection" and "eternity"), appearing after the Cross/Grail motive, are found only once in this movement but appear frequently in the pivotal finale (about which more below). In this earlier context, they seem to lift the hero to a victory over death, but the phrase that began with the eternity motive abruptly concludes with the *Dies Irae* incipit, leading to a *fortississimo* dissonant climax at rehearsal 18. As with every other manifestation of the hero's power in this movement, the death decree proves to be stronger. The movement ends with a typically Mahlerian moment: an abrupt shift from a major triad to its parallel minor via a lowering of the third (2 mm. before reh. 27), followed by a two-octave, chromatic stepwise descent featuring the Infernal triplets. The tragic *mythos* is confirmed by the death of the hero, but the society itself has lost its youthful vitality and power.

Ironic Mythos (Second Symphony, Second and Third Movements)

The third narrative stage found in the *Wunderhorn* symphonies is irony. Irony lies at the other end of the spectrum from the wish fulfillment of romance: its primary role, in fact, is to parody the ideals and conventions of the romance, which is only able to cast the world according to standards of good and evil by excluding certain critical elements of reality (Frye 1957: 223). Ironic writers or composers may have different social goals, ranging from a call for flexibility in an otherwise acceptable society to a desire to supplant or overthrow society. Unlike romance, in which undesirable elements are seen as lying outside society, as threatening to it, irony targets society itself as the villain (224). Mahler is well known for his capacity to look beyond the veil of appearances to the reality underneath; his music is thus ironic in the most general sense. This was observed above in the third movement of the First Symphony, where irony served to undermine somewhat the romantic framework of the work as a whole. In the First Symphony, however, the *Totenmarsch* only casts a momentary cloud over the valorization of the hero.

The ironic *mythos* proper, depicting a truly flawed world and the futility of improving it, does not truly emerge into the open until the third movement of the Second Symphony, having been prepared by the death and exclusion of the hero.

Because irony is essentially anti-systemic, the primary Western models for this *mythos* do not tend to be found in the biblical tradition but rather in the literature and drama of the West and the classical era: in the satirical plays of Aristophanes, in the novels of Charles Dickens, in *Gulliver's Travels* and *Brave New World*. The emphasis of irony, according to Frye, is on the apprehension of truth by the juxtaposition of the ideal with the real. It is the narrative of hopelessness, ossification, and hypocrisy.

Irony involves a particular combination of the protagonist's function in society (seeking a desired order from a social hierarchy that does not possess it) and the narrative outcome (the repudiation of that attempt), in conjunction with the particular symbolic constellations described above. In the Second Symphony's "myth," a social ideal is set up (second movement) and then dashed to pieces by the destruction of the illusions that support it. The hero, now "dead" to society, and therefore existing outside society (despite having emerged from it), is in a perfect position to critique it, to attempt a reformulation. In the world of irony, no successful reformulation is yet possible, but weaknesses are exposed and cracks widened.

The second movement of the Second Symphony is not ironic in itself. Mahler, in light of a March 1896 letter to Max Marschalk, apparently understood this movement as a memory: "some long-forgotten hour of shared happiness suddenly rose before your inner eye, sending as it were a sunbeam into your soul—not overcast by any shadow" (Martner 1979: 180). If, based on this remark, we approach this movement as being a happy recollection of youth and innocence, then it also serves to provide the ground and context by which the ironic effect of the third movement is made even more pointed. The second movement, although not overly rich in symbolism, makes use of various dance topics, from the stylized Ländler at the beginning to the elfin, Mendelssohnian scherzo first heard at rehearsal 3. The spectrum of emotive connotation includes both naïve contentment and sad wistfulness, but the prevalence of dance music has the effect of calling attention to the *stylistic, socially constructed character* of music. Music associated with dance, appearing both as a ritual act and a product of culture (as opposed to nature), is a genre that most strongly illuminates the artifice of music and its necessary foundation on social context.

The milieu of the dance carries over into the third movement, but here its cultural basis is turned back on itself as a weapon, using musical and extra-musical symbolism to lay bare the superficial character of bourgeois culture. This movement is a reworking of the *Wunderhorn* song "St. Anthony of Padua Preaches to the Fish," with its *perpetuum mobile* accompanimental character. In the song the aforementioned saint, discovering the church to be empty, instead delivers a powerful sermon to the fish in a nearby stream. The sermon is apparently well received by its aquatic audience, but the fish ultimately change nothing about their sinful behavior. On the surface, then, this movement is ironic in two ways: first, the textual reference highlights the futility of true spiritual growth within modern society; and, second, the character of endlessness established by the dance music renders that very society grotesque.

Enough has been said about these two aspects of the third movement; in fact, Mahler's own comments about the piece clearly center on the themes of senselessness, spiritual futility, and existential doubt.[26] Instead, let us examine the two basic symbols of this movement: the dance as mythic expression and the fish as representative of mankind.

The dance has always symbolized the wordless expression of, and urge to, a kind of collective transcendence, an attempt to align the group with the rhythms of creation and existence. As such, it embodies many of the ideals and conflicts of society: the desire for freedom and creativity as manifested in bodily motion is countered by the ritualized form of this manifestation. Also, just as trance music transports the listener into a new ecstatic awareness, so, too, does the dance transport the dancer. This connection is made explicit by Mahler in the repetitive rhythms and undulating phrases of the third movement. Many traditional religions make use of ceremonial dances to achieve access to the world of the spirit, from which spiritual insights or physical cures can be obtained. Dance, then, lies both within society, as an embodiment of its artistic codes, and outside it, as a means to an expression of the Other. In the third movement, Mahler evokes this ideal but repudiates its conclusions, in effect declaring that the mannered dances of nineteenth-century Europe may be cultural constructs, but they point only to themselves and not to the beyond.

Fish have several symbolic connotations in Western culture. First, they are water dwellers and therefore embody certain characteristics of the aquatic realm: activity below the threshold of consciousness partaking of primordial chaos and lack of differentiation. In this sense, the fish is a revitalizing symbol; it refuses to be bound by the moral strictures and religious mores of any one culture. Saint Anthony's attempt to preach to the fishes reveals the great gulf between morality and ethics, on the one hand, and instinct and human nature, on the other. In this gulf lies irony, since reality is always larger than any attempt to describe and encompass it.

The fish in Christianity is a symbol of the Christian *in potentia*. Christ, the fisherman, is responsible for casting out his net and drawing in the souls of humanity. In this reading (which reveals the multivalent character of mythic interpretations), St. Anthony's failure to radically alter the behavior of his listeners is an indictment of the religious system itself. The Church is not Christ; it has forfeited the redemptive power of the Trinity in favor of a moralizing preachiness. In either case, Mahler's censure is not directed at the fish but at the social entity that believes it can or should attempt to reform them. In light of the previous movements of the *Wunderhorn* symphonies, the culture that kills Mahler's hero does not have the spiritual authority to offer redemption, which must be found elsewhere. Mahler does not, in the third movement, indicate what kind of society *would* be endowed with this authority (that statement is left to the Third and Fourth Symphonies).

Clearly, however, Mahler's sympathy is with the fishes, base instincts and all. These symbols of fecundity and intuitive wisdom prefigure, in this third movement, the utopian employment of animal symbolism in the later *Wunderhorn* symphonies.

Comic Mythos (Second Symphony, Fourth and Fifth Movements; Third and Fourth Symphonies)

The final narrative *mythos* found in the *Wunderhorn* symphonies is the comedy, its use here in a sense comparable to Dante's *Divine Comedy*. The comedy displays a dialectic of regeneration and rebirth, a reconstitution or re-creation of society, a victory of a new, more responsive order over an older, unresponsive one (Frye 1957: 163). Again, there is often a clear separation of "good" and "evil," but the latter, as embodied in the initially prevailing society, might better be understood as misguided or outmoded. The comedy is the successful quest *from without*, the emergence of a new, more inclusive and comprehensive society, often resulting in the reconciliation of previously opposing factions (164). In this new society, the downtrodden become powerful, and the mighty are brought down. In the Western world, the primary models are classical, biblical, or Christian/mythological: the creation of the Roman state in the *Aenead*, the redemption of the Israelites from bondage in Egypt, the resurrection of Christ, the healing of the Grail King, and the wasteland by Parsifal. The emphasis of the comedy, according to Frye, is on the creation of a new, more effective mode of relationship with the divine, in the face of opposition from tradition and an ossified culture (167). It is the narrative of rebirth, reawakening, and revitalization.

Comedy arises from a particular combination of the protagonist's place in society (largely outside the social hierarchy or on its margins) and the narrative outcome (the replacement of that hierarchy by a new, more inclusive order), in conjunction with the particular symbolic constellations described above. In the Second Symphony's "myth," Mahler's hero, perhaps because of his former role as defender of society, not only participates in a global resurrection, a refashioning of the hierarchies that govern creation, but also *initiates* and contributes to this work of re-creation. Here, again, we see the symbols and language of Western, classical, and especially biblical tradition but inflected against the grain of this tradition in the particular understanding of the individual's directive role in rebirth, of love through suffering as the key to salvation, and the cosmological-natural hierarchy of the reconstituted divine society.

The first "act" of Mahler's Divine Comedy is the *Urlicht* movement from the Second Symphony. Having leveled his sharp critique against society, Mahler's hero now begins the process of healing and constructing it anew. The fourth movement is a setting for alto voice of one of the *Wunderhorn* poems, "Primal Light." The text expresses a powerful longing for an end to loneliness, pain, and separation and a re-union with God in eternal life. This, of course, is a typical Christian theme, but the *Urlicht* text contains, in germinal form, a theology that has more to do with the Romantic spirit of the times and with Mahler's own predilections than with traditional Christian doctrine. The last five lines show us a hero who is not content to let God (or at least his angelic representative) pronounce judgment upon him:

> Da kam ein Engelein und wollt mich abweisen,
> *Ach nein, ich ließ mich nicht abweisen,*
> Ich bin von Gott, ich will wieder zu Gott,
> Der liebe Gott *wird* mir ein Lichtchen geben,
> *Wird* leuchten mir bis in das ewig selig Leben. [emphasis mine][27]

Note the confidence with which Mahler's hero speaks of not letting himself be sent away and the use of "wird" ("will") to mark his future salvation as a fact and not as speculation. This might be explained away as hopefulness that overreaches reality, but the subsequent movement bears out the interpretation. Mahler's hero, having been defender, victim, and critic, has acquired the power to determine his own fate. Later, in the final movement, Mahler himself will pen the words that justify this moment.

At this point in the drama, the resurrection has not taken place; the sacrificed victim who judges from the grave has not been redeemed. *Urlicht* is a presage of events to come in the final movement. Note that chorale topics return prominently in this movement, recalling the last significant appearance of this topic in the first movement, during the brief appearance of the Cross/Grail motive after rehearsal 17. There, the victim's strivings were thwarted, but the apotheosis of the chorale in the last two movements (along with other effects) marks a turning point in the fortunes of the hero and society. Obviously the chorale topic is intended to introduce a religious tone and authenticity to the events being described, along with a subtext of simple, direct expression (in opposition to convoluted theological discourse of the type found in the third movement).

Note also that Mahler, for the first time in the *Wunderhorn* symphonies, turns to the word to express himself. The reason for this is clear: musical and visual symbols are products of a centuries-long accretion of meanings and associations, and Mahler intends to turn these images on their head. Mahler's *creative mythopoesis* requires textual elaboration in order to clarify the significance of the reworked symbols, to show how the traditional symbols are not, in fact, *employed* traditionally (see below).

The final, fifth movement of the Second Symphony divides dramatically into three large sections, preceded by a short introduction (up to reh. 3) which serves to return the listener to the scene of activity last visited at the end of the first movement. The "fright fanfare" (Floros 1994: 68) is the hero's death cry revisited but seen from the other side, at the threshold of judgment. The three large sections correspond roughly to Prophecy or Annunciation (rehs. 3–14), Last Judgment (rehs. 14–27), and Resurrection (rehs. 29–end; rehs. 27–29 form a link between the last two sections). As in the First Symphony, this program seems to invoke a traditional Christian religious theme, in this case the Apocalypse as presented in the book of Revelation. This movement, however, has to respond to what has preceded it dramatically (the sacrifice of the culture-hero), so the resolution of the symphony cannot blithely reestablish the socioreligious status quo. For Mahler to affirm the

Table 7.2. Symbolic Taxonomy of Mahler, Symphony No. 2, Fifth Movement

1. Prophecy/Annunciation
   a. The Caller (horn theme emphasizing the interval of the fifth) (rehs. 3, 6, 11)
   b. Triplet motives (associated with the Caller, perhaps as response to the Call; rehs. 3, 5, 6, 11–13)
   c. Recitative, fanfare topics (rhythmic fluidity)

2. Judgment
   a. "Fright fanfare" recalling first movement (beginning, reh. 20; 7 mm. after reh. 26)
   b. Fear motive (ascending dissonant leap using large intervals, especially minor 9th) (reh. 14; 10 mm. after reh. 15)
   c. Dies Irae (from first movement, ritualized expression of judgment) (8 mm. before reh. 5; rehs. 10, 14; 10 mm. after reh. 15; reh. 20)
   d. Sigh motive (Entreaty using musical motive from "O Glaube" text) (rehs. 7, 21, 39)
   e. March, chant, fanfare topics

3. Resurrection
   a. Resurrection theme, chorale (music set to opening text of Klopstock's Resurrection Chorale) (reh. 5; 10 mm. after reh. 15; rehs. 31, 35, 42, 48)
   b. Eternity motive (short, descending leap followed by stepwise ascent) (rehs. 2, 27, 33, 37, 46 [Floros 1994: 70])
   c. Ascension motive (stepwise descent with undulating triplet ending (rehs. 2, 11, 33, 37, 46 [Floros 1994: 70])
   d. Bird of the Night (see below, announces resurrection) (rehs. 29–30)
   e. Fanfares of the Apocalypse (carries over theme of judgment from group 2) (reh. 22)
   f. Chorale topics

Christian cosmological order in every sense would retrospectively justify the absurd sacrifice of the first movement. (This position is possible, of course, based on the argument of the inscrutable will of God, but clearly Mahler had little patience with this idea.)

Just as the final movement divides into three large sections, so do the musical and visual symbols group themselves into broad categories corresponding to each section (Table 7.2; symbol labels from Floros 1994: 67–78).

These symbols do not always confine themselves to the corresponding section but are associated with it and represent that semantic network whenever they appear. For example, both the *Dies Irae* melody and the Resurrection theme appear in the first section of the finale (8 mm. before reh. 5; reh. 5), but they are the prophetic events spoken of by the "voice calling in the wilderness," prophesying judgment followed by redemption.

Likewise, the appearance of the Entreaty motive at rehearsal 7, within the Prophecy section, occurs after Caller material and functions as a response to prophecy, a human outcry of doubt and fear. The fears expressed by this motive seem to be realized at rehearsal 21, in the context of the Last Judgment and accompanied by trumpet fanfares blowing the arrival of the Apocalypse. Because of the dysphoric character of this motive, it associates most comfortably with the other Judgment material. The answer to the Entreaty, however, comes in the Resurrection section of the finale, when the text "Oh, believe, my heart, oh believe, Nothing will be lost to you!" uses the Entreaty motive as accompaniment. The particular combination of words and music seems incongruous here unless the text is seen as a response to the Entreaty motive, the appearance of which here serves as a reminder.

There are also interesting uses of symbolic material in the finale that represent a progression from previous movements. The most important of these is the use of the fanfare, and it is interesting to trace the shifting correspondences of this topic throughout the symphonic cycle. It was first used in the first movement of the First Symphony as an expression of the socially constructed world within the primordial world, then as a manifestation of the hero's power and vitality as defender of society, and then in the Second Symphony as representing society's decree of death for the hero. Now, in the finale, the fanfare shifts its locus of meaning several times. As embodied in the fifths of the Caller motive, it retains the character of decree from earlier in the movement, but its power is withdrawn from society to its margins (from the "wilderness"): it will be those with no apparent cultural power who possess true power. The fanfare character of the Caller becomes more pronounced until the *fortissimo* horn passage at rehearsal 11, when the prophetic force is most strident and when the Last Judgment itself is most imminent. In the Judgment passages, the fanfares assimilate the symbolic associations of the trumpets of the Apocalypse; the bitonal clashes with the Entreaty material and polytempo at rehearsal 21 mock the orderly, seemingly comprehensible fanfares of previous movements, as though this vital force had once more regained its full primordial potency. The last significant appearance of the fanfare is at the beginning of the Resurrection material (reh. 29), with the final appearance of the Caller motive. Here, we are reminded that this event is both inevitable and foreordained: the fanfare-as-decree ushers in the expected resurrection.

However, as the fanfare topic gives way, the chorale topic comes into its own. It had previously appeared in the finale in the context of the *Dies Irae*, providing religious undertones. Recall that, in the first movement, the Resurrection theme (among others) gave way to the *Dies Irae* as a sign of defeat and death (reh. 17). In the finale, this process is reversed, first at rehearsal 5, when the Resurrection theme interrupts the *Dies Irae* as part of the Caller's prophecy, then before rehearsal 16 during the Last Judgment passage, to remind the listener that this Day of Judgment is a necessary precursor to salvation. The chorale takes center stage at rehearsal 31 with the first entry of the chorus proclaiming the resurrection. The complex character of the chorale—communal, solemn, religious in the sense of supplication and assurance and in contrast to judgment and decree—lends this passage its legitimacy.

As previously mentioned, however, the anticipated resurrection does not correspond entirely to Christian doctrine. There are elements on both a small and large scale that comprise our creative mythopoesis of the redemption archetype. The descent that has taken us through two symphonies reaches the lowest depths in the finale at rehearsal 29, when the Judgment has taken place and eternity supplants time (reh. 27). At this point, however, an unusual birdcall motive makes its appearance. Floros has documented the linkage between this passage and the "Bird of the Night" from the *Mitternacht* movement of the Third Symphony, and has alluded to its connections with the music of Weber and German Romanticism (Floros 1977b: 204–205). The origin of the "Bird of the Night," however, can be traced back to Ovid's *noctis avis*, from his Metamorphoses 2.564. The *noctis avis* is clearly meant to be an owl, which was understood to be both a symbol of wisdom (as a representative of Athena) and an omen of death (because of its nocturnal activity and its mournful shriek [Ferber 1999: 146–47]). The Bird of the Night appears at the turning point of the symphony, initiating the ascent from death to life. Mahler portrays the darkest moment in the cosmic drama with this enigmatic, classical symbol, and then echoes the avian imagery later in the movement with this text: "With wings that I won in the passionate strivings of love I shall mount to the light to which no sight has penetrated." Notice that the wings represent that which has been won, a spiritual treasure and source of power. Mahler's use of bird imagery in the *Wunderhorn* symphonies is extremely significant, beginning with the cuckoo in the First Symphony (which Shakespeare, in the final song of *Love's Labour's Lost*, juxtaposes with the owl as the bird of spring versus that of winter). In the finale of the Second Symphony, the hero becomes embodied by the owl, who will fly to salvation in the Third and Fourth Symphonies. The Fourth Symphony was often described by Mahler in terms of images of flying through Paradise, and there is a musical link between the musical setting of the above text and the third movement of the Fourth Symphony. The qualities of wisdom found in the Bird of the Night emerge in the *Mitternacht* movement of the Third Symphony, when the poet asks "What says the deep midnight?" and we learn that the world is more profound than it appears to be.

The most striking aspect of Mahler's own text for the finale is the emphasis placed on the hero, as opposed to the mechanism of judgment/rebirth. From Mahler's standpoint, *no intercessor is required to achieve salvation*. It is apparently within the ability of the seeker to attain his or her own enlightenment, assuming that he or she is confident enough to claim it and has suffered in the cause of a transcendent love: "Everything is yours that you have desired, yours, what you have loved, what you have struggled for." The notion that the divine is within us is an ancient concept, but it is expressed succinctly in the formula of Loren Eiseley: "Since in the world of time every man lives but one life, it is in himself that he must search for the secret of the Garden" (1962: 140). This is a critical feature of the comic archetype: the transgressor is the agent through which the old order is overturned. Mahler's text reinforces the notion that the hero has embarked upon a quest in which he has actively striven to achieve his own goal, and that the obstacles overcome are in some sense inner ones.

The reason for undergoing a great ordeal, for forcing oneself to change, is to achieve a new orientation, to gain a reward. In the case of the *Wunderhorn* symphonies, the triumph is won when the hero, freed from a conventional identification with societal goals, is sacrificed and set free to dissolve the old boundaries and create new ones.[28]

Epilogue: Third and Fourth Symphonies

The finale to the First Symphony, "From Inferno to Paradise," invokes Dante to clarify the terms of the musical drama; we are presented with the criteria for distinguishing the blessed from the damned as defined by society, with the hero acting as both tour guide and defender of the sacred. This highly "romantic" tableau is in marked contrast to Mahler's re-valued (and apparently preferred) hierarchy of the Third and Fourth Symphonies. In the Third and Fourth, Mahler's hero refashions the cosmic and social hierarchy, the power for which task he has been equipped by the events of the First and Second Symphonies. Mahler gradually unfolds the implications of his hero's victory over the course of ten movements, as we ascend through the much-discussed layers of being or self to an experience of the divine.[29] Mahler himself makes clear the link between the self and the levels of being portrayed in the Third Symphony in remarking that "I imagined the constantly increasing articulation of feeling, from the muted, rigid, merely elemental form of existence (the forces of Nature) to the delicate structure of the human heart, which in its turn reaches further still, pointing beyond (to God)" (Martner 1979: 266). We are justified, then, in seeing the progress of the Third Symphony as both an inner ascent (as a psychological transformation) and as an outward ascent (as a cosmological transformation). The Third Symphony expresses the relatedness, even the unity, of the natural (mvts. 1–3), human (mvt. 4), and divine (mvts. 5–6) spheres. There is no longer any impassable boundary between these layers; rather, they are seen as different facets of the whole.

As the hero ascends, the implications of his rebirth become clear. The movement titles, in the form of "What *x* tells me," make sense only when we do not view these movements as mood paintings or pictorialisms but as a particular arrangement of symbols expressing a transcendent message, sometimes made more explicit by textual elaboration. In the fourth movement, perhaps the nexus of the whole symphony, a new realization of life's meaning is achieved: "The world is deep, and deeper than the day has imagined." (Note also the references to awakening in this movement.) In the fifth movement, Mahler provides his own twist to the Christian tradition, with the notion that, through love, we can cast away our *own* sorrow and sinfulness. We do not need to wait for salvation, but instead the *Wunderhorn* text tells us: "Only love God forever! Thus will you attain heavenly joy, the holy city, the heavenly joy that has no end." We are given a view of this heavenly joy without end in the final movement.

The transformation has not yet been fully accomplished, however, and in the Fourth Symphony, the cycle's goal is reached. Mahler's dream excursion into "an exceedingly cheerful, distant, wondrous sphere" (Lindt 1969: 50) leads the hero to the revelations he has been seeking throughout the cycle. In the second movement, interestingly, we return to the symbol of Death from the Second Symphony, but

Example 7.7. Mahler, Symphony nos. 3 and 4, melodic link
   a. Symphony no. 3, fifth movement, mm. 58–64
   b. Symphony no. 4, fourth movement, mm. 36–38

now this symbol is presented in a friendly guise, as a guide (note the title, "Friend Death is Striking Up the Dance"). After what has gone before, Death, like the other sorrows of the world, has been transvalued and no longer has power over the hero.

   The final movement is clearly meant to present us with the desired object, the image of Paradise. Unexpectedly the goal of Mahler's hero is that from which he sprang in the First Symphony and that which was mourned as lost in the third movement of the Second: the symbol of the child. It is striking that Mahler should, consistently and throughout his oeuvre, associate childhood, the banquet, and the divine. These elements also appeared in the angelic boys' choir in the Third Symphony (note the similarity of motives between this movement [example 7.7a] and the finale of the Fourth [example 7.7b]). We should perhaps not be surprised by this symbolic correspondence: it is the vitality of the primordial state that gave the hero his power and made him suitable for the defense of society. Its appearance here emphasizes that Mahler's hero has always had the means to effect his own renewal, and that he had only to return to his true source to find it. Furthermore, the child's image of the inexhaustible banquet carries echoes of Valhalla and Germanic myth, of the revels of Mt. Olympus, and of the New Jerusalem.[30] In Mahler's scene of redemption, he contrasts the ephemeral piety of his society to a deeper piety that transcends it, that can be understood through the image of the child. That this image itself is a social construct is unavoidable. The process of breaking out of the network of meanings established by society cannot be fully achieved; one can only reconfigure a part of this network through the shifting and revaluing of its symbols. This, then, is what Mahler's hero will return to the world.

   As an afterthought, it should be noted that a hero-quest typically ends with a return to society, but this is not found in the *Wunderhorn* cycle. It is striking, however, that with the Fifth Symphony (which carries over several musical motives and symbols from the previous works), Mahler saw himself as emphasizing the "bright light of day," the "zenith of life" (Bauer-Lechner 1984: 193). Here we see the "earthy" musical styles of the waltz, the march, and the serenade. Perhaps, having completed his own creative mythopoesis, his own quest, he felt free to write about the world in which he lived.

Mythic readings of Mahler's music of the sort undertaken above are useful in that they enrich several dimensions of current research. With respect to "depth," they amplify the symbols and semantic references gathered through historiographic research beyond the time frame of the music in question, illuminating the "biography" of these symbols, the fundamental associations that had previously attached to them over centuries. With respect to "breadth," they organize the disparate symbols taken from many sources into a coherent and archetypal narrative schema (uncovered here via the contributions of Northrop Frye). Finally, with respect to "density," they reflect and refract the musical and semantic material in new and unconventional ways, bringing other interpretations to light on the relationship of music and society. If it is often important to situate a musical work with respect to the culture it arose from, or with respect to the way it is viewed by our own culture, it is also important to examine its place in the larger lattice of history to discover what is constant and universal in art.

Notes

This chapter is dedicated to the memory of A. Peter Brown, whose encyclopedic knowledge of, and passion for, the symphonic music of Mahler was of great inspiration to me. He was also extremely helpful in reviewing an earlier draft of this study, and the discussion of Mahler's *Wunderhorn* symphonies in his recently published fourth volume on the symphonic repertoire (2003: 551–634) is an excellent summary of his conception of these works, a conception that represented for me a conceptual starting point. Sincere thanks are extended also to J. Peter Burkholder and my co-editor Edward Pearsall, whose comments and suggestions strongly influenced the final versions of this chapter.

1. See Floros 1977a; 1977b; 1994. The 1994 text is the English translation of volume 3; volumes 1 and 2 are not yet available in English.
2. See, especially, Youens 1986; Birchler 1991; Floros 1994; Buhler 1995; Mitchell 1995; and Abbate 1996.
3. See also Almén 2003, for an extended treatment of Frye's narrative archetypes with respect to music analysis. We might also mention the tetralogy's employment of a typical hero-quest schema, which models cyclically the stages of the primary theme-actor's transformation from both an external/social and an internal/psychological perspective (Campbell 1968).
4. See note 1 above.
5. James Jakob Liszka (1989: 133) notes that "each of Frye's four *mythoi* can be reclassified as a certain tendency between a hierarchy and its disruption." He observes that

the four literary categories can be, firstly, divided into those which emphasize the victory of one hierarchy over another (comedy, romance), and those which emphasize the defeat of one hierarchy by another (tragedy, satire/irony).

Second, the remaining pairs are distinguished by those types in which the initial order triumphs (romance, tragedy) and those in which the transgressive elements prevail (comedy, satire/irony).

6. A facsimile of this program can be found in de La Grange 1973: Ill. 47.

7. Reproduced in de La Grange 1973: Plates 46, 47.

8. Frye identifies six different phases for each of the four *mythoi*—these phases represent different phenomenal manifestations of the *mythoi*. In keeping with Frye's notion that the four *mythoi* lie along a cyclic continuum (Romance, Tragedy, Irony, Comedy, then back to Romance, and so on), the first three phases of each *mythos* have elements in common with the previous *mythos,* in decreasing degrees, while the latter three phases have elements in common with the subsequent *mythos,* in increasing degrees. In the cited example, then, the second phase of Romance has elements in common with Comedy, particularly a degree of innocence lacking in tragic Romance phases.

9. Frye (1957: 187–88) equates summer, not spring, with the romance, but the first movement of the First Symphony is establishing the mythical preconditions for the romantic drama to follow, so a reference to spring is not inappropriate.

10. See note 5 above.

11. See also the discussion of the germinal function of the "theme of fourths" in Brown 2003: 560–61.

12. Campbell (1990: 167) observes that "in many lands the soul has been pictured as a bird, and birds commonly appear as spiritual messengers."

13. This appellation derives from its motivic similarity to the descending, chromatic motive from the Inferno movement of Liszt's *Dante Symphony.* See Brown 2003: 569.

14. Eero Tarasti (1994) uses "premodalization" to describe the process by which the character of a musical passage is partly formed by the character of material that prepares it.

15. See Floros 1994: 47; and Brown 2003: 569. Although the relationship between Mahler's motive and Wagner's Cross and Grail motives is somewhat tenuous, even so it participates in the current symbolic network within which the *Wunderhorn* symphonies are situated. Since my analysis concerns the symbols that have become attached to these symphonies over time, not Mahler's intentional employment of certain symbols, any potentially spurious symbolic connections that nevertheless have a wide currency can and should be considered in the present context.

16. See Campbell 1968: 77–89. I have omitted discussion of the *Blumine* movement, which Mahler had originally included in this symphony. The nature symbolism of *Blumine* is not inappropriate to the *mythos* under consideration, but the expectations generated in the first movement tend to be diluted by the lyrically static atmosphere of *Blumine.*

17. See de La Grange 1973: Ill. 47.

18. Campbell (1968: 90–95) has illustrated the prevalence of the "night-sea journey" as a typical manifestation of this stage of a hero-quest.

19. The excerpt from *Lieder eines fahrenden Gesellen* quoted in the third movement of this symphony recalls the following text (translated):

> A linden tree stands by the roadside,
> there I rested and slept for the first time.
> Under the lime tree which covered me with its blossom
> I lay in oblivion of life's bustle,

and all, oh! all was well again!
All, all! Love and sorrow,
world and dream!

Susan Youens (1986: 264) has pointed out the relationship between the linden tree and death or dream in the German Romantic tradition. Notice also the specific references to oblivion and dream in the succeeding lines of the poem.

20. There is a useful discussion of the importance of liminal figures in ritual in Doty 2000: 351–60.

21. See also Brown 2003: 568–69.

22. See Floros 1994: 43–48, for a fuller discussion of the motives and themes in the finale.

23. Blaukopf 1980: 39–40; translated and quoted in Floros 1994: 43.

24. This can be inferred from Mahler's own comments to Natalie Bauer-Lechner. Brown (2003: 578–79) summarizes the various programmatic accounts given by Mahler in conversations and program notes.

25. The Cross/Grail variants and most of the subsequent symbolic and associative features are discussed in Floros 1994: 57–61.

26. There are a number of summaries and discussions of these quotations; for example, see Floros 1994: 63–65.

27. There came an angel and wanted to send me away.
    Ah no! I did not let myself be sent away!
    I am from God, I want to return to God.
    The loving God will grant me a little light,
    Will light my way to blissful life eternal and bright.

28. Through this process, as Campbell (1968: 148) observes, "the world is no longer a vale of tears, but a bliss-yielding, perpetual manifestation of the Presence."

29. See Floros 1994: 88–91, for a summary of Mahler's cosmology.

30. Campbell (1968: 177, 181) remarks that,

It is obvious that the infantile fantasies which we all cherish still in the unconscious play continuously into myth . . . as symbols of indestructible being. . . . The prodigious gulf between those childishly blissful multitudes who fill the world with piety and the truly free breaks open at the line when the symbols give way and are transcended. . . . The gods and goddesses then are to be understood as embodiments and custodians of the elixir of Imperishable Being but not themselves the Ultimate in its primary state. What the hero seeks through his intercourse with them is therefore not finally themselves, but . . . the power of their sustaining substance.

8 Contingencies of Meaning in Transcriptions and Excerpts: Popularizing *Samson et Dalila*

Jann Pasler

"Music and Meaning"—An Introduction

The main character in a recent filmed version of *Howards End,* Helen, becomes agitated in the middle of a lecture on "Music and Meaning."[1] The middle-aged male speaker was haughtily describing the impressions that Beethoven's Fifth Symphony suggested to him, as if they were the composer's own and should be the audience's as well.

> You can hardly fail to recognize in the development section of the first movement a mighty drama and struggle of a hero beset by perils, riding to magnificent victory and ultimate triumph.

The audience at the Ethics Society at first listened, perched slightly forward, motionless and unblinking. They were balding older men and the occasional young amateur, male and female, those who could afford to idle on a rainy afternoon—a group of mixed social classes as the story later reveals.

> In the third movement, we no longer hear a hero but a goblin, a single solitary goblin [Helen looks at her watch] walking across the universe, from beginning to end.

At this point the camera shifts from the hands of the speaker's elderly mother who is playing the period piano, to Helen's hand as she takes the umbrella beside her and prepares to leave, and then to an old man's hand raised with a question for the speaker. As Helen walks out, the old man asks,

> *old man:* Why a goblin? Why a goblin?
> *speaker:* The goblin is the spirit of negation.
> *old man:* But why specifically a goblin?

The speaker stutters, a young man, Leonard Betts, gets up to follow Helen, and the piano drowns out the speaker's words. The orchestra takes over as he runs out into the rain, and we never get an answer to the question.[2]

In the following scene, a rain-soaked Leonard appears at Helen's richly appointed bourgeois house to ask for his tattered umbrella that Helen had taken by mistake. They engage in conversation.

Leonard: What do you think of the lecture?
Helen: I don't agree about the goblins, do you? But I do about the hero in ship-wreck. You see, I've always imagined a trio for elephants dancing at that point, but he obviously didn't.
Her sister: Does music have meaning, of the literary kind?
Her brother: That's pure slush.
Helen: How boring it would be if it were only the score.
Her brother: Only the score? [they rush off in conversation]

Near the end of the film, just before Helen and Leonard steal away on a boat and make love, Leonard explains why he had married a crass, insensitive woman he obviously didn't love—

Leonard: I didn't think people like you exist except in books and books aren't real.
Helen: But they are more real than anything else. When people fail you, there's still music and meaning.
Leonard: That's for rich people to make them feel good after their dinner.

In this tale, music reveals itself as much more, something dangerous but not an-archic that subverts social hierarchy regardless of age, background, or status. In this case, it brings together a landed bourgeois woman and a poor working-class clerk. Music may encourage flights of imaginative fancy, but when its interpreta-tion goes too far or someone wishes to impose their reading of it on others, listeners protest. In its polyvalence, music resists any person's claim to absolute authority.

But this was the turn of the century, before, as Peter Bürger (1984: 80) put it, the avant-garde denied the signifier its signified, some might say for reasons with which Leonard Betts might sympathize. In the context of that period's widespread preoccupation with increasing literacy, many believed music was legible, like illus-trated magazines and newspaper supplements, even if its narratives were abstract or multivalent. Audiences "read" music as they might have a novel of the time, whether coded with many layers of meaning or utterly straightforward. They saw comprehending and appreciating it, especially its beautiful form and harmonious proportions, as prerequisites to feeling its beneficial effects.

Scholars and critics have long understood meaning as a function of a com-poser's intentions, a conscious relationship between signifiers and signifieds. More recently, under the influence of postmodernist concerns, we are becoming more attuned to the role played by a listener's predilections. The nineteenth century pre-sents a rich domain for exploring how music not only represents but also gener-ates meaning for listeners. Even if music has its own structural coherence, it was understood as fair game in the bricoleur's search for experiences to facilitate self-definition, to help make sense of life, and to understand what is essential for sur-vival. Music stimulates emotion, reveals one's emotions to oneself, and, for better or worse, as in *Howards End*, evokes impressions different for each listener. It provides frameworks on which to hang beliefs, keep alive memories, or envisage destinies. For example, the goblins represented to Helen "the phantoms of cowardice and unbelief." (Projecting her own feelings, Forster noted, "she had felt the same and had seen the reliable walls of youth collapse . . . the music summed up to her all that had happened or could happen in her career" [1910: 34].) In France, politicians wished to tap into music's capacity for meaning for a very different purpose. They looked to music to play a significant role in the formation of citizens, the health of the democracy, the unity of the French people beyond and against class distinctions, and the struggle over cultural identity—how their international peers and future generations would remember them, regardless of social, economic, religious, and political differences in the population. In the words of Mikhail Bakhtin (1981 [1935]: 276, 278), music was widely recognized as "an active participant in social dialogue," its "dialectics . . . interwoven with the social dialogue surrounding it."

I sympathize with listeners' tendency to see themselves mirrored in artworks, to project their own concerns onto those of the composer, and, in opera, to seek enlightenment (or catharsis) through the feeling that the performer is portraying the listener and the work represents the listener's own reality. That a female character like Dalila or Carmen is "strong," at least strong enough to bring a male under her spell, and her male counterpart "weak," or at least willing to submit to female charm, may seem today to reflect fear that liberated women threaten the social order, or to suggest that the character was indeed created to evoke misogynistic feelings. But an interpretation rooted in feelings about our own realities too often essentializes the artistic experience, reducing it to one's current concerns, and this rarely involves sensitivity to paradoxes inherent in a work's possible meanings and to other "plausible intersubjective interpretations."[3] What if characters like Dalila and Carmen, for example, were covers for other kinds of oppositions, even the inverse of what we might expect today?[4]

Listening to music is rarely just a private affair, and the experience is rarely separate from the form and format in which we perceive it. In the film *Howards End*, Helen and Leonard heard Beethoven in a piano transcription played by an old woman during a lecture to a motley crowd in a Victorian hall. All the audience heard was an excerpt. In this chapter I take such experiences seriously and suggest that the discourse, or meanings, generated by *Samson et Dalila* involve not just the opera itself but also the many forms and contexts in which it became known. Focusing on important determinants of the musical experience that have been ignored by scholars, I offer a methodology for decentering the work and studying meanings that arise from excerpts and transcriptions of it. If we have only reviewers to tell us how audiences responded to orchestral excerpts, and virtually no one besides the fictional characters of novels to document the perception of transcriptions, we must interrogate the kind of expectations encouraged by fragments, especially when placed in certain contexts, and seek to widen our understanding of a listener's "horizon of expectation."

As in perception, conscious attention, especially to works of art, "is only possible upon a background, or horizon, of distraction."[5] This horizon includes not only the personal preoccupations of individual listeners but also that which might affect understanding its relative value, and in Aristotle's terms, its final purpose. With this in mind, I investigate myriad concerns that may have informed interpretations of *Samson et Dalila*, starting with the political context in which the opera was conceived, the musical issues being explored, the composer's possible attitude toward the characters, and what the work itself allowed the composer to accomplish. These concerns not only shed light on the composer's possible intentions and the meanings he may have wished to encourage, but also lead to an interpretation of what the characters may represent that is more ambiguous than the work's Orientalist binarisms suggest.

Because *Samson et Dalila* was not produced onstage in France for fifteen years, I then examine the forms and contexts that rendered it popular. I argue that because so much music was presented in excerpts or transcriptions—whether in orchestral concerts, piano recitals, or outdoor wind-band performances—this created certain perspectives on the work and made possible meanings distinct from those associated with the staged opera. Transcribers, music publishers, and concert organizers brought their own intentions to bear on how the work might be perceived. The first two determined what excerpts were available to the public, thereby establishing boundaries on what was heard and imagined; the third placed these fragments in meaningful relationships with the music surrounding them on concerts, and thus set the terms for comparison and comparative judgments. In the case of transcriptions and excerpts, then, one should consider how their means, manner, and mode contributed to the audience's experience: the instruments used and skills needed of the performers, whether professional or amateur; the context in which the performance was heard, whether serious or popular, whether performed alone or surrounded by other works; and the relationship of their narrative configuration—their plot, thought, and character—to those of the opera in its original form.

All these factors imply that meaning is contingent, conditioned by certain frameworks, and affected by a sometimes disjunct, sometimes cumulative layering of meanings. Developing a "horizon of expectation" for understanding these entails a "passage from the individual to the collective or social aspects" of what is being heard and analyzed, and acceptance of meanings as socially constructed (de Man 1986: 58–60). By socially constructed I mean that the choice of which fragments became known was influenced by certain social, political, and cultural forces, including public taste, and in turn conditioned audience response to the first complete performances of the opera. French society, besides having its experience of the opera shaped by excerpts and transcriptions, changed significantly between 1877, the premiere of *Samson et Dalila* in Weimar, and 1890, its French premiere. That in the 1890s critics shifted their emphasis from the exotic charms of Dalila to the strength and virility of Samson suggests that meaning was not a stable category even when it came to the opera as a whole.

My hope is that this chapter sheds light on how excerpts and transcriptions in the late nineteenth century can shape the perception of meaning in a work, how we can trace changes in musical meaning over time, and how we think about meaning even in postmodern appropriations and recontextualizations, including those used in film and various new media.

Conception and Creation: The Hermeneutics of Charm

Under the photograph of Saint-Saëns facing the title page of the piano-vocal score of *Samson et Dalila* is a short citation in the composer's hand from the opening of its most famous air, "Mon coeur s'ouvre à ta voix comme s'ouvrent les fleurs" (My heart opens to your voice like flowers open at the kisses of dawn) (figure 8.1). Early sketches for the opera begin with the consequent of this melody, "Réponds à ma tendresse" (Respond to my tenderness).[6] The air refers to the central plot of the opera, Dalila's seduction of the enemy Samson for the sake of her people, the Philistines. Placed here it also functions as an emblem of the composer and the opera.

To understand its significance for Saint-Saëns, it is important to examine both the musical and political context in which he conceived the opera between the late 1850s and the late 1860s. What led him to begin *Samson et Dalila* has often been explained as a response to a competition for a prize in oratorio writing. Handel's music was very popular in Paris in the late 1850s. Excerpts from Handel's *Samson* were performed at the Paris Conservatoire in April 1857, February 1860, and April 1861, and Saint-Saëns subscribed to the 1861 Gesellschaft edition.[7] The Société des Oratorios and amateur choruses also performed Handel oratorios in the late 1860s and early 1870s. In this context, Katharine Ellis has argued that Handel evolved into a republican icon, his music representing much that republicans thought French society should embrace—robustness, solidity, healthy energy, and virility.[8] Was Saint-Saëns, a committed republican, playing into Handel's appeal and signaling the meaning associated with Handel's music when he wrote a Handelian-influenced Hebrew chorus in 1859 and later incorporated it as the opening of his own *Samson et Dalila*? Scholars have also pointed to another possible inspiration for the opera: Voltaire's *Samson* set to music by Rameau in 1732. The lyrics of Samson's hymn, "Israel! Romps ta chaîne! O peuple, lève toi!" echo Voltaire's air, "Peuple, éveille-toi . . . romps tes fers," set to music by Gossec and performed with the proclamation of the Constitution in 1791 and 1795. In both, the Hebrews call for reviving their grandeur and pride, important republican concerns in the 1860s.[9]

Still another motivation may have contributed to the decision to write this opera. Saint-Saëns began his career as a composer of instrumental and sacred music. Even though critics praised him for his knowledge of timbres and the clarity of his forms, acknowledging him as one of the lively forces in modern music, some criticized his earlier music for its lack of individuality and charm. In 1872, a reviewer of his first opera, *La princesse jaune*, commented:

> I told myself that what I had [before me] was a very extraordinary pianist, an organist from the best school, a conductor full of promise, a harmonist [who knew as much] as possible, a doctor in music, a memory full of all the masterpieces from all periods; but in the middle of all this wealth, I was forced to admit, like the cock in the fable, that

Figure 8.1. Saint-Saëns photo with "Mon coeur" sketch, from the piano-vocal score

the least millet seed would have been better. The millet seed that Saint-Saëns lacks is individuality, it's charm.[10]

If Saint-Saëns was sensitive to such a perspective, did this contribute to his decision, just after this premiere, to return to the opera he had begun to compose earlier on Dalila, a woman most known for her charm? His original title, in fact, was *Dalila*. The subject was popular in the late 1850s, especially Octave Feuillet's three-act *Dalila*, and was used in the 1866 Prix de Rome competition.[11] The next year Saint-Saëns began sketching his opera with the second act, which features Dalila and the two other main characters in solos and duets.[12] His inspiration included Italian melodic expression; one reviewer pointed to the fourth act of Verdi's *Aida*.[13] After setting the opera aside for years, did the composer see the work as an opportunity to seduce us with his voice, as Dalila seduced Samson with hers? In pencil and purple ink, Saint-Saëns created drawings of flowers over the sketches for the opening of act 3, "Look at my misery . . . have pity on my weakness," probably composed in 1873. Was he thinking of the power of the lady of the lilacs (*des lilas*), the flowers Voltaire's Dalila used to "enchain" Samson, or his music as the musical flowers of his imagination?

In many ways the composer charms audiences by means of Dalila, the only female singer in the opera, who, despite her exotic appearance, leads listeners to take her perspective. We often get her point of view; she is the primary agent of the drama. To engage her seductive charms and her "*puissance enchanteresse*," Dalila destabilizes Samson with music reminiscent of the "weakness" which he says she sees in him in act 1. Like the chromatically descending tritone (E♯ to B) he uses to symbolize his anguish and his pleasure (perhaps also foreshadowing his surrender to her), Dalila sings a long sequence of chromatic half-steps spanning a tritone from A down to D♯, when, after he tells her he loves her, she asks him to remember "these beautiful days spent on one's knees before a lover." (Similar descending chromaticisms permeate the instrumental music at the beginning of act 2, when we first see her house, surrounded by "Asian flowers and lush vines.") In exchange for her song and "in hopes of learning the secret of his strength," she then asks to possess not his body but his voice which is the key to his power: "My heart opens to your voice . . . let your voice speak again."

With curves and chromaticisms carefully controlled and manipulated in their every nuance, Dalila gives voice to Saint-Saëns's notions of desire and musical charm. "To enslave" Samson and "enchain" him to herself, she musically links the memory of his "caresses" with her idea of love. Starting on the pitch D♭ where he left off singing "I love you," she goes on to entreat him in one of the most powerful moments of the opera: "Respond to my tenderness, give me ecstasy [*ivresse*]." This is symbolized musically by three interlocking chains of chromatically descending lines that end on the tritone G♭–C (figure 8.2). Unfortunately for Samson, she does not have to be sincere for her charms to take effect. In the duo that follows, a strophic variation of this section, he responds to her descending lines and the "tenderness" she offers him in three ways: with a rising arpeggio as if to console her as he sings, "With my kisses, I want to dry your tears"; by echoing the descending

Figure 8.2. *Samson et Dalila,* excerpt, piano-vocal score, "Ah, réponds à ma tendresse"

chromaticisms and singing with her a third lower; and finally by moving into unison with her at the end of the stanza as she pleads for ecstasy. Musically this is the surrender love calls for—Samson's music follows Dalila's, the man loses his will to the woman's. Love indeed has rendered the Other vulnerable and submissive, but in this case the Other is male.

The opera is also a story of the struggle for individuality, as represented by Samson. In her analysis of the biblical story, Mieke Bal sees, as the main themes, the problem of the hero and those associated with love rather than heroism or love itself. "Redeem us from love" is the theme of this myth. From Bal's perspective, based on a reading of Lacan, Dalila is there to help Samson "reach awareness."[14] She holds up a mirror that allows him to "discover" himself and ultimately to escape his symbiotic bond with God (and himself), to "be reborn" (1987: 65–66).

At some point after writing act 2, Saint-Saëns changed the title of his opera to reflect the importance of both Dalila and Samson, or, one might say, the need for both charm and individuality in his music. In a way they represent what Bal (1987: 45) calls the "riddle about strength and sweetness" that runs through Samson's life, beginning with his secret encounters with the lion.[15] What Saint-Saëns does with such a story offers an answer to this riddle. As French culture was trying to think about race and gender in increasingly essentialist terms, he focuses on the anti-essentialist aspects of his two main characters. Both are complicated, neither reducible to stereotypes. Dalila is not particularly weak (in the Bible she is depicted as socially successful and independent, having her own house). Samson is mostly passive and ends up in chains, hardly the proud hero; the libretto omits any reference to his slaying of the lion and one thousand Philistines. Saint-Saëns's answer to the riddle is both to foreground the confrontation of "sweetness" (or charm) and "strength" (or individuality) as conflicting forms of power, and to suggest that pleasure (sexual as well as other kinds) lies in their coexistence or comingling.

Through performers who would draw attention to the complexities of gender in the story, Saint-Saëns could also de-essentialize the notion of who is speaking through them and what they represent. Dalila's voice is central in the opera, but her charms are not those of a typical light soprano. Saint-Saëns conceived such a role for the mezzo-soprano Pauline Viardot and dedicated the opera to her. He once referred to her voice as "of enormous power and prodigious range . . . made for tragedy," and to the singer as one who lent "incomparable grandeur" to whatever she performed. At the first performance of excerpts, another woman known for her strength and virile music, the composer Augusta Holmès, sang the part. Through such a character the composer could both address his critics and explore what he may have coveted, not only her power of seduction but also her unrepressed sexuality, attraction to strength in others, and desire to dominate it—in short, her will and ability to get what she wants.

Saint-Saëns's description of the tenor voice of Henri Regnault, a painter friend who sang the role of Samson in the private premiere with Mlle Holmès, suggests that neither was his idea of Samson that of the stereotypical male hero. The composer appreciated a certain feminine-like charm in his friend, calling his voice "exquisite" with "an enchanting timbre" and "an irresistible seduction." Perhaps he saw himself that way or sought to explore those aspects in himself, for he explains, "as we loved and admired the same things, the good feelings that united us were very natural" (Ratner 1985: 110, 120 n. 18). In Samson, Saint-Saëns had a hero who was weak in many ways, helpless, surrendering, and responsive rather than initiating—stereotypically feminine—while maintaining a physical strength of mythic proportions.

The main characters in the opera speak almost incessantly of their voices, yet often it is as a medium for something else, the source of their power. Beyond the role of religion in defining this, what Samson and Dalila signify is ambiguous. The historian Michel Faure understands their opposition as the class conflict underlying French society at the time. In the late 1850s, he explains, Samson would have been understood as a lion symbolizing the "people," and his story "the myth of the left," with workers enslaved to a corrupt bourgeois society. After the Paris Commune, however, this image was easily reversed.[16] The composition of the opera amid war with Prussia, the siege of Paris, and the reassertion of power by the Third Republic adds further ambiguities, particularly to the possible meaning of Dalila. France was forced by the war to give up its imperialist pride and to accept its relative weakness vis-à-vis its neighbors. With these changes came a return in politics to female allegories, not just Marianne crowned with a phrygian cap but also Liberty wearing a lion's muzzle.[17]

Women have long served as allegories in France, particularly political allegories, whether of democracy, monarchy, liberty, or anarchy.[18] Exotic women, too, I would argue, allowed the French to explore their attitudes about their colonies, the woman standing in as the quintessential Other, desirable but potentially dangerous. Susan McClary (1991) and Ralph Locke (1992) have eloquently shown that women the likes of Carmen and Dalila are often victims of misogyny and the racist, imperialist climate of the times.[19] But as Paul Robinson (1985: 65) pointed out, these women are "rarely experienced as victims" and, in any case, "their vocal assertiveness places them on an absolutely equal footing in many love duets and gives lies to the notion that women are inferior creatures." Moreover, in the early 1870s the focus of public attention was not the colonies but rather the humiliating defeat of the Franco-Prussian War and the fall of the Paris Commune. In this context, some French saw the value in learning from other societies, such as those "bound by ties of deference, status, and a sacred union of the human and natural orders."[20] Those who preferred to concentrate French resources on recuperating Alsace and Lorraine (largely conservatives and monarchists) protested the country's imperialist ventures bitterly and with some success.

In the 1870s and 1880s the stereotype of the exotic woman relied on a certain ambivalence critical to its function.[21] To the extent that Dalila seduces audiences into the illusion, listeners are given the opportunity to explore what existentially weak women call on to survive, learn about the nature of their charm, its uses, and the limits of its power. They could consider what it means to be the weaker in a dyad, what kind of relationship is possible with stronger Others, how they might appropriate these tactics (as the composers do) as a way to empower themselves. A Dalila could stimulate reflection about how the French viewed themselves, their strengths and weaknesses, perhaps also their repressed desires, fantasies, hopes, and dreams related to France's political position in Europe.

To the extent that Voltaire's Dalila influenced Saint-Saëns's concept of the woman or audience reception of the character, other interpretations are also possible, especially given that a new edition of Voltaire's *Samson* was published in 1877 (the year *Samson et Dalila* was premiered in Weimar). Voltaire's Dalila is a pacifist. She tells the Hebrews to "forget combat" and prays to Venus to instruct her on the "charming art of pleasing and seducing" for the purposes of bringing "peace on earth." She sees her duty as love. If love is dangerous, as the prologue points out, Voltaire's Dalila also suffers, a victim of following the orders of the High Priest. When she learns her actions have betrayed Samson, she commits suicide.

Operas featuring exotic women are thus not convincing principally because of their predictable plots—the women usually die. I argue they are occasions to ponder the nature and meaning of musical charm and its power, an illusive magic as untranslatable as the foreignness of the exotic women. The importance the women give to their ability to "enchant" and the consciousness with which they call on it suggest that feminine charm was not considered entirely pejorative, an instrument of "the devil" leading to a man's ruin—but instead, at least in some cases, could be desirable and worthy of developing especially if it gives voice, as it does in many of these operas, to the will of an older male. The role charm plays in this music suggests that, whether consciously or not, composers thought it an essential element to explore, understand, and promote in French music.[22]

First Performances: Meaning from Excerpts

Critics by the late 1870s were largely enthusiastic about Saint-Saëns, but the composer did not have an easy time getting the opera staged. When he proposed it to the Opéra in the mid-1870s, after the private performance of excerpts arranged by Pauline Viardot in 1874 and later with Holmès and Regnault, he was rebuffed by the theater's director, Olivier Halanzier. Halanzier objected to the lack of melody and found it more oratorio than opera, even though oratorio was in fashion.[23] He also thought the Old Testament and the image of Samson with a shaved head would not appeal to audiences.[24] Instead, in 1876 the Opéra chose to put on Mermet's *Jeanne d'Arc*. Mermet's *Roland et Roncevaux* (1864) was having a "triumphant tour" in the provinces. Its blatant patriotism portrayed the Francs as militarily successful, and Roland, their hero, celebrated in marches and dancing, was probably closer to what French audiences wanted to hear after their 1871 defeat.[25] Saint-Saëns wrote to the Minister of Public Instruction and Fine Arts asking for help in getting his opera performed in Paris. He was again told that the work was inappropriate for the stage. The composer later confessed that he had received "such hostility" whenever he spoke of it and that, had it not been for Liszt (who said he would arrange a performance in Weimar in 1877), he would have "renounced" finishing it.[26]

Other than concert performances of the individual acts and various transcriptions, *Samson et Dalila* onstage was not known to the French public until the 1890s. Yet by the time the Opéra finally produced it in 1892, it was already hailed as the composer's most popular work.[27] The story of how this paradox emerged helps us to understand how music generates meaning in the absence of the original form of the work and in contexts different from those envisaged by the composer.

Table 8.1 shows in what forms the French public was able to hear the opera. Orchestras performed excerpts in the 1870s and 1880s. Transcriptions and fantasies were made available for piano and voice. Wind bands, made up of soldiers or working-class amateurs, gave their own versions in public parks, and singers presented airs in private salons.

This proliferation of genres raises certain questions. If part of Dalila's charm comes from the insistent repetition of recurring themes and entire sections within scenes, and from act to act, what happens to the meaning of the work—and to the whole project of charm in *Samson et Dalila*—if listeners come to know the work only through excerpts and transcriptions, most of them without the voice? And what happens when a work is cut into pieces, especially *Samson et Dalila,* whose scenes are largely through-composed and whose vocal writing integrates short, unaccompanied recitatives with bel canto singing? In short, what is the nature, meaning, and value of a work of art when it is presented in something other than its original form?

In his book *Music in the Moment,* the philosopher Jerrold Levinson (1997) suggests that people listen and comprehend music perfectly well without necessarily being aware of large-scale form. Like the nineteenth-century psychologist Edmund Gurney (1880), who inspired his ideas, Levinson believes that meaning derives principally from the moment-to-moment process of a work's unfolding. This thesis should give us pause. If the value of a work is a function of its individual parts, what kinds of meaning do parts generate in the absence of the whole to which they belong? Parisian orchestras occasionally performed an act or a selection of fragments from a new opera hoping that these would generate interest in a recent work. Eventually, however, some excerpts and not others entered the orchestral repertoire, suggesting that fragments could be appreciated as self-sufficient.

What happens to the meaning of a fragment when one hears another composer's music before and after it? Gurney and Levinson contend that meaning arises when a listener grasps connections to immediately neighboring music, thus concatenating what is heard. This suggests a resonance from one musical moment to the next. Gurney may very well have arrived at his emphasis on temporal succession as a source of meaning by observing the nineteenth-century taste for aesthetic contrast. Nineteenth-century music often creates contrast through what we now call masculine and feminine themes. This principle also dominated the structure of late-nineteenth-century concert programs in France. Many achieved balance through the juxtaposition of diverse genres. Even if these genres may have been understood as distinct parts of a musical meal, with the beginning and end serving functions different from those served by the middle, they were also seen as opportunities for comparison, digested as part of the same experience and valued for teaching

Table 8.1. Selected Performances and Publications of *Samson et Dalila*

Opera	Orchestras	Wind Bands	Publications
	Act I, CC, 26 Mar. 1875 "Danse des prêt," CC, 16 Jan. 1876 "Danse des prêt," CC, 11 Nov. 1877 "Bacchanale," CP, 23 Nov. 1877		Durand acquires the opera (Apr. 1875) "Danse des prêtresses," pf (Durand, 1876) "Danse des prêtresses," *JM* (11 Aug. 1877) pf, v [German and French] (Durand, 1877) H. Cramer, *Reminiscences* (Durand, 1877) Orchestral parts (Durand, 1878) "Bacchanale," pf; pf à 4 (Durand, 1878) 11 detached numbers, pf, v (Durand, 1879)
Weimar, 2 Dec. 1877 Brussels (concert) May 1878	"Bacchanale," CP, 17 Nov. 1878 "Danse," "Bacch," CC, 25 Jan. 1880 Act III, CC, 26, 28 Mar. 1880 "Danse," "Bacch," CC, 23 Jan. 1881		
Hamburg, 1882	"Danse," "Bacch," CL, 21 Dec. 1884 Air, CL, 1 Feb. 1885 Air, CC, 22, 29 Nov. 1885 "Danse," CC, 15 Apr. 1887		F. Spindler, *Fantaisie brillante*, pf (Durand, 1882)
Liège, 1888	Duo, 1889 Exposition, 31 May 1889 "Danse des prêt," CL, 17 Nov. 1889 "Danse des prêt," CC, 15 Dec. 1889		
Rouen, 3 March 1890		*Military bands* (Paris): 24 Sept., 12 Oct. 1890	
Paris, Théâtre-Lyrique (Eden) 31 Oct. 1890	"Danse," "Bacch," CC, 19 Oct. 1890 "Bacchanale," CC, 23 Nov. 1890 Air, SdC (Strasbourg), 4 Feb. 1891		"Chant de Dalila," v, pf *Le figaro* (19 Mar. 1890) G. Bull, *Fantasie*, pf facile (Durand, 1890) A. Lefort, *Fantasie*, pf, vln (Durand, 1890) L. Roques, *Illustrations*, pf à 4 (Durand, 1890)

Geneva, Dec. 1891		*Bon marché*: 6 June, 25 July 1891	G. Meister, *Fantasie*, wind band (Evette, 1891)
Bordeaux, Toulouse, Nantes, Dijon, New York (concert) Algiers,	Air, CC, 27 Mar. 1892	*Military bands* (Paris): 1892–94: **68 times** incl. 3, 5, 7, 24 July; 4, 11 (2x), 14 Aug.; 9, 29 Sept. 1892;	pf, v (New York, 1892) "Bacchanale," pf, vc (Durand, 1892)
Montpellier, Florence, March 1892	Air, SdC (Strasbourg), 26 Oct. 1892		L. Roques, "Mon coeur," Duo, Hymn, pf à 4, vln, vc (Durand, 1892)
Monte Carlo	Paris zoo, 14 Aug., 2 Oct. 1892		"Danse des prêtresses," pf, Le figaro (23 Nov. 1892)
Paris, Opéra, 23 Nov. 1892			
New Orleans, Jan. 1893		16, 18, 19, 21, 31 May; 1 June (2x), 7, 8 (2x), 6 July 1893	
Milan, Cairo, Feb. 1893			
		Military bands (Algiers): 5 Mar., 6 Apr., 22 June 1893	
London, Sept. 1893			
Antwerp, Dec. 1893		*Bon marché*: 24 June, 12 Aug. 1893; 21 July 1894 8 July, 10 Aug. 1895	pf, mandoline or guitar (Durand, 1894)
Moscow, St. Petersburg, Brussels, 1894	"Danse," "Bacch.," CC, 28 Oct. 1894		Fantasie, military band (1894) Fantasie, pf, fl (1894)
New York, 1895		*Military bands* (Paris): summer 1895 9, 25 June, 2,4 July 1896	L. Roques, 2 Suites faciles, pf à 4 (Durand, 1895)
Buenos Aires, 1896	Air, Jardin, 4 Oct., 8 Nov. 1896		G. Papin, pf, vc (Durand, 1896)
Barcelona, Jan. 1897			

Continued on the next page

Table 8.1. *Continued*

Opera	Orchestras	Wind Bands	Publications
Paris Opéra, June 1897 100th performance		27 May (2x), 4, 8 July 1897	E. Kosieck, Grand duo, pf (Durand, 1897)
Rio de Janeiro, 1898 Paris Opéra, 30 Oct. 1898, Free performance		10 July, 2, 7, 14, 21, 25, 28 Aug. 1898 4, 11 June, 23, 30 July, 4, 20, 27 Aug., 3 Sept., 8, 15 Oct. 1899	A. Luigini, Fantasie, pf orch (Durand, 1898)

Note: CC = Concerts Colonne; CP = Concerts Populaires; CL = Concerts Lamoureux; Jardin = Jardin zoologique d'acclimatation; JM = *Le journal de musique*; v = voice; pf = piano; pf à 4 = piano, four hands; vln = violin; vc = cello.

judgment, a crucial attribute for training citizenship. In other words, a certain meaning was attached to where excerpts were placed on concerts and what surrounded them.[28]

Conductors played an important role in how audiences would encounter musical fragments. Edouard Colonne knew how to market new music to Parisian audiences and program it appealingly. Even before its staged premiere in Weimar in 1877, he tried to get audiences interested in *Samson et Dalila* by performing the premiere of its first act in March 1875 on a concert that always used a chorus and took place on what was often the most popular day of the year: Good Friday. This performance featured the premiere of Gounod's *Jésus* and ended with an audience favorite, the finale of Beethoven's Ninth Symphony. The concert was indeed well attended, and ticket sales at the door were the highest for the season.[29] Ironically, however, it was not the allusions to Judeo-Christian religiosity that appealed to the public, even on Good Friday. Nor did reviewers compare it to the excerpts from Handel's *Samson* by the Concerts Pasdeloup that were warmly received the previous month. Instead, they noted that listeners found Saint-Saëns's style inaccessible, elevated, and too complicated, but admired his orchestral colors, even the bizarre ones. They especially appreciated the strikingly original "Dance of the Priestesses," the music in which Dalila begins to work her magic on Samson.[30]

Colonne's success with this trope of musical charm led him in January 1876 to excerpt the "Dance of the Priestesses." In many ways, he treated it as a new independent work, placing it second on the program, a position often reserved for new music. It may have appeared to audiences as the next in Saint-Saëns's series of tone poems. Like *Phaeton* (which Colonne premiered in 1874), followed by *Le rouet d'Omphale* and the *Danse macabre* (which he premiered in 1875), it was "descriptive music," its exotic narrative inspiring imaginative uses of the orchestra.[31] It also had a memorable theme and a clear structure that was easy to follow.

In January 1880 Colonne moved the "Dance of the Priestesses" to fourth on the program, the position of new work in their repertoire, and paired it with another dance from the opera, the equally exotic "Bacchanale," first excerpted by Pasdeloup in 1878 (figure 8.3). This introduced his audience to material from act 3, which he presented later that March. Colonne again chose Good Friday. As with the premiere of act 1 five years earlier, audiences preferred the instrumental music, particularly the brilliant orchestration of the "Bacchanale."[32] It is significant that the Handelian-influenced choruses and music that revealed Samson's fate on having been seduced, and his courage in resisting his chains, apparently held little interest for audiences of this period.

The reception of these excerpts may surprise us, especially since scholars in recent times have pointed out how unstable the music is harmonically and rhythmically. To what extent did the context in which conductors placed the excerpts encourage audiences to embrace this music despite the absence of the dancers for whom they were written? In the first three performances, the excerpts were twice adjacent to Mozart and Beethoven. Colonne performed the 1875 premiere of act 1 before Mozart's funeral march, a work he had paired with Saint-Saëns's Second Piano Concerto on 13 December 1874. This choice is striking, and not just for the

DIMANCHE 25 JANVIER 1880, A 2 HEURES PRÉCISES

15ᴹᴱ CONCERT ᴅᵤ CHATELET

PROGRAMME

1. SYMPHONIE en *fa mineur* (1ʳᵉ audition)................ TSCHAÏKOWSKY

  Introduction et moderato — Andantino — Scherzo — Finale.

2. SCÈNES D'ENFANTS orchestrées par B. GODARD......... R. SCHUMANN

  a. Des pays mystérieux.
  b. Colin-Maillard.
  c. Bonheur parfait.
  d. Rêverie.
  e. Sur le cheval de bois.
  f. L'enfant s'endort.
  g. En songe.

3. CONCERTO pour violon............................... BEETHOVEN

  Allegro e cadenza — Larghetto — Rondo.
  M. Camille SIVORI.

4. SAMSON ET DALILA............................... C. SAINT-SAËNS

  a. Danse des prêtresses de Dagon.
  b. Bacchanale.

5. PRÉLUDE DE LA REINE BERTHE.................... V. JONCIÈRES

6. POLONAISE DE STRUENSÉE....................... MEYERBEER

L'Orchestre sera dirigé par M. Ed. COLONNE.

CE PROGRAMME DOIT ÊTRE DÉLIVRÉ GRATIS.

Premières Loges, Baignoires et Fauteuils de Balcon 4 fr. — Fauteuils d'Orchestre, 3 fr. — Première Galerie, 2 fr. — Stalles d'Orchestre et Pourtour, 1 fr. 50 — Partorre et Premier Amphithéâtre, 1 fr. — Deuxième et troisième Amphithéâtre, 75 c.
En location : Premières Loges, Balcon et Baignoires, 5 fr. — Fauteuils d'Orchestre, 4 fr. — Galerie, 2 fr. 50. — Stalles et Pourtour, 2 fr. — Parterre et Premier Amphithéâtre, 1 fr. 25.

On trouve des Billets : Au THÉÂTRE DU CHATELET, *tous les jours (excepté le Lundi),* de 1 heure à 5 heures, et le Dimanche de 10 heures à midi 1/2 ; à l'OFFICE DES THÉÂTRES, boulevard des Italiens, 15 ; — AGENCE DES THÉÂTRES, avenue de l'Opéra, 60 ; — chez BRANDUS, rue Richelieu, 103 ; — DUPUIS, rue de Rivoli, 146 ; — DURAND, SCHŒNEWERK et Cⁱᵉ, place de la Madeleine, 4 ; — GREGH, chaussée d'Antin, 10 et boulevard des Italiens, 17 ; — HEUGEL, rue Vivienne, 2 bis ; — KATTO, rue des Saints-Pères, 17 ; — MACKAR, passage des Panoramas, 22 ; — MASCLET, rue du Bac, 43 ; — O'KELLY, faubourg Poissonnière. 11 ; — TELLIER (ancienne maison GÉRARD), boulevard des Capucines, 12 ; TRAUVIN, boulevard Saint Michel, 38. — A la salle des dépêches du *Figaro*, rue Drouot, 22.

Dimanche 1ᵉʳ Février 1880, 16ᵉ Concert

3604 Imp. Vᵛᵉ RENOU, MAULDE & COCK, R. Rivoli, 144, à PARIS.

Figure 8.3. Concerts Colonne, program of 25 January 1880

reuse of the Mozart. Why did Colonne not juxtapose Saint-Saëns's act 1 with Handel, whose choruses had served as a model? Two months earlier, on 24 January 1875, he had programmed an excerpt from Handel's *Saul* before the premiere of Saint-Saëns's *Danse macabre*. In 1876 the "Dance of the Priestesses" again followed Mozart. Beethoven, of course, was on many Colonne programs, but what is noteworthy is the Violin Concerto he performed adjacent to this dance twice on 16 January 1876 and 25 January 1880. On 19 December 1880 Colonne had programmed the premiere of Saint-Saëns's *Suite algérienne,* also between a Mozart symphony and Beethoven's Violin Concerto.[33] Did Colonne hope listeners would hear a sympathetic resonance between Saint-Saëns's music and that of Mozart and Beethoven? Saint-Saëns was recognized as a pianist for his interpretations of classical music. Germans appreciated his Mozart, and Parisians his virtuoso renditions of Beethoven. Saint-Saëns performed Beethoven's Fantasy for Piano, Chorus, and Orchestra regularly in Paris, including with the Conservatory orchestra the week after the premiere of act 1 from *Samson et Dalila.* He also composed his own Variations on a Theme of Beethoven (1872), which audiences could have heard at the Concerts Colonne on 31 January 1875, three months before their rendition of act 1, and again on 3 April 1876. Might listeners have appreciated the similar phrase structures and formal clarity? Would the influence of the French violin school on the work have made it good for comparison, or might the virtuosity of Beethoven's solos have drawn attention to that of Saint-Saëns's orchestration? If the violinists incorporated Saint-Saëns's cadenza for the concerto, might audiences have compared the work to the composer's approach to Beethoven's music?[34] In some ways the German masters set a high standard. When the performance of the dances after Beethoven's Violin Concerto in January 1880 was well received, the comparison worked to Saint-Saëns's advantage, for reviewers suggested that he was on the way to becoming a "grand maître."[35]

With Saint-Saëns next to Mozart and Beethoven, the Frenchman's orchestral colors (especially in the "Bacchanale") offered audiences the kind of contrast that made for instructive comparisons. The novelty of the dances' exoticism not only enhanced the distinction of Saint-Saëns's music but also led audiences to associate his music with progress and regeneration, even if he did not challenge the principles and structures of classical music. The organization of concert programs in the 1870s would have contributed to this conclusion, for on many of them German classical music and French contemporary music alternated, with the former framing and creating a reassuring context for the innovations of the latter.

That alternating pattern began to change, however, in the 1880s, as conductors programmed less German classical music and more contemporary music. On 25 January 1880, Colonne began with Tchaikovsky's Symphony in F minor, and after the excerpts from *Samson et Dalila* came the prelude from another recent French opera, Joncières's *La Reine Berthe* (Opéra, December 1878) (figure 8.3). On 29 February Colonne's audiences heard two excerpts from Charles Lefebvre's opera, *Dalila,* and, in March, act 3 of *Samson et Dalila* was followed by excerpts from act 3 of Massenet's *Le roi de Lahore* (Opéra, April 1877). The latter would have allowed audiences to compare two concepts of the Orient (the temple of Dagon versus a Hindu paradise), two versions of Orientalist choral singing and dance music (the Philistine's "Bacchanale" as against the Hindu "Divertissement des esclaves persanes"), and two styles of conducting (as Saint-Saëns and Massenet conducted their own works).

Colonne's orchestra performed excerpts from *Samson et Dalila* a dozen times from the 1870s through the 1890s. Their success as distinct works made them as popular with Colonne's audiences as the tone poems given about the same number of times (see table 8.1). The excerpts provided opportunities for audiences to increasingly compare Saint-Saëns with his French contemporaries. For example, in 1885 and 1887 the "fine and delicate" orchestration of the "Dance of the Priestesses" provided contrast with that of Berlioz's *Roméo et Juliette* and his powerful *Marche troyenne*. In 1885 Colonne, focusing on vocal style, twice put an air from *Samson et Dalila* after melodies by Edouard Lalo and placed the dances next to music by Franck, Bizet, and Tchaikovsky. Beginning with Colonne's premiere of his "Ride of the Walkyries" in 1881, Wagner appeared on four of the remaining eight Colonne concerts with Saint-Saëns's dances but only once was Saint-Saëns's music adjacent to Wagner's. The prelude from *Lohengrin* came after an intermission, as if direct comparison between the two would not be fruitful. The dances from *Samson et Dalila* allowed audiences to situate Saint-Saëns's exoticism in a variety of musical contexts and to test his accomplishments against those of his peers. Colonne thus played an important role in predisposing his audiences to considering a succession of possible meanings.

Transcriptions and Their Meanings

These orchestral successes also had practical functions. With such performances often preceding publication of the musical scores, it is possible that Saint-Saëns used them as opportunities to hear his works before finalizing them for publication.[36] Also, and perhaps more important, one week after Colonne's premiere of act 1 in 1875, Durand acquired the score. A year later he published Saint-Saëns's piano transcription of the "Dance of the Priestesses," the selection Colonne had excerpted.[37] When Weimar agreed to produce the opera in 1877, Durand published Saint-Saëns's piano-vocal score of the entire opera in French and German, and an eleven-page piano fantasy based on the work "Reminiscences" by Henri Cramer.[38] In August 1877, partly to draw attention to the premiere abroad, *Journal de musique,* a family magazine sympathetic to living composers and whose editor had attended the Weimar premiere, reproduced Saint-Saëns's three-page piano transcription of the "Dance of the Priestesses" (figure 8.4). The following year Ernest Guiraud, a professor at the Paris Conservatoire, made a version of this and the "Bacchanale" for piano, four hands.

Why so many transcriptions, particularly for piano, and why by 1877 had both publishers and performers perceived the "Dance of the Priestesses" and the "Bacchanale" as excerpts capable of achieving popularity without the dancers or the orchestra? Transcriptions were certainly a mode of transmission and dissemination. They allowed access of the work to a wider public, somewhat like recordings

Figure 8.4. "Dance of the Priestesses," reproduced in *Journal de musique* (August 1877)

except one had to perform them oneself. Listeners who heard them at orchestral concerts may have purchased them as a reminder of these performances and their musical experiences. Except for those who could afford a subscription at the Opéra or Opéra-Comique or who produced operas in their own homes—the musical manifestation of luxury—most people became familiar with art music only through some virtual representative. Transcriptions blurred the boundaries between classes, as did consumer goods at department stores that likewise helped domesticate luxury products and encourage desire for them. Most Parisians could only afford to purchase cheap imitations of the real thing, be it furs, jewelry, or music.

Transcriptions allowed audiences to get to know a work in a variety of formats. Saint-Saëns made piano transcriptions of all his major pieces and often published them simultaneously. He also made them of works by J. S. Bach, Gluck, and Beethoven as well as Berlioz, Gounod, and Wagner, which suggests that he found the exercise useful and satisfying. Sabina Ratner sees them as part of the broader practice of self-borrowing that characterizes Saint-Saëns's compositional output.[39] Transcriptions contributed to the repertoire of professional pianists who, following the example of Liszt, were expected to give renditions of works popular in other media, such as opera.[40] More important, they also allowed Saint-Saëns to try out new works for his peers, such as at the Société Nationale, well before orchestras performed them.[41] Often audiences heard his piano transcriptions first and sometimes found them as satisfying as the original form.[42] To augment the genre, Saint-Saëns, like other composers, looked to friends he could trust. That illustrious composers such as Fauré and Guiraud would make transcriptions of Saint-Saëns's music suggests that this was not considered lowly work. In becoming coauthor of a work by Saint-Saëns, they would have had to take the genre seriously.[43]

For publishers, composers, and transcribers, transcriptions were a way to make money and build reputations even if a work never caught on. They were not cheap. While Saint-Saëns's piano-vocal score of the whole opera cost fifteen francs, piano fantasies based on the work, such as Cramer's *Reminiscences*—all produced by the same publisher, Durand—cost from five francs for a five-page version (the price of the best seats at the Concerts Colonne) to nine francs for a thirteen-page *Suite facile* for piano, four hands. Few composers failed to take advantage of the opportunities offered by transcriptions.

Of particular interest in this study is how transcriptions mediate and shape the meanings associated with a work. What happens, for example, when the medium changes? For some, such as Busoni, a great work is always great even if in transcription. Its meaning comes from its essence, not necessarily the medium in which one hears it.[44] To the extent that transcriptions neutralize the specificity of the original instruments, they encourage the transcriber to act *through* the new medium to communicate something beyond the transcription. The piano is ideal for this kind of work for, as Joseph Kerman (1999: 41, 69) points out, it can mimic human voices, strings, woodwinds, and even the orchestra. From this perspective, the meaning of a transcription can be tied to its function as a sign to the original work or to some essence perceived in it. In this sense, for Busoni and others, transcriptions are not very different from the original work since both are signs to the originating idea.[45]

French composers learned this skill at the Conservatory. Transcribing one's cantata for voices and piano was a required part of the Prix de Rome competition. In most cases and except for the orchestral performance of the winning cantata each year, the piano-vocal transcriptions would be the only form in which these works were heard. It was crucial, therefore, that their essence be perceivable through the medium of transcription and that they stay as close as possible to the original, with no major cuts or rearrangements.

To the extent that transcriptions allow for fragmentation of the original work and presentation of excerpts out of the original context, however, they did not always signify their origins in a simple and straightforward manner. Yes, transcribed excerpts were often used to draw attention to a recent production of a work, particularly those published around the time of its premiere and appearing in newspapers and music magazines. Transcriptions could be used to keep the work in the public ear, in the case of opera, even before it was staged. As reviewers suggest in writing on the orchestral excerpts from *Samson et Dalila,* they also could add pressure on officials to stage it.[46]

But the piano transcriptions of the two opera fragments from *Samson et Dalila* point to a problem in assuming that they signified the opera. Without the orchestra and unable to appeal through their timbres, it is not obvious how these piano transcriptions were understood. Both are dance pieces easily excerpted from the opera, capable of being listened to without the larger context. Neither was difficult for amateurs to perform, with their two-bar gestures, repetition of short passages, and consistent left-hand pattern for long stretches. Perhaps with their grace notes, accented weak beats, and augmented seconds, they brought to mind the charms of exotic culture in general. Like other piano pieces published in *Journal de musique* in 1876–77—songs and dances from Serbia, Peru, Montenegro, Turkey, and Israel— they allowed French audiences to bring the exotic into their homes, to study it up close and become comfortable with it. By performing this music, amateurs could domesticate its exoticism. For republicans advocating an imperialist agenda based on assimilation, such music may have helped French families contemplate the benefits of cultural assimilation without forcing them to consider the social and political consequences of assimilating exotic peoples.

Transcriptions are also a mode of translation and critique, a reading of the original representing a will and desire to convert one kind of order into another, foregrounding what is important.[47] As such, they represent a distinct form of creativity, more like wood-cut engravings than photographs. They give musical form to the way the transcriber heard or understood the original work, constituting what recent scholars have called an "écriture de l'écoute," a "composition de l'écoute," or an "interpretation composée."[48] In this sense, the medium of the transcription and its means are less significant than what the transcriber chose to include or exclude, embrace or resist in the original.

Leaving aside the virtuosity that often bathes the borrowed tunes, the piano fantasies on *Samson et Dalila* from 1877, 1882, and 1890 embody what the transcribers thought were its most salient elements. Because these authors sometimes reordered, expanded, and contracted fragments of the original, their fantasies offer various readings of the essence and meaning of *Samson et Dalila,* some of them quite different from what either the composer may have envisaged or one might construe upon seeing the whole opera staged. As such, transcriptions call into question opera as a fixed system of representation. They are neither simple signs to some original nor mere objects of consumption. They have their own authenticity giving them the power to produce meaning and to legitimize perspectives on the work that could change over time. Since transcriptions affect the experience of the work, the transcriber's choices establish boundaries on not only what listeners hear of the work but also what they are likely to imagine. That certain excerpts were repeatedly used in these fantasies attests to their popularity over others that could have been chosen.

Three of the fantasies based on *Samson et Dalila* and published by Durand— Henri Cramer's *Reminiscences* (1877), Georges Bull's *Fantasie* (1890), and Léon Roques's *Illustrations* (1890)—concentrate on music associated with the opera's two main characters (see table 8.2).[49] What is marked and unmarked in the music derives from the exotic and non-exotic elements underlining this gender opposition. These fantasies start with Samson's hymn from act 1 in which he expresses his strength and associates himself with the Hebrew God: "Israel, let us rise once again. . . . In the Lord follow me." This returns in the middle of his act 2 duo with Dalila, when he explains why he must leave her. His "call to duty" creates the context for her quintessential air, "My heart opens," the musical representation of charm in which she draws Samson's voice into unison with her own. The three fantasies culminate with the "Bacchanale," a celebration of Dalila's victory over Samson.

The choice of these excerpts is significant, as is the order in which they appear. Samson's music represents his commitment to his people before his seduction by Dalila, not his defeat nor his moment of triumph when he breaks the chains. Dalila's music expresses love, not betrayal or anything that reveals her other side. (Music that shows Dalila as unambiguously evil is not included.) The juxtaposition of love with duty was a classic theme in French drama since Corneille. In this fantasy, however, love for a woman does not function as a foil to underline how great is a man's love for his God or his country. By ending with the "Bacchanale," the transcriber, like the orchestral audiences of this music, seems more interested in the musical power of exoticism and thus in the appeal of Dalila's charm, even if in the opera this ultimately results in the male's defeat. Moreover, the excerpts suggest that the two characters are not irreconcilable antagonists. Samson's four-square rhythms and tonal harmonies function as baseline expectations that make Dalila's virtuoso display that follows seem extraordinarily effective. In this sense, the music associated with Dalila and the Philistines provides occasions for transcriber and performer alike to push on the boundaries of the expected, exploring musical equivalents for the exotic Other.[50]

The placement of the "Bacchanale" in these three fantasies implies another message as well. Even if eight of the eleven pages of Cramer's *Reminiscences* are Dalila's

Table 8.2. Piano Fantasies

H. Cramer, *Reminiscences* for piano (Paris: Durand, 1877), eleven pages
1. Act 1/2 Samson's hymn
2. Act 2   Dalila, "Pourquoi repousser ma tendresse?" "Mon coeur s'ouvre"
3. Act 1   Dalila, "Printemps"
4. Act 1/3 Female Philistine chorus, "Voici le printemps"
5. Act 3   "Bacchanale"

F. Spindler, *Fantaisie brillante* for piano (Paris: Durand, 1882), nine pages
1. Act 1/3 Philistine Chorus, "Voice le printemps"
2. Act 3   "Bacchanale"
3. Act 1   Samson's hymn
4. Act 2   Dalila, "Mon coeur s'ouvre"
5. Act 1   Samson's hymn

G. Bull, *Fantaisie facile* for piano (Paris: Durand, 1890), five pages
1. Act 1   Samson's hymn
2. Act 1   Dalila, "Printemps"
3. Act 2   Dalila, "Mon coeur s'ouvre"
4. Act 3   "Bacchanale"

L. Roques, *Illustrations* for piano, four hands (Paris: Durand, 1890), nine pages
1. Act 1   Samson's hymn
2. Act 2   Samson, Dalila, duo, "Pourquoi repousser ma tendresse?"
3. Act 2   Dalila, "Mon coeur s'ouvre"
4. Act 1   Dalila, "Printemps"
5. Act 1/3 Female Philistine Chorus, "Voici le printemps"
6. Act 3   "Bacchanale"

L. Roques, *Suite facile*, No. 1 for piano, four hands (Paris: Durand, 1895), thirteen pages
1. Act 1   Philistine Chorus, "Voici le printemps"
2. Act 1   "Danse des prêtresses"
3. Act 1   Dalila, "Printemps"
4. Act 1   Samson's hymn

L. Roques, *Suite facile*, No. 2 for piano, four hands (Paris: Durand: 1895), thirteen pages
1. Act 2   High Priest, Invocation to Dagon
2. Act 2   Samson, Dalila, duo, "O toi bien-aimé"
3. Act 2   Dalila, "Mon coeur s'ouvre" (eight to nine pages)
4. Act 3   "Bacchanale" (two pages)

airs and excerpts from the female Philistine chorus, the transcribers encircle the feminine music with masculine music, with Samson's hymn first and the "Bacchanale" last. The "Bacchanale," too, shares this shape, incorporating static but oscillating material within the framework of its aggressive, energetic sections. This suggests that the masculine frames the feminine, even within the context of exoticism. Musical structure thus draws attention to the fact that, as in the opera, Dalila neither acts independently nor has the last word; she follows the orders of the High Priest who creates the context for understanding her actions. This interpretation of the musical sequence supports Levinson's and Gurney's notion of meaning as affected by what comes before and after a given section. At the same time it strengthens the proposition that some overall sense of form is necessary for a more complete musical comprehension.

The three fantasies also interject Dalila's air, "Here comes spring bringing hope to loving hearts," with which she begins to enact her charm. In the opera this follows the "Dance of the Priestesses" and ends act 1. Unlike "My heart opens," this tune is neither exotic nor chromatic. Instead, it shows another side of the character presented here as lyrical and loving, even naïve, with no suggestion of her manipulative nature. Such an excerpt, with the main character stripped of her difference and excessive exoticism, may have been considered more accessible to traditional opera audiences whom concert organizers wished to attract to the new production, for the excerpt appeared in the newspaper *Le figaro* on 19 March 1890, just two weeks after the French premiere of the opera in Rouen.

Cramer and Roques also include two more excerpts. Before Dalila's seductive air, both insert part of the duo in which Samson tries to resist Dalila's entreaty, "Why push away my tenderness?" and eventually comes to recognize his love for her. Later, before the "Bacchanale," they incorporate the Philistine chorus, "The voices of spring." The overall structure of this fantasy thus differs from that of Bull's in ignoring temporal succession in the opera. Here Dalila's two airs come in reverse order. This makes some sense if one hears the fantasy in two parts. The first builds from Samson's hymn of duty and his expressions of resistance to Dalila's successful seduction. The second interjects the Philistines' spring song—music that appears both before Dalila's spring song in act 1 and before the "Bacchanale" in act 3—as a bridge between these two sections, thereby representing both male and female Philistines, the sensuous and the warrior in their culture. In these two fantasies, therefore, exotic music associated with Dalila and the Philistines far outweighs music associated with Samson in quantity and importance. Its first half culminates in Dalila's conquest of Samson, and its second half consists entirely of music associated with the Philistines.

Fritz Spindler's 1882 *Fantaisie brillante*, published the year of the Hamburg premiere of the opera, presents a more balanced relationship between feminine excerpts (five pages) and masculine material (four pages). It begins with the female Philistine chorus and ends with Samson's hymn. However, while reiterating the same excerpts, it more or less reverses their order. The result suggests a different interpretation of the opera's meaning. With the Philistine chorus and "Bacchanale" first, their music serves as the frame for perceiving the couple. This could suggest that Dalila's culture and its exotic difference are the context for understanding her power over Samson. Perhaps not surprisingly, the longest and the most virtuoso section is Dalila's seduction aria, the very notion of seduction inspiring the transcriber's "brilliant" pianism.[51]

These fantasies suggest that, until the work was known as an opera in France,

Saint-Saëns's publisher and these transcribers judged that audiences were more interested in the charms of the exotic woman and her culture than any other aspect of the opera. Undoubtedly they were also addressing the fantasies and desires of those who would have performed these pieces. Most likely it was women, for they dominated the world of amateur pianists and singers. Excerpts from Saint-Saëns's opera appeared regularly in private salons in the 1880s.[52] By 1888 teachers at the Conservatory were assigning their students vocal excerpts for the annual exams.[53] Dalila's airs soon became "classics" among "all female singers."[54]

Understanding charm was important to young French women. In an 1887 speech to a women's high school, Eugène Spuller, the Minister of Public Instruction and Fine-Arts, told women that they should nurture "grace, charm, and delicacy," and at the same time "develop a virile character" so that they can also be like fathers to their children if their husbands die. The country, he told them, wants "useful women" (i.e., good wives and mothers), not "useless ornaments to society" (Spuller 1888: 246–49). Certainly Dalila was both charming and useful to her people, and the French public apparently enjoyed reading about her and listening to her music.[55] After 1890, however, this attitude changed subtly as a profoundly conservative current began to influence republican leaders. As the feminist movement began to gain force, there was a predictable backlash. In 1894 Spuller (1895: 93, 96) told those at another women's school that "feminine education" must not be confused with "virile education." Women "are not made to command, but to inspire." Their role is to bring "a spirit of sweetness and reconciliation into the Republic . . . not to do battle with the opposite sex, but to unite and complete one another." With this new spirit of hostility toward strong women, it should be no surprise that the reception of Dalila would change dramatically, and that in 1890 singers would begin to perform the act 2 air "Love, come help my weakness," in which Dalila plots her betrayal and assumes that Samson's force will be "in vain." In this context, the meanings associated with Saint-Saëns's opera could not remain the same.

Staging the Opera: New Contexts and New Meaning in the 1890s

On 3 March 1890 the French premiere of *Samson et Dalila* at the Théâtre des Arts in Rouen stimulated a new wave of interest in the opera, as did the Parisian premiere on 31 October. The director Henry Verhurt had been looking for a work that was "recognized and at the same time unknown to Parisians" to inaugurate a new lyric theater.[56] His recent production of it was ideal to bring to Paris, as was the venue he envisaged. The Eden-Théâtre, just a block from the Opéra, had been used by the Concerts Lamoureux for performances in the mid-1880s, and otherwise produced exotic spectacles and ballet. It was therefore an appropriate place to stage a work known so far for its orchestral excerpts and exoticism. For the new venture, the theater was transformed, its promenade gallery removed, and some seats in the balcony taken away to make space for boxes. Like the Théâtre des Arts, the Théâtre-Lyrique (Eden) attracted the musical cognoscenti to *Samson et Dalila,* but few others.

Critics embraced the opera immediately, calling it Saint-Saëns's best for the theater. Henri Bauer asserts that the "freshness, charm, and delicacy" of the "justly famous" romantic duo would "attract all those who had not yet heard it as well as all those who know it and would like to hear it again."[57] Another praises this duo in which the composer deploys "all the richness of his inspiration, all his art of declamation, and all the nuances of his so colorful orchestral palette."[58] At the same time reviewers begin to explore a new perspective on the opera's meaning. Camille Bellaigue emphasizes the work's "virile poetry," "male severity," and "style that eschews all affectation, all refinement that is too picturesque, almost all Oriental color."[59] This suggests that, for him, the story is less about charm—the woman's wickedness and the man's entrapment—than it is about strength, virility.[60] Ernest Reyer, too, explains that it is not just about an exotic seductress; it overflows with choruses and music for men. His focus is almost entirely on Samson, the "Jewish Hercules." In the first act Samson "revives the courage of his brothers, promising to lead them to battle"; in the second he resists Dalila's charms three times, "always master of his secret"; in the third he "shatters the pillars of the temple." Arthur Pougin notes that the librettist modified the character of Dalila to render her more theatrical and make her seem "a ferocious fanatic" rather than a "perverse and self-interested woman." His point is that she stands for religion rather than women. Like Reyer, he prefers the first act, praising "the purity of its lines" and the choruses "of grand allure" influenced by Bach and Handel. He considers this the composer's "most powerful and noble" work. In their annual review of Parisian performances, Edouard Noel and Edmond Stoullig also focus on Samson. They point out that, although he was an "imprudent" man who was betrayed, Samson saw his strength return while his enemies were making fun of him, unaware that his hair was growing back.[61] This shift of focus from Dalila's charm and the exoticism of the second and third acts to Samson's strength, along with the more severe style of the first act, signals a significant evolution in public taste.

Publishers and performers helped draw attention to these premieres. Besides Dalila's spring song published in *Le figaro* on 19 March, Colonne reprogrammed the "Bacchanale" the same day and twice again that fall. And as we have seen, two more fantasies for piano were published. Increasingly there were also fantasies, sometimes called "mosaics," for other instruments, including the wind band. In the fall of 1890, even before the Parisian premiere of the opera, military bands performed one such transcription in Paris. The following summer on 6 June the amateur wind band of the department store Bon Marché opened its 1891 season with a similar transcription of the opera, repeating it again on 15 July.

Like opera fantasies in military band concerts, this wind-band transcription was placed in the middle of the program, typically the fifth of six pieces, as if it were a main course of the musical meal that often began with a march and ended with a polka or waltz. Thousands attended these concerts on Saturday nights in the square outside the store, as well as the late afternoon concerts given by military

SAISON D'ÉTÉ

CONCERT DU SAMEDI 21 JUILLET

5ᵐᵉ Audition

dans le Square

à 8 heures ¼ du soir

PAR

L'HARMONIE

DU

BON MARCHÉ

SOUS LA DIRECTION

de M. Paulus ✻ *ex-chef de musique de la Garde Républicaine*

PROGRAMME

1º **Marche du Figaro** . . . . G. Wittmann.

2º **Samson** et **Dalila**. . . . . Saint-Saëns.

3º **Anna Bolena** . . . . Donizetti.

4º Fragments de **Rienzi**. . . . . R. Wagner.

5º **Solo de Cornet,** par M. Prialoux . . J. Mellé.

6º **Mystères des bois** . . . . L. Itasse.

FINALE

La prochaine audition aura
lieu le Samedi 4 Août

Figure 8.5. Concert of the Bon Marché's Harmonie in the Square

Figure 8.6. Meister's Fantasy for wind-band, introduction

bands throughout the city several days a week. Wind-band transcriptions not only provided access to those who could never afford to see the opera but also whetted appetites and recalled the memories of those who could attend the Opéra.

The 1891 wind-band fantasy by George Meister, conductor of the first regiment of the military engineers' band, is a large compilation of music from the opera comprising thirty-one pages in the conductor's score (cf. tables 8.2 and 8.3).[62] Even if Durand authorized its publication, the fantasy does not respect the original order of the excerpts in the opera.[63] In a strange sort of way, however, it does signify one of the work's origins, a fully orchestrated "Marche turque" in MS 545 at the Bibliothèque Nationale in Paris. This march, reused as the main section of the "Bacchanale," is a prime example of Saint-Saëns's self-borrowing. He either wrote it in 1859, around the same time as his "choeur d'Israel" later used in the opening of *Samson et Dalila,* or more likely around the time of the "grand march," *Orient et occident,* dated October 1869.[64] Like *Orient et occident,* the "Marche turque" was written for *grande harmonie* in twenty-seven to thirty-two parts—flutes, clarinets, oboe, saxophones, cornets, trumpets, trombones, and saxhorns of all sizes.[65]

Meister's fantasy resembles the "Marche turque" especially in its tune and texture. The woodwinds articulate the tune in staccatos (clarinets in the "Marche turque"; flutes, oboe, and E♭ clarinet in the "Bacchanale" of the fantasy and opera), although the phrase accent in the "Marche" falls on the tonic whereas in the fantasy and the opera it comes on the repeat of the dominant. As in the opera, the fantasy deletes the grace notes drawing attention to the syncopated beats in the opening measures. But otherwise it creates a similar texture. The bare accompaniment of repeated eighth notes on and off the beat creates a static background, also as in the opera. With successive iterations of this tune, the intensity also builds similarly, although the opera adds strings. A valved cornet joins the woodwind tune, together with other brass (saxhorns in the "Marche" and an alternation between bugle and contraltos in the fantasy); a quartet of saxophones, doubled by flutes in the fantasy, adds a layer of alternating sixteenth notes; and the rest of the brass reinforce one or another of the alternating eighths. As such, the wind-band transcription of the "Bacchanale" forges almost an equivalence between the sign and the opera's signified, bypassing the mediating role of the opera.

The organization of this fantasy—Meister's choices from the opera and the order in which he presents them—echoes the critics' focus in 1890 on Samson and the male choruses. Whereas in the earlier piano fantasies the music of Samson provides a horizon against which to judge and enjoy the difference of Dalila's music, in this arrangement the music of men dominates. The work begins and ends with fragments from Hebrew choruses. In the opening segment from act 1, scene 1, the chorus expresses distrust of Samson when he refers to God's action in freeing the people from Egyptian bondage, "That happened long ago . . . now we suffer." Then, in a last excerpt from act 1, scene 2, they shift to faith in his leadership and God's mercy. Besides including two of Dalila's songs, the middle sections focus on the Hebrews' oppressors, both the lascivious, pleasure-seeking Philistines and the aggressive Philistine soldiers. These choices, of course, may reflect the fact that the performers would be male wind-band players, many of them soldiers or men play-

Table 8.3. Wind-band Fantasies

Samson et Dalila, arr. G. Meister (Paris: Evette et Schaeffer, 1891) for harmonie (in thirty-five parts); also performed by military bands, thirty-one pages

1. Act 1	Opening bars
	Hebrew Chorus fragment, "Ils ne sont plus, ces temps"
2. Act 1/3	Philistine Chorus, "Voici de printemps"
3. Act 3	Récit *for oboe*
	"Bacchanale"
4. Act 1	Dalila, "Printemps" for *contralto*
5. Act 2	Philistine soldiers preparing to ambush Samson:
	their theme with Abimélech and the High Priest's curse
6. Act 2	Dalila, "Mon coeur s'ouvre" *for cornet*
	Duo, "Réponds" *for cornet and trombone; tutti*
7. Act 1	Hebrews' response to Samson's hymn

Samson et Dalila, arr. Grossin, mosaic for military band, perf. 1899,
as described in *Le petit poucet* (August 1899)

1. Act 2	Prelude, Durand score pp. 94–95
2. Act 1	Hebrew Male Chorus, pp. 71–73
3. Act 1	Philistine Female Chorus, "Voici le printemps," pp. 73–76
4. Act 1	"Danse des prêtresses," pp. 84–88
5. Act 2	Dalila, "Mon coeur s'ouvre," pp. 147–56 *for bugle*
	Duo, "Réponds" *for bugle and trombone*
6. Act 3	Samson, p. 224
7. Act 1	Samson's hymn and the Hebrews' response, pp. 48–57 *for trombone and tutti*

Samson et Dalila, arr. A. Luigini (Durand, 1898), fantasy for orchestra with piano conductor, nine pages

no "Bacchanale"

ing for civic occasions. But other factors may also have contributed to these choices and the fantasy's structure.

Of utmost significance is the principle of aesthetic contrast, characteristic of much military music. The opening excerpts pit the Hebrew and Philistine choruses against each other, the "majestic" followed by the "mellow [*moelleux*]."[66] After the Philistines' spring song that ends on "Let us always remember . . . love alone endures and will never die," the "Bacchanale" comes next, as it does in the opera. However, whereas the Spindler piano fantasy has Dalila's seductive music following the passion of the "Bacchanale," as if a female response to the masculine frenzy, this wind-band transcription presents her spring song of soft, lyrical simplicity and manipulative naïveté after the "Bacchanale," an andante after an allegro. Moreover, since Meister truncates the "Bacchanale" somewhat, her song functions in part as a continuation of its more languorous middle section, albeit without the exoticism.

What follows Dalila's song is another allegro propelled by dotted rhythms, music again associated with the Philistines.

The choice of the Philistine soldiers' music situated in the middle of the fantasy is significant. In the opera we hear their first theme when protecting Abimélech in act 1, scene 2, and their second one initially sung by the High Priest cursing the Hebrews in act 1, scene 4. But the counterpoint of these themes comes only at the end of act 2, that is, *after* Dalila's seduction and Samson's revelation of his secret. Placed by Meister *before* "My heart opens," the temporal reversal has narrative implications. With the Philistine soldiers waiting in the wings, we are reminded of the intended betrayal and so hear the seduction scene differently. After "My heart opens" and the romantic duo, the return to music from act 1 is also salient. Ending with the Hebrews' response to Samson's enthusiastic hymn, "Let us rise and be free," their dotted rhythms and leaping fourth foreshadow Samson's call for God's strength at the end of the opera, and the fantasy seems to suggest that, despite the seduction, the will of Samson and his God would prevail. With Samson promising victory, the fantasy thereby concludes on an optimistic tone that, if played by soldiers, could have been meant to uplift both the army when going into battle and the French back home still demoralized by the Prussian defeat.

The alternation of solos and tutti in the fantasy contributes to these musical contrasts. As in the opera, a short cadenza for oboe, *récitativo ad libitum,* accompanied by a long chord in the trombones (horns in the opera) intervenes between the Philistine chorus and the "Bacchanale." The "Bacchanale" then rapidly builds to a long tutti. After this, a solo contralto (with a bugle sometimes substituting) presents Dalila's spring song. It was typical in military and wind-band fantasies of the time for operatic music sung by a female to be performed by the bugle or valved trumpet. The tone remains sweet for this love song as woodwinds eventually double the melody and saxophones add an arpeggio accompaniment reminiscent of lieder. After the basses introduce the aggressive music of the Philistine soldiers and the whole ensemble takes part in the counterpoint of their two themes, the "tumult leads to the calm of Dalila's tender phrase," the valved cornet playing Dalila's seductive air.[67] Samson and Dalila's love duo follows, "Respond to my tenderness," split between the cornet (leading two clarinets, alto saxophone, and contralto) and the trombone (doubled by the flute, oboe, soprano and tenor saxophones). Building to its climax, the entire band joins in. The duo, however, stops short of including Samson's declaration of love and surrender. Perhaps the transcriber thought this would make the return to the theme of duty in his optimistic hymn at the end seem more plausible. Without the surrender, the bombastic tutti of the final section could also function as an expression of continued resistance.

The inclusion of these solos serves other purposes as well, some related to their function as signs to the opera. Of particular interest are the words for "Here comes spring" and "My heart opens," printed under Dalila's airs as if to suggest that performers have them in mind while playing (see figure 8.7). Was Meister hoping that listeners grasp the iconic nature of the sign and the meaning of the words? He also indicated performance instructions, asking the cornet player to interpret the female airs just as in the opera, "*dolce*" and then "*dolcissimo e cantabile.*" In asking

Figure 8.7. Meister's Fantasy for wind-band, Dalila's air

soloists to imitate the human voice, to play as the characters sing, Meister was challenging them to explore operatic expressivity, including sentiments and music associated with women. Listeners could reap the benefits without the luxury of women or opera singers. Organizers of military-band performances considered the contributions of these soloists important enough to list their names in the programs.

Meister's tempo choices also imitate those of the opera:

Moderato;
Allegretto ($\downarrow$ = 76) for the Philistine chorus;
Allegretto ($\downarrow$ = 120) for the "Bacchanale";
Andante ($\downarrow$ = 84) for Dalila's spring song;
Allegro moderato ($\downarrow$ = 116) and animato poco a poco for the Philistine soldiers preparing to ambush Samson;
Andante ($\downarrow$ = 66) for the seduction air, Un peu plus lent for the duo; and
Allegro ($\downarrow$ = 76) for the Hebrew chorus and finale.

This, too, contributes to the sense of contrast from one section to the next. At the same time it sheds light on the work's organization and integrity as distinct from its capacity to signify the opera. The middle sections, framed by the male choruses and extending from the "Bacchanale" through the seduction scene, are a balanced A–B–A'–B' in terms of texture and tempo. In order for the rhythmic proportions of these sections to mirror this structure, Meister may have truncated the strophic repetition of "My heart opens" and the romantic duo. At the same time he incorporates intact both Dalila's spring song and the Philistines' ambush of Samson. The result is sections of roughly the same length.

This compositional structure gives much more weight both to Dalila's spring song and the music accompanying the Philistines' ambush than the opera does. Several motivations might have led to this. In much military music, assertive, upbeat sections that are meant to rouse and inspire soldiers alternate with lyrical sections that provide relief and a respite from the demands of energetic display. This could symbolize the juxtaposition not only of the masculine and the feminine but also of military service and private, civilian life that soldiers were there to protect. In Meister's fantasy, the docile, hypnotic rhythms and melodic tenderness of the love song serve the function of difference well. Here it is not the allure of the Oriental, as in the opera, but rather the stereotypical feminine and the expression of love. The section functions musically as if it were a trip home to one's beloved in the middle of a life filled with battles and men. The words written under its notes suggest the soldiers' feelings, their anxiety about their beloveds waiting for "their return," their nostalgia for spring as a time of "hope for hearts in love," and their "memories of past happiness." In this context, Dalila's song probably would have been heard as expressing universal sentiments with which soldiers or their beloveds might identify.

Meister's choices also reflect his desire to challenge performers in their ensemble playing. Indeed, while some considered wind-band transcriptions of art music "travesties," those promoting them believed they would have a positive effect on both performers and audiences.[68] Renewing the concert repertory for military musicians with works using different scales and harmonies, more complicated melismatic ornaments, quicker rhythms, and more subtle textures helped soldiers grow as musicians. The coordination demanded by this music undoubtedly also helped to make them better soldiers. In the Philistines' spring song, three chamber groups alternate and come together, creating the need for subtle balance in the performing forces. Accompanying Dalila's spring song and her seductive air, the clarinets and saxophones would have to hold long notes quietly and play extended, delicate repeated staccatos in unison and sweet arpeggios, like the strings and harp in the opera. From this perspective, it is perhaps understandable that Meister would devote so much attention to the music for the Philistines' ambush, otherwise a minor part of the opera. Not only does it extend the chamber groups in alternation to more instruments and tighter, closer juxtapositions, its difficult counterpoint requires precision and clarity from the whole band. Such music thus not only helped composers and theaters to attract attention to new works but also gave band members opportunities for different kinds of playing, using the complexities of contemporary music to stretch their skills and capacities.

Another year would go by before the Paris Opéra produced *Samson et Dalila*, even with pressure from productions in the provinces (Bordeaux, Toulouse, Nantes, Dijon, and Montpellier) and abroad (Geneva, Monte Carlo, Algiers, Florence, and a concert version that March in New York). Meanwhile, in July and August 1892, Parisians could hear eleven performances of the wind-band fantasy by the military bands of three infantry regiments as well as the zoo orchestra performing all over the city, from the Champ-de-Mars in the prestigious seventh district and the centrally located Tuileries and Luxembourg gardens to three sites in the working-class eastern part of town.

When the Opéra did schedule it for 23 November, they spent very little on the decor and costumes and, although Colonne conducted it from memory, Mme Blanche Deschamps-Jehin, the wife of the well-known conductor, was unconvincing as Dalila, her powerful voice a bit overwhelming and her talents perceived as "a little too bourgeoise."[69] Moreover, the opera evidently started thirty minutes late because there was so much talk in the corridors, possibly about problems in Dahomey and Tunisia that were dominating the news.[70] One critic noted that since the story had become "trop connu," especially with Reyer's *Salammbô* performed at the Opéra all that year, the listener could become "absorbed in the exclusive admiration of the art." Critics were divided over the dramatic qualities of the outer acts, some praising the "grandiose effect" of its choruses and "skillful simplicity" of its style, and others bemoaning the influence of oratorio on the lack of dramatic movement. At the same time they observed that the public preferred the second act not just because of its theatrical color and intimate beauty but also because of the ease with which the air and duos had been excerpted and made known through performances in homes and on concerts.[71] As in 1890, it was anticipated that the "irresistible intertwining, the freshness, charm, and delicacy" of the romantic duo would attract to the production those who had not heard it as well as those who already knew it well.[72] For its part, on the day of the premiere, *Le figaro* responded conservatively, publishing a piano transcription of the ever-popular "Dance of the Priestesses," while Roques, addressing the renewed interest of audiences in the duo, made new transcriptions of it for piano, four hands, and for violin and cello.

Throughout December 1892, the Opéra performed *Samson et Dalila* after another work of far less significance by an unknown composer, Alix Fournier's one-act opera, *Stratonice* (1892), as if to discourage audiences.[73] Still, sixty-one performances of the opera followed in two years, as did transcriptions for other instrumental combinations (see table 8.1). Compilations published after the opera was staged, however, treat it somewhat differently than those from the 1870s and 1880s. Roques's first *Suite facile* for piano (1895) contains only excerpts from act 1 and, unlike all previous piano fantasies based on the opera, follows the example of Meister's 1891 wind-band version: it ends rather than begins with Samson's hymn. Dalila's and the Philistines' languorous music, including the "Dance of the Priestesses," establishes the context for what Samson stands up for when he proclaims, "Israel, break your chains! O people, rise up." In his second *Suite facile* with excerpts from acts 2 and 3, Roques for the first time incorporates music expressing Dalila's duty to her people. Placed before the love duo with Samson, "O, you beloved, for whom I've been waiting," and the seduction air, "My heart opens," it plants betrayal as the central motivation for Dalila's behavior. Coming after these, the "Bacchanale" reinforces the image of depravity and decadence.

After being produced as an opera, *Samson et Dalila* left the repertoire of major orchestras but joined that of military and wind bands (see table 8.1). Their performances interwove closely with those at the Opéra. For example, between performances at the Opéra on 3 and 26 May 1893, military bands played the work on 16 May at the Tuileries, 18 May at Passy, 19 May at the Palais Royal, 21 May in the Luxembourg gardens, and 23 May again in the Tuileries. Anticipating the 9 June performance at the Opéra, these bands repeated it on 31 May at the Palais Royal, 1 June at both the Champ-de-Mars and out where workers lived, the Buttes Chaumont, as well as on 7 June at the Palais Royal and on 8 June at the Champ-de-Mars. From 1892 through 1894, over sixty military-band performances were given in more than a dozen Parisian gardens, and this continued through the turn of the century.

These concerts had programs and notes published for them in *Le petit poucet*, a magazine of military-band music. Whereas the notes for Meister's fantasy performed by Garde Républicaine in 1896 featured only a description of the excerpts from the opera, those for Grossin's military-band arrangement of *Samson et Dalila* performed in 1899 included a short performance history of the opera, an outline of the excerpts with reference to the analogous pages in the published piano-vocal score, and a narrative linking them to the opera. These cite the texts from the Chorus of the old Hebrews from act 1, the first stanza of the Philistine chorus, "Here comes spring," and two stanzas of the text for Dalila's seduction air and duo for bugle and trombone:

Bugle: My heart opens to your voice. . . .
Ah, respond to my tenderness . . .

Trombone: Dalila! Dalila! I love you!
Bugle: Wooed by the summer breeze . . .
Bugle and trombone: Ah, respond to my tenderness . . .

In this case the performance clearly was intended to point to the opera as a theatrical production and musical score, perhaps even creating a desire to hear it at the Opéra. Why then, one might ask, does this fantasy present the excerpts out of their original order (see table 8.3)? As in Meister's fantasy, the organizing principle seems to be aesthetic contrast and an overall tripartite structure resembling that of military music, with the Hebrew male choruses framing music associated with Dalila and the priestesses. The mosaic begins with the highly chromatic prelude from act 2, a tone poem suggesting the fall of night in an exotic locale. Next come two choruses: the harmonically and melodically static male chorus of old Hebrews singing in praise of their God and foreshadowing their deliverance by Samson, followed by the more supple arabesques of the female Philistines' spring song. This leads to Dalila's entreaty for Samson to follow her, as played by the bugle—the "Dance of the Priestesses" used for the first time in such a setting—and Dalila's seductive air. Love appears as an interlude in a piece about men. Perhaps most significant, as in the fantasy for orchestra published in 1899, there is no "Bacchanale" to distract listeners with its charm. Like other fantasies from the 1890s, Samson has the last word. The composer ends, perhaps addressing the French, with a call for the Hebrews to return to their previous grandeur.

Such a reading of the opera may have been self-serving, with military band conductors using Saint-Saëns as a pretext to expand the boundaries of military music without questioning its conventional structures. But if we take history as a set of practices and music as important *lieux de mémoire,* places that remind us of the ambiguities underlying our treasured monuments, this interpretation makes some sense. After 1889, "the year of exoticism," many French were tiring of exotic Others. A decade of extensive colonization wrought with troubles had also made them less naïve about their "*voyages imaginaires.*" Some began to question seriously France's civilizing mission and its "great idea of raising up the races." As the French had to come to grips with conquering and governing their colonies—particularly Dahomey, in the 1890s, with its ferocious female Amazons—works portraying women as willful, rebellious, and even capable of treason began to challenge the conventions associated with exotic female characters, to imbue them and what they may have stood for with increasing ambivalence. At the same time, with the first stage of the Franco-Russian alliance completed in August 1891, the country was feeling a renewed sense of strength as a nation, encouraging a celebration of their virile qualities. Increasingly in the 1890s transcriptions as well as critics drew attention to these qualities in the opera, planting the seeds for misogynist interpretations. By the one-hundredth performance at the Opéra in 1897, reviewers were calling Dalila "treacherous," her voice "hypocritically caressing."[74] Studying the contingencies of meaning implied in opera fantasies thus helps to draw our attention to how music can express the flux of national identity. As Pierre Nora (1984: vii, ix) has pointed out, it is sometimes "places without glory, little frequented by research and disappeared from circulation that make us most realize what the place of memory is."

Conclusion

The aesthetic of authenticity and the value we ascribe to the apparent intentions of a composer have often blinded us to how an opera reaches diverse audiences and generates meaning. In this chapter I have shown why we should reevaluate our assumptions about the composer's or the Opéra's hegemony. When works were written to tolerate fragmentation and reproduction in many formats and contexts, it was not possible to control the uses to which they could be put and the ensuing meanings they could generate. Some, as I have suggested, emerged from choices made by transcribers and from juxtapositions with the music surrounding them on concerts. Orchestral and vocal excerpts, piano and wind-band transcriptions, and a wide range of popular venues led to pressure on theaters to produce *Samson et Dalila* and played an important role in popularizing it; but they also helped to shape listeners' "horizon of expectation." Before the work was staged, these focused principally on Dalila, feminine charm, and the work's exotic elements. After it reached the Opéra in 1892, they shifted to celebrating Samson and virile strength. This tells us much about the flux in French taste and French identity during this period. Excerpts and transcriptions are thus important for the perspective they offer on the history of reception and public taste.

Such practices were not unique to *Samson et Dalila*. From the Second Empire through World War 1, many operas in France, both foreign and contemporary French works, went through this process. Beginning in the 1860s, the Garde républicaine's conductor A. Sellenick composed and performed wind-band fantasies on not only popular operas by Meyerbeer and Verdi but also Gounod's *Roméo et Juliette* in 1867, the year of its Théâtre-lyrique premiere. Also in the 1860s, long before the opera was staged at the Eden Theater in 1887, audiences heard the march and prelude of *Lohengrin* in Parisian concert halls, and fantasies on *Lohengrin* for piano or wind band. Orchestral concerts and wind bands in public parks played excerpts from new works such as Massenet's *Hérodiade* and Reyer's *Salammbô* before their staged premieres in 1882 and 1892.[75] Even if an opera was produced on stage soon after its composition, such as Delibes's *Lakmé* in 1883, Saint-Saëns's *Henry VIII* in 1883, and his *Proserpine* in 1887, most large-scale works were heard most often and by the most people in some partial form. In 1899 the editor of *Le petit poucet* claimed that without the help of wind-band transcriptions, "the glory of Saint-Saëns, Massenet, and Reyer would not have penetrated as easily into the provinces [where there were not always symphony orchestras] and works of theirs that cannot be adequately played by the solo piano would have remained completely unknown."[76] In making a work available to amateurs as well as professionals, provincials as well as Parisians, and in diverse private and public venues, transcriptions and excerpts broke down meanings tied to the class, education, politics, and location of Opéra audiences.[77]

Such a study leads us to interrogate the compositional consequences of such contingent meanings. Did the knowledge that their work would inevitably be transcribed and perhaps become known largely through excerpts and transcriptions in turn influence composers' choices of what and how they wrote? The "Dance of the Priestesses," for example, was appreciated for its orchestral effects in part because its main theme could so easily be fragmented and played by a wide range of instruments. What effect did such consideration have on works that became part of the canon? Did some composers feel it was necessary at the end of the nineteenth century to inhibit the performance of excerpts and the medium of transcription by writing music that could not move easily among different formats, venues, and performers? From this perspective, Debussy's focus on timbral specificity and formal ambiguity in his *Prelude to the Afternoon of a Faun* and other works takes on a new light, as does his desire for musical meaning that was immanent rather than transcendental. Debussy and other French modernists embraced an aesthetic of difficulty to distance music from the general public, reversing the practice of making it accessible.[78] Schoenberg, too, wished to get beyond pianistic writing that was really just a transposition of orchestral music. Even if his colleagues at the Association for Private Musical Performances made chamber transcriptions of many contemporary works, including Debussy's *Faun,* Schoenberg told Busoni that transcriptions made him fearful of losing control over his own work.[79] Modernism, then, may have arisen partly as a reaction to the processes I have outlined here, sacrificing all that this tradition brought to audiences in terms of meaning as well as access to the contemporary music of their times.

Notes

For a fuller discussion of the issues raised in this chapter, see my *Useful Music, or Why Music Mattered in Third Republic France,* to be published by the University of California Press. I am grateful to Marianne Wheeldon and Byron Almén for their kind invitation to participate in the symposium, "Music and Meaning," at the University of Texas at Austin on 27 January 2003; to Jim Webster for inviting me to present this to the music department at Cornell University on 9 October 2003; and to colleagues and students for their helpful comments on these occasions as well as at the University of California, San Diego, on 8 February 2005.

1. *Howards End* (1992) was directed by James Ivory and produced by Ismail Merchant. The screenplay, based on a novel by E. M. Forster, was written by Ruth Prawer Jhabvala.

2. All this is ironic, for in E. M. Forster's novel upon which the film is based, it is Helen, not the lecturer, who imagines the goblins. Moreover, she is listening to an orchestral performance of Beethoven's Fifth Symphony, not a piano transcription.

3. This expression comes from Robert Hatten (1994: 5).

4. If we take gender to be what S. Žižek (1989: 87) has called a "floating signifier" whose "literal signification depends on metaphorical surplus-signification," we can use it to consider a network of possible meanings generated by a work. Gender is one element of the "ideological field" discussed in Žižek's *Sublime Object of Ideology.* For him, such elements

"are structured into a unified field through the intervention of a certain 'nodal point' (the Lacanian *point de capiton*) which 'quilts' them, stops their sliding and fixes their meaning."

5. In his *Resistance to Theory* Paul de Man (1986: 58–60) discusses "horizon of expectation," derived from Husserl's phenomenology of perception and used by Hans Robert Jauss to explain the nature of historical consciousness. See Jauss 1982a: 79; 1982b: chap. 5.

6. Ms 545, Bibliothèque Nationale, Département de Musique, Paris.

7. Moreover, Saint-Saëns's friend, Pauline Viardot, sang an air from this work at the Conservatoire in 1862. See Servières 1930: 171.

8. See Katharine Ellis 2005, chap. 6.

9. Gossec also set this to music to accompany the transfer of Voltaire's ashes to the Panthéon in 1791. See Constant Pierre 1899: xxviii.

10. Paul Bernard, *Revue et gazette musicale* (16 June 1872).

11. Feuillet's *Dalila* was published in many editions including in 1855, 1857, 1860, 1870, 1876, and 1892. Two other dramas on the topic were also published in 1857: Armand Lapointe's *Dalila et Samson* and Fransicque Tapon Fougas's *La princesse Dehli-la ou Des lilas*, a parody in five acts.

12. According to James Harding, an excerpt from act 2 was performed in a salon in 1867. In his entry, "Samson et Dalila," Hugh Macdonald suggests that Saint-Saëns abandoned his opera after sharing aspects of act 2 with his friends and "only after the appearance in 1872 of his third opera, *La princesse jaune*, did he feel sufficiently encouraged to resume *Samson et Dalila*" (*New Grove Dictionary of Music Online*, ed. L. Macy, http://www.grovemusic.com; accessed 16 Sept. 2003). The sketches, ending with those for act 3, were completed on his first trip to Algeria in 1873, the orchestral parts in January 1876. See Servières 1930: 34; and Ratner 1985.

13. Victor Wilder, "Premières représentations," *Gil blas* (2 Nov. 1890).

14. Mieke Bal (1987: 65) writes, "Delilah's role could ultimately be compared to the analyst's. It is only when she reproaches Samson for not feeling real love in the sense of surrender that he realizes that surrender is what he seeks, that he understands the real nature of his love and the anxiety that knowledge evokes in him. She is the instrument of, or the partner in, his talking cure."

15. In the Bible, chapter 16 of the Book of Judges, this riddle comes from Samson. During a bachelor party before his first marriage, he asks it in the form of a declarative sentence: "Out of the eater came forth a meat and out of the strong came forth sweetness" (14:14). Later the Philistines answer it in the form of a question, "What is sweeter than honey? and what is stronger than a lion?" Bal (1987: 42, 45) interprets this as the relationship between pleasure and strength in sexuality.

16. Michel Faure 1985: 117–19.

17. See the bust of Liberty reproduced in Maurice Agulhon 1981: 97.

18. See Agulhon 1981: 12–13.

19. Also see McClary 1992 and Locke 1991 for excellent bibliographies on this subject.

20. According to Debora Silverman (1989: 127), scholarly writers on the arts and crafts of Japan were particularly attracted to such values.

21. According to Homi K. Bhabha (1986), this insures the replicability, predictability, and thus understandability of stereotypes.

22. I develop this thesis more fully in volume 2 of my *Useful Music, or Why Music Mattered in Third Republic France*, to be published by the University of California Press.

23. Oratorio was declared in fashion in "Paris et départements," *Ménestrel* (7 Feb. 1875): 78.

24. As reported in Victorin Joncières, "Revue Musicale," *La liberté* (21 June 1897).

25. See Henri Collet 1922: 37. Note that Roland was another hero of French history, also commemorated with a "Hymne de Roland" by Rouget de Lisle written around the same time as his more famous "Marseillaise."

26. Letter to Jules Combarieu of 8 November 1901; cited in Ratner 1985: 114.

27. See Henry Bauer, "Les premières représentations," *Echos de Paris* (25 Nov. 1892).

28. Among today's conductors, Pierre Boulez is one of those who arrange their concerts with a keen ear for how one work affects the perception of another on the same program.

29. The concert earned 4,806 francs in part because ticket prices were increased somewhat for the concert (Concerts Colonne Archives, Paris).

30. Octave Fouquet, *Revue et gazette musicale* (28 Mar. 1875): 100–101.

31. Audiences preferred these to *La jeunesse d'Hercule*, which Colonne premiered on 28 January 1877. Auguste Morel, in "Concerts annoncés," *Ménestrel* (4 Feb. 1877): 79, found that, in trying to express abstract and philosophical ideas, this piece "required too much" of music.

32. The vocal music was far less successful partly because of the singers. See A. M. [Auguste Morel], "Concerts et soirées," *Ménestrel* (4 Apr. 1880): 143.

33. The Société des Concerts du Conservatoire chose similar works to pair with Saint-Saëns's music. On 27 February 1876 they performed a "very noble and elevated" chorus from *Saul* immediately before *Le rouet d'Omphale,* and "par piquant contraste déjà très marqué" followed this with Beethoven's Violin Concerto. See Aug. [Auguste] Morel, "Concerts et soirées," *Ménestrel* (5 Mar. 1876): 110.

34. Saint Saëns's cadenza for Beethoven's Violin Concerto was not always well received. A reviewer of Marguerite Pommereuil's performance at the Concerts Pasdeloup wrote in the *Revue et gazette musicale* 44/5 (4 Feb. 1877): 36–37, "Pour faire quelque chose d'aussi spécial qu'un point d'orgue de concerto, de même qu'une étude, il faut de toute nécessité pratiquer l'instrument et le bien posséder. M. Saint-Saëns est un compositeur de premier ordre, un admirable musicien et un grand pianiste: il a échoué, completement échoué dans cette cadence pour le violon, dont le style même est étranger à celui de l'oeuvre." I am grateful to Maiko Kawabata for directing me to this.

35. *Ménestrel* (1 Feb. 1880): 70.

36. Colonne also performed *Phaeton* before the orchestral score and parts were published in 1875 and *Danse macabre* nine months before their publication that October.

37. "Paris et départements," *Ménestrel* (4 Apr. 1875): 143.

38. In 1876 Cramer had also done a transcription of Saint-Saëns's *Danse macabre* for easy piano.

39. These included compositions reworked for different instrumental combinations, works extracted from larger ones and adapted for a new usage, and the reemployment of melodic material from one composition in a subsequent composition. See Ratner 1997: 243–56; see also the transcriptions listed for each work in Ratner 2002.

40. Sabina Ratner pointed this out to me in a telephone conversation on 23 February 2003.

41. Furthermore, according to Brian Rees (1999: 164), composers submitted their works in piano versions for consideration by their peers and for secret voting.

42. A. M. [Auguste Morel], "Concerts et soirées," *Ménestrel* (5 Mar. 1876): 111.

43. Guiraud produced transcriptions for piano, four hands, of *Le rouet d'Omphale, Danse macabre, La jeunesse d'Hercule,* and *Hymne à Victor Hugo,* as well as one for two pianos, eight hands, of *Danse macabre.* Fauré transcribed for piano, four hands, Saint-Saëns's *Suite algérienne* and his overture to *La princesse jaune.*

44. See Ferruccio Busoni 1922: 147–53.

45. For further discussion of this attitude, especially in the music of Schumann, Liszt, and Busoni, see Peter Szendy 2000a, 2000b.

46. E. de Bricqueville, "Nouveaux concerts," *Ménestrel* (28 Dec. 1884): 31.

47. Hugues Dufourt 1991: 179.

48. See Szendy 2000a: 15; Brice Pauset 2000: 131–40; Szendy 2001; and Zender 2002: 36. Zender used the latter term to describe his orchestration of Schubert's *Winterreise*. This work, performed at the Cité de la musique in November 2002, was part of a series of concerts dedicated to transcriptions, twenty-five of them focusing on piano transcriptions.

49. Jean-Léon Roques took first prize in counterpoint and fugue at the Conservatory in 1862, composed operettas (*La rosière d'ici* for Anna Judic), and was later accompanist at the Théatre des Bouffes-Parisiens, conductor, and organist. Besides his numerous transcriptions of many composers' works, he orchestrated Offenbach airs for café-concert performances.

50. Here I am using virtuosity to mean not just bravura but also what Kerman (1999: 67 ff.) calls "virtù," or power and capacity.

51. Because Dalila sings remnants of this aria mockingly after the "Bacchanale," one could hear the aria placed here as tinged with her treacherous intentions.

52. For Mme Brunet-Lafleur's performance of a Dalila air in April 1884, Countess Elizabeth Greffulhe paid more than one thousand francs. This was a large sum, supporting the interest it held for her. At this concert Saint-Saëns's music was paired with an air from *Tannhäuser* sung by Jean-Baptiste Faure.

53. Exam presented by a vocal student in the class of M. Boulanger, 14 January 1888. Notes taken during the annual exams at the Conservatory in the 1880s (AJ37.239, Archives Nationales, Paris).

54. Intérim, "Chronique musicale," *figaro* (1 Nov. 1890); Ernest Reyer, "*Samson et Dalila*," *Journal des débats* (9 Nov. 1890). There were also occasional performances of transcriptions of the entire opera. According to "Concerts et soirées," *Ménestrel* (20 June 1880): 231, a singing teacher in Bordeaux organized a performance of the opera by his students, accompanied by two pianos and harmonium, and later students of Mme Bosquet-Luigini performed a four-hand piano version of the opera, possibly Roques's *Illustrations,* in their recitals of 7 May 1891 and 2 June 1892. In the second context, *Samson et Dalila* was surrounded by short works of Chaminade and Chabrier as well as four-hand versions of Wagnerian operas. These included Chaminade's "Fileuse," "Sévillane," and "Idylle arabe," Wagner's overture to *Tannhaüser,* a fantasy on *Lohengrin,* and a chorus from *Vaisseau fantôme,* most of them for piano, four hands, as well as Beethoven's Eroica Symphony for two pianos, eight hands.

55. Subsequent editions of Feuillet's *Dalila* appeared in 1870, 1876, 1882, and 1892.

56. Intérim, "Chronique musicale." According to their review of the 1890s performance at the Eden-Théâtre in their *Les Annales du théâtre et de la musique,* Edouard Noël and Edmond Stoullig (1892: 513) suggest that it was they who suggested *Samson et Dalila* to Verdhurt.

57. Henri Bauer, "Les premières représentations," *Echos de Paris* (2 Nov. 1890).

58. Intérim, "Chronique musicale."

59. Camille Bellaigue, writing in *Le figaro* (26 Jan. 1889). In spite of such praise, he goes on to say that he prefers the composer's oratorio *Le deluge.*

60. In his review of the Rouen premiere, Léon Kerst, too, noted that the composer treated the subject with "unusual vigor" ("*Samson et Dalila*," *Le petit journal* [4 Mar. 1890]).

61. Reyer, "*Samson et Dalila*"; Arthur Pougin, "Semaine théatrale: *Samson*," *Ménestrel* (9 Nov. 1890): 354–56; Noel and Stoullig 1892: 513–15.

62. This is the earliest wind-band version of the opera in the collection of the Bibliothèque Nationale. Besides his wind-band transcriptions of waltzes, polkas, and marches,

Georges Meister had already produced important band fantasies of operas soon after their premieres, such as Saint-Saëns's *Prosperine* (1888; Opéra-Comique 1887), Chabrier's *Le roi malgré lui* (1890; Opéra-Comique 1887), and Messager's *La Basoche* (1891; Opéra-Comique 1890). As with *Samson et Dalila,* he made a fantasy of Reyer's *Salammbô* (1890) *before* its Opéra production in 1892. In 1892 he also published military-band fantasies of Bizet's *La jolie fille de Perth,* revived in 1887, and Berlioz's *Les Troyens,* premiered in Karlsruhe in 1890 and performed in Paris at the Opéra-Comique in 1892. Meister continued to produce fantasies of such works throughout the 1890s.

In response to an earlier version of this paper delivered at University of Texas at Austin, on 27 January 2003, Robert Hatten encouraged consideration of how these fantasies might resemble overtures. In the case of *Samson et Dalila,* however, there is no overture and the short introduction does not announce the work's subsequent themes.

63. Durand's explicit authorization is noted on the bottom of the first page of the conductor's score.

64. Sabina Ratner (1997: 246 n. 11) notes that the handwriting and paper of this manuscript "strongly resemble that of an early 'choeur d'Israel' dated 1859 by Saint-Saëns." In a telephone conversation with the author on 23 February 2003, Ratner noted that MS 545 is a compilation of the composer's manuscripts which he gave to the Opéra archivist Charles Malherbe who probably bound them in the order the composer indicated.

65. What makes it a "musique turque" is the inclusion of a large drum, cymbals, a triangle, and a tambour de basque. See George Kastner 1848: 332.

66. "Programme analytique," *Le petit poucet* (9 June 1896): 3–4.

67. Ibid.

68. In an editorial comment, Henry-Abel Simon writes that "the genius does not shine through less" in them and that the "practical result" of performing such music would be "the modification of the repertoire of our music societies that is so much desired and the elevation of taste" (*Orphéon* [Jan. 1882]). Efforts to improve the quality of military music had begun with discussions at the Chambre des députés in 1882 and culminated in new laws in 1898 calling for additional training and status assigned to directors of military bands. See the Annex no. 1507 for the 13 December 1882 session of the Chambre des députés A.N., S.E. t.4, 312–13.

69. F. Régnier, "Premières représentations. Opéra. *Samson et Dalila,*" *Le Journal* (24 Nov. 1892).

70. Bicoquet, "La soirée parisienne. *Samson et Dalila,*" *Echos de Paris* (25 Nov. 1892).

71. Régnier, "*Samson et Dalila*"; Henri Bauer, "Les premières représentations," *Echos de Paris* (25 Nov. 1892).

72. Henri Bauer, "Les premières représentations," *Echos de Paris* (2 Nov. 1890).

73. Emile Eugène Alix Fournier (1864–1897), a pupil of Delibes, had won a Deuxième Second Grand Prix de Rome in 1889. Louis Gallet wrote the libretto of his one-act opera, *Stratonice,* published by Paul Dupont in 1892. With a subject echoing that of Méhul's *Stratonice* (1792), the work had recently won the Crescent competition. In his review, "Paris au théâtre," in *Le petit journal* (10 Dec. 1892), Léon Kerst called it "antimusical," a work of "pretentious incoherence" without "any ideas" whose reception was "less than zero." Still, it was performed fourteen times until the last one on 4 March 1893.

74. Victorin Joncières, "Revue musicale," *La liberté* (21 June 1897).

75. Léon Chic published a fantasy on *Hérodiade* for musiques militaires in 1882, just after the world premiere in Brussels in December 1881, but two years before the Opéra produced it. The Concerts Colonne featured excerpts of it sung by M. Faure on 17 February 1884, only two weeks after its Opéra premiere on 1 February, and Salomé's air sung by Mme

Fides-Devriès there on 11 April 1884, Good Friday. Likewise G. Meister published a fantasy on *Salammbô* for musiques militaires in 1890, coinciding with the world premiere in Brussels; Théodore Dureau did one for harmonie militaire in 1891; and Gabriel Parès published a "Second Fantasy" on *Salammbô* in 1892, the year the work premiered at the Paris Opéra.

76. "A nos lecteurs," *Le petit poucet* (2 May 1899).

77. In this sense, transcriptions and excerpts challenge the direction, tempo, and dynamics of Georg Simmel's trickle-down theory. Simmel (1904) argues that when "subordinate social groups" have tastes resembling those of "superordinate groups," they result from the former imitating the latter in search of new status claims, a process he interprets as unidirectional. For a fuller discussion of this, see my article "Material Culture and Postmodern Positivism: Rethinking the 'Popular' in Late 19th c. French Music" (2004: 356–87).

78. Debussy may have preferred that listeners hear his music in his chosen genres, but in the Selznick Archives of the Humanities Research Center, University of Texas at Austin, there is an agreement dated October 1948 in which, for a license fee, the Debussy heirs allowed for "unlimited usage of special orchestration, provided these arrangements are dignified concert versions, without burlesque, swing, or jazz." I am grateful to Sarah Reichardt for drawing my attention to this.

79. See François Nicolas 2000: 48–49.

References

Abbate, Carolyn. 1991. *Unsung Voices: Opera and Musical Narrative in the Nineteenth Century.* Princeton, N.J.: Princeton University Press.

Abbate, Elizabeth. 1996. "Myth, Symbol, and Meaning in Mahler's Early Symphonies." Ph.D. dissertation, Harvard University.

Adamowicz, Elsa. 2000. "Hats or Jellyfish? André Breton's Collages." In Ramona Fotiade (ed.), *André Breton: The Power of Language,* 83–95. Exeter: Elm Bank.

Adorno, Theodor W. 1976. *Introduction to the Sociology of Music.* Trans. E. B. Ashton. New York: Seabury.

———. 1992a. *Mahler: A Musical Physiognomy.* Trans. Edmund Jephcott. Chicago: University of Chicago Press.

———. 1992b. "Music and Language: A Fragment." In *Quasi una Fantasia: Essays on Modern Music,* trans. Rodney Livingstone, 1–6. London: Verso.

Agawu, V. Kofi. 1991. *Playing with Signs: A Semiotic Interpretation of Classic Music.* Princeton, N.J.: Princeton University Press.

Agulhon, Maurice. 1981. *Marianne into Battle: Republican Imagery and Symbolism in France, 1789–1889.* Trans. Janet Llody. Cambridge: Cambridge University Press.

Allanbrook, Wye Jamison. 1983. *Rhythmic Gesture in Mozart:* Le Nozze di Figaro *and* Don Giovanni. Chicago: University of Chicago Press.

Almén, Byron. 2003. "Narrative Archetypes: A Critique, Theory and Method of Narrative Analysis." *Journal of Music Theory* 47.1 (spring): 1–39.

Bakhtin, M. M. 1981 [1935]. *The Dialogic Imagination: Four Essays by M. M. Bakhtin.* Ed. Michael Holquist. Trans. Caryl Emerson and Michael Holquist. Austin: University of Texas Press.

Bal, Mieke. 1987. *Lethal Love: Feminist Literary Readings of Biblical Love Stories.* Bloomington: Indiana University Press.

Barry, Kevin. 1987. *Language, Music, and the Sign.* Cambridge: Cambridge University Press.

Barthes, Roland. 1977. *Image, Music, Text.* Trans. Stephen Heath. London: Fontana.

Bauer-Lechner, Natalie. 1984. *Gustav Mahler in den Erinnerungen von Natalie Bauer-Lechner.* Ed. Herbert Killian. Hamburg: K. D. Wagner.

Bennett, Tony. 1995. *The Birth of the Museum: History, Theory, Politics.* London: Routledge.

Bertinetto, Pier Marco. 1994. "Temporal Reference, Aspect, and Actionality: Their Neutralization and Interactions, Mostly Exemplified in Italian." In Carl Bache et al. (eds.), *Tense, Aspect and Action: Empirical and Theoretical Contributions to Language Typology,* 113–37. Berlin: Mouton de Gruyer.

Bhabha, Homi K. 1986. "The Other Question: Difference, Discrimination and the Discourse of Colonialism." In Frances Barker et al. (eds.), *Literature, Politics, and Theory,* 148–72. London: Methuen.

Birchler, David. 1991. "Nature and Autobiography in the Music of Gustav Mahler." Ph.D. dissertation, University of Wisconsin–Madison.

Blaukopf, Herta, ed. 1980. *Gustav Mahler—Richard Strauss. Briefwechsel 1888–1911.* Munich/Zurich: Piper Verlag.

Bloch, Ernest. 1976 [1933]. "My Sacred Service: Ernest Bloch." In Suzanne Bloch and Irene Heskes (eds.), *Ernest Bloch: Creative Spirit,* 11–16. New York: Jewish Music Council of the National Jewish Welfare Board.

Bloom, Harold. 1973. *The Anxiety of Influence: A Theory of Poetry.* New York: Oxford University Press.

Bonds, Mark Evan. 1996. *After Beethoven: Imperatives of Originality in the Symphony.* Cambridge, Mass.: Harvard University Press.

Boretz, Benjamin. 1977. "Two Replies." *Perspectives of New Music* 15.2: 239–42.

Boulez, Pierre. 1999 [1952]. "Schoenberg Is Dead." In Stephen Walsh (ed.), *Composers on Modern Musical Culture: An Anthology of Readings on Twentieth-Century Music,* trans. Stephen Walsh, 145–51. New York: Schirmer.

Bowman, Wayne D. 1998. *Philosophical Perspectives on Music.* New York: Oxford University Press.

Brooks, Jeanice. 2004. "Performing Autonomy: Nadia Boulanger's Concert Programmes as Music-Historical Texts." Paper presented at the symposium "Music in France (1930–1940)," University of Melbourne, July.

Brown, A. Peter. 2003. *The Second Golden Age of the Viennese Symphony: Brahms, Bruckner, Dvořák, Mahler, and Selected Contemporaries.* Vol. 4, *The Symphonic Repertoire.* Bloomington: Indiana University Press.

Budd, Malcolm. 1992. *Music and the Emotions: The Philosophical Theories.* New York: Routledge.

Buhler, James. 1995. "'Breakthrough' as Critique of Form: The Finale of Mahler's First Symphony." *19th-Century Music* 20.2: 236–56.

Bürger, Peter. 1984. *Theory of the Avant-garde.* Trans. Michael Shaw. Minneapolis: University of Minnesota Press.

Burghardt, Gordon M. 1973. "Instinct and Innate Behavior: Toward an Ethological Psychology." In J. A. Nevin and G. S. Reynolds (eds.), *The Study of Behavior: Learning, Motivation, Emotion, and Instinct,* 322–400. Glenview, Ill.: Scott, Foresman.

Burke, Richard. 1999. "Film, Narrative, and Shostakovich's Last Quartet." *Musical Quarterly,* 83: 413–29.

Burkholder, J. Peter. 1983. "The Evolution of Charles Ives's Music: Aesthetics, Quotation, Technique." Ph.D. dissertation, University of Chicago.

———. 1991. "Berg and the Possibility of Popularity." In David Gable and Robert P. Morgan (eds.), *Alban Berg: Historical and Analytical Perspectives,* 25–53. Oxford: Clarendon.

———. 1995a. *All Made of Tunes: Charles Ives and the Uses of Musical Borrowing.* New Haven: Yale University Press.

———. 1995b. "Rule-Breaking as a Rhetorical Sign." In Thomas J. Mathiesen and Benito V. Rivera (eds.), *Festa Musicologica: Essays in Honor of George J. Buelow,* 369–89. Stuyvesant, N.Y.: Pendragon.

———. 2001. "Intertextuality." In Stanley Sadie (ed.), *The New Grove Dictionary of Music and Musicians.* 2nd ed. London: Macmillan.

Busoni, Ferruccio. 1922. "Wert des Bearbeitung." In *Von der Einheit der Musik. Verstreute Aufzeichnungen,* 147–53. Berlin: Max Hesses.

Butler, Judith. 1990. *Gender Trouble: Feminism and the Subversion of Identity.* New York: Routledge.

Cage, John. 1961. *Silence: Lectures and Writings by John Cage*. Middletown, Conn.: Wesleyan University Press.

Campbell, Joseph. 1968. *The Hero with a Thousand Faces*. 2nd ed. Princeton, N.J.: Princeton University Press.

———. 1990. *The Flight of the Wild Gander*. New York: HarperPerennial.

Campbell, Patricia Shehan. 1998. *Songs in Their Heads: Music and Its Meaning in Children's Lives*. New York: Oxford University Press.

Canty, Captain Daniel J. 1916. *Bugle Signals, Calls & Marches: For Army, Navy, Marine Corps, Revenue Cutter Service & National Guard*. Bryn Mawr, Pa.: Oliver Ditson.

Caplin, William E. 1998. *Classical Form: A Theory of Formal Functions for the Instrumental Music of Haydn, Mozart, and Beethoven*. New York: Oxford University Press.

Chatman, Seymour. 1978. *Story and Discourse*. Ithaca, N.Y.: Cornell University Press.

Chevalier, Jean, and Alain Gheerbrant. 1994. *A Dictionary of Symbols*. Trans. John Buchanan-Brown. Oxford: Blackwell.

Chua, Daniel K. L. 1999. *Absolute Music and the Construction of Meaning*. Cambridge: Cambridge University Press.

Clifton, Thomas. 1983. *Music as Heard: A Study in Applied Phenomenology*. New Haven: Yale University Press.

Coker, Wilson. 1972. *Music and Meaning: A Theoretical Introduction to Musical Aesthetics*. New York: Free Press.

Colby, Elbridge. 1942. *Army Talk: A Familiar Dictionary of Soldier Speech*. Princeton, N.J.: Princeton University Press.

Collet, Henri. 1922. *Samson et Dalila de C. Saint-Saëns: Etude historique et critique, analyse musicale*. Paris: Mellottée.

Cone, Edward T. 1968. *Musical Form and Musical Performance*. New York: Norton.

———. 1974. *The Composer's Voice*. Berkeley: University of California Press.

———. 1992. "Poet's Love or Composer's Love?" In Steven Paul Scher (ed.), *Music and Text: Critical Inquiries*, 177–92. New York: Cambridge University Press.

Cook, Nicholas. 1990. *Music, Imagination, and Culture*. Oxford: Clarendon.

———. 2001. "Theorizing Musical Meaning." *Music Theory Spectrum* 23.2 (fall): 170–95.

Copland, Aaron. 1957. *What to Listen for in Music*. Rev. ed. New York: McGraw-Hill.

Corbett, John. 2000. "Experimental Oriental: New Music and Other Others." In Georgina Born and David Hesmondhalgh (eds.), *Western Music and Its Others: Difference, Representation, and Others in Music*, 163–86. Berkeley: University of California Press.

Cox, Arnie Walter. 1999. "The Metaphoric Logic of Musical Motion and Space." Ph.D dissertation, University of Oregon, Eugene.

Crist, Elizabeth Bergman. 2000. "Aaron Copland's Third Symphony (1946): Context, Composition, and Consequence." Ph.D. dissertation, Yale University, New Haven, Conn.

Cumming, Naomi. 2000. *The Sonic Self: Musical Subjectivity and Signification*. Bloomington: Indiana University Press.

Dauenhauer, Bernard P. 1980. *Silence: The Phenomenon and Its Ontological Significance*. Bloomington: Indiana University Press.

Davies, Stephen. 1994. *Musical Meaning and Expression*. Ithaca, N.Y.: Cornell University Press.

Del Mar, Norman. 1962. *Richard Strauss: A Critical Commentary on His Life and Works*. 2 vols. London: Barrie and Rockliff.

Deliège, Célestin. 1989. "On Form as Actually Experienced." *Contemporary Music Review* 4: 101–15.

———. 2000. "The Musical Work as Discourse and Text." *Musicae Scientiae* 4.2: 213–23.

Dempster, Douglas. 1998. "Is There Even a Grammar of Music?" *Musicae Scientiae* 2: 55–65.

Denham, Robert D. 1978. *Northrop Frye and Critical Method.* University Park: Pennsylvania State University.

Diel, Paul. 1966. *Le symbolisme dans la mythologie grecque.* 2nd ed. Paris: Payot.

Doty, William G. 2000. *Mythography: The Study of Myths and Rituals.* 2nd ed. Tuscaloosa: Alabama University Press.

Downes, Olin. 1976. "A Great Composer at 75." In Suzanne Bloch and Irene Heskes (eds.), *Ernest Bloch: Creative Spirit,* 21–23. New York: Jewish Music Council of the National Jewish Welfare Board.

Dufourt, Hugues. 1991. "L'Artifice d'écriture dans la musique occidentale." In *Musique, pouvoir, écriture,* 171–90. Paris: Bourgeois.

Eagle, Herbert. 1981. *Russian Formalist Film Theory.* Ann Arbor: Michigan Slavic Publications, University of Michigan.

Eiseley, Loren C. 1960. *The Firmament of Time.* New York: Atheneum.

Eisenstein, Sergei. 1949. *Film Form: Essays in Film Theory.* Ed. and trans. Jay Leyda. London: Dennis Dobson.

———. 1988. *Selected Works.* Vol. 1, *Writings 1922–34.* Ed. and trans. Richard Taylor. London: British Film Institute.

———. 1991. *Selected Works.* Vol. 2, *Towards a Theory of Montage.* Ed. Michael Glenny and Richard Taylor. Trans. Michael Glenny. London: British Film Institute.

———. 1998. *The Eisenstein Reader.* Ed. Richard Taylor. Trans. Richard Taylor and William Powell. London: British Film Institute.

Ellis, Katharine. 2005. *Interpreting the Musical Past.* Oxford: Oxford University Press.

Ernst, Max. 1956. *La femme 100 têtes.* Paris: Editions de l'Oeil.

Everett, Yayoi Uno. 2004. "Intercultural Synthesis in Postwar Western Art Music: Historical Contexts, Perspectives, and Taxonomy." In Yayoi Uno Everett and Frederick Lau (eds.), *Locating East Asia in Western Art Music,* 1–21. Middletown, Conn.: Wesleyan University Press.

Fauconnier, Gilles. 1997. *Mappings in Thought and Language.* Cambridge: Cambridge University Press.

Faure, Michel. 1985. *Musique et société du Second Empire aux années vingt.* Paris: Flammarion.

Feldman, Morton. 1985. "Lectures/Vorträge 1984." In Walter Zimmerman (trans.), *Morton Feldman Essays,* 143–80. Köln: Beginner Press.

———. 2000 [1984]. "The Future of Local Music." In B. H. Freidman (ed.), *Give My Regards to Eighth Street: Collected Writings of Morton Feldman,* 157–95. Cambridge: Exact Change.

Ferber, Michael. 1999. *A Dictionary of Literary Symbols.* Cambridge: Cambridge University Press.

Fish, Stanley. 1980. *Is There a Text in This Class? The Authority of Interpretive Communities.* Cambridge, Mass.: Harvard University Press.

Floros, Constantin. 1977a. *Gustav Mahler I: Die geistige Welt Gustav Mahlers in systematischer Darstellung.* Wiesbaden: Breitkopf & Härtel.

———. 1977b. *Gustav Mahler II: Mahler und die Symphonik des 19. Jahrhunderts in neuer Deutung.* Wiesbaden: Breitkopf & Härtel.

———. 1994. *Gustav Mahler: The Symphonies.* Trans. Vernon Wicker and Jutta Wicker. Portland: Amadeus.

Forster, E. M. 1910. *Howards End.* London: Arnold.

Foucault, Michel. 1970. *The Order of Things: An Archaeology of the Human Sciences.* London: Tavistock.

Freud, Sigmund. 1953. "The Uncanny." In James Strachey (ed. and trans.), *Standard Edition of the Complete Psychological Works of Sigmund Freud,* 219–52. London: Hogarth.

Frye, Northrop. 1957. *Anatomy of Criticism.* Princeton, N.J.: Princeton University Press.

Fulcher, Jane F. 1995. "Musical Style, Meaning, and Politics in France on the Eve of the Second World War." *Journal of Musicology* 13: 425–53.

———. 1999a. "The Composer as Intellectual: Ideological Inscriptions in French Interwar Neoclassicism." *Journal of Musicology* 17: 197–230.

———. 1999b. *French Cultural Politics and Music: From the Dreyfus Affair to the First World War.* New York: Oxford University Press.

Genette, Gérard. 1980. *Narrative Discourse: An Essay in Method.* Trans. Jane E. Lewin. Ithaca, N.Y.: Cornell University Press.

———. 1988. *Narrative Discourse Revisited.* Trans. Jane E. Lewin. Ithaca, N.Y.: Cornell University Press.

Gide, André. 1949. *Notes on Chopin.* Trans. Bernard Frechtman. New York: Philosophical Library.

Girard, René. 1977. *Violence and the Sacred.* Trans. Patrick Gregory. Baltimore, Md.: Johns Hopkins University Press.

Goswami, Roshmi. 1995. *Meaning in Music.* Shimla: Indian Institute of Advanced Study.

Gould, Eric. 1981. *Mythic Intentions in Modern Literature.* Princeton, N.J.: Princeton University Press.

Graves, Robert. 1992. *The Greek Myths: The Combined Edition.* London: Penguin Books.

Greimas, Algirdas Julien. 1983. *Du sens II: Essais sémiotiques.* Paris: Seuil.

Gurney, Edmund. 1880. *The Power of Sound.* London: Smith, Elder.

Hanslick, Eduard. 1986. *On the Musically Beautiful: A Contribution to the Revival of Musical Aesthetics.* Trans. Geoffrey Payzant. Indianapolis: Hackett.

Hatten, Robert S. 1985. "The Place of Intertextuality in Music Studies." *American Journal of Semiotics* 3.4: 69–82.

———. 1994. *Musical Meaning in Beethoven: Markedness, Correlation, and Interpretation.* Bloomington: Indiana University Press.

———. 1997. "Music and Tense." In Irmengard Rauch and Gerald F. Carr (eds.), *Semiotics around the World: Synthesis in Diversity,* 627–30. Proceedings of the Fifth Congress of the International Association for Semiotic Studies, Berkeley, 1994. Berlin: Mouton de Gruyter.

———. 2004. *Interpreting Musical Gestures, Topics, and Tropes: Mozart, Beethoven, Schubert.* Bloomington: Indiana University Press.

Hatten, Robert S., and Charls Pearson. Forthcoming. "Aspect in Music." Proceedings of the Seventh International Congress on Musical Signification, Imatra, Finland, 2001.

Heile, Björn. 2001. " 'Transcending Quotation': Cross-Cultural Musical Representation in Mauricio Kagel's *Die Stücke der Windrose für Salonorchester.*" Ph.D. dissertation, University of Southampton, U.K.

Hertz, David Michael. 1993. *Angels of Reality: Emersonian Unfoldings in Wright, Stevens, and Ives.* Carbondale and Edwardsville: Southern Illinois University Press.

Higgins, Kathleen Marie. 1991. *The Music of Our Lives.* Philadelphia: Temple University Press.

———. 1997. "Musical Idiosyncrasy and Perspectival Listening." In Jenefer Robinson (ed.), *Music and Meaning,* 83–102. Ithaca, N.Y.: Cornell University Press.

Hodge, Joanna. 1993. "Aesthetic Decomposition: Music, Identity, and Time." In Michael Krausz (ed.), *The Interpretation of Music: Philosophical Essays,* 247–58. Oxford: Clarendon.

Hooper-Greenhill, Eilean. 2000. *Museums and the Interpretation of Visual Culture.* London: Routledge.

Hueß, Alfred. 1933. "Die kleine Sekunde in Mozarts g-moll Sinfonie." *Jahrbuch der Musik- bibliothek Peters* 40: 54–66.

Husserl, Edmund. 1991 [1893–1917]. *On the Phenomenology of the Consciousness of Internal Time (1893–1917).* Trans. John Barnett Brough. Dordrecht, Germany: Kluwer.

Ives, Charles E. 1953. Foreword to *The Unanswered Question.* New York: Southern Music.

James, William. 1977. "Necessary Truths." In John J. McDermott (ed.), *The Writings of William James,* 74–133. Chicago: University of Chicago Press.

Jauss, Hans Robert. 1982a. *Aesthetic Experience and Literary Hermeneutics.* Trans. Wlad Godzich. Minneapolis: University of Minnesota Press.

———. 1982b. *Toward an Aesthetic of Reception.* Trans. Timothy Bahti. Minneapolis: University of Minnesota Press.

Johnson, Eric. 1976. "A Composer's Vision: Photography by Ernest Bloch." In Suzanne Bloch and Irene Heskes (eds.), *Ernest Bloch: Creative Spirit,* 29–34. New York: Jewish Music Council of the National Jewish Welfare Board.

Jones, Mari Riess, and Susan Holleran, eds. 1992. *Cognitive Bases of Musical Communication.* Washington, D.C.: American Psychological Association.

Jung, C. G. 1990. *Collected Works of C. G. Jung.* Vol. 5, *Symbols of Transformation.* Princeton, N.J.: Princeton University Press.

Juslin, Patrick N., and John A. Sloboda, eds. 2001. *Music and Emotion: Theory and Research.* Oxford: Oxford University Press.

Kaemmer, John E. 1993. *Music in Human Life: Anthropological Perspectives on Music.* Austin: University of Texas Press.

Karbusicky, Vladimir. 1983. "Intertextualität in der Musik." In Wolf Schmid (ed.), *Dialog der Texte: Hamburger Kolloquium zur Intertextualität,* 361–98. Vienna: Institut für Slawistik der Universität Wien.

Kassler, Jamie C., ed. 1991. *Metaphor: A Musical Dimension.* Sydney: Currency.

Kastner, Georges. 1848. *Manuel générale de musique militaire à l'usage des armées françaises.* Paris: Firmin Didot.

Kerman, Joseph. 1980. "How We Got into Analysis, and How to Get Out." *Critical Inquiry* 7.2: 311–31.

———. 1999. *Concerto Conversations.* Cambridge, Mass.: Harvard University Press.

Kershaw, Baz. 1992. *The Politics of Performance: Radical Theatre as Cultural Intervention.* London: Routledge.

Kinderman, William. 1995. *Beethoven.* Oxford: Oxford University Press.

Kivy, Peter. 1980. *The Corded Shell: Reflections on Musical Expression.* Princeton, N.J.: Princeton University Press.

———. 1990. *Music Alone: Philosophical Reflections on the Purely Musical Experience.* Ithaca, N.Y.: Cornell University Press.

Kolb, Barbara. 1978. Program Notes. *Appello*. Bryn Mawr, Pa.: Boosey & Hawkes.

Korsyn, Kevin. 1991. "Towards a New Poetics of Musical Influence." *Music Analysis* 10: 3–72.

Kramer, Jonathan D. 1973. "Multiple and Non-linear Time in Beethoven's Opus 135." *Perspectives of New Music* 11: 122–45.

———. 1988. *The Time of Music*. New York: Schirmer Books.

Kramer, Lawrence. 1990. *Music as Cultural Practice*. Berkeley: University of California Press.

———. 1991. "Musical Narratology: A Theoretical Outline." *Indiana Theory Review* 12: 141–62.

———. 1995. *Classical Music and Postmodern Knowledge*. Berkeley: University of California Press.

———. 2002. *Musical Meaning: Toward a Critical History*. Berkeley: University of California Press.

Krausz, Michael, ed. 1994. *The Interpretation of Music*. Oxford: Clarendon.

Kuenzli, Rudolf E. 1983. "The Nazi Appropriation of Nietzsche." *Nietzsche-Studien* 12: 428–35.

La Grange, Henry-Louis de. 1973. *Gustav Mahler*. Vol. 1. New York: Doubleday.

Lanoé-Villène, G. 1926–35. *Le livre du symboles*. Vol. 3. Bordeaux and Paris: Bossard.

Lautréamont, Comte de [Isidore Ducasse]. 1970. *Lautréamont's* Maldoror. Trans. Alexis Lykiard. London: Alison and Busby.

Lavedan, P. 1931. *Dictionnaire illustré de la mythologie et des antiquités grecques et romaines*. Paris: Hachette.

Laws, Catherine. 1998. "Morton Feldman's *Neither*: A Musical Translation of Beckett's Text." In Mary Bryden (ed.), *Samuel Beckett and Music*, 57–83. Oxford: Clarendon.

Leach, Maria, ed. 1984. *Funk and Wagnall's Standard Dictionary of Folklore, Mythology, and Legend*. New York: Harper and Row.

Lehrer, Adrienne. 1983. *Wine and Conversation*. Bloomington: Indiana University Press.

Lerdahl, Fred, and Ray Jackendoff. 1983. *A Generative Theory of Tonal Music*. Cambridge, Mass.: MIT Press.

Levinson, Jerrold. 1997. *Music in the Moment*. Ithaca, N.Y.: Cornell University Press.

Leydon, Rebecca. 2001. "Debussy's Late Style and the Devices of the Early Silent Cinema." *Music Theory Spectrum* 23: 217–41.

Ligeti, György. 1983a. "György Ligeti Talking to Péter Vánai." In Babor J. Schabert (trans.), *Ligeti in Conversation*, 13–82. London: Eulenburg Books.

———. 1983b. "György Ligeti talking to Josef Häusler." In Sarah E. Soulsby (trans.), *Ligeti in Conversation*, 83–110. London: Eulenburg Books.

Lindt, Walter Lotte, ed. 1969. *Bruno Walter: Briefe 1894–1962*. Frankfurt am Main: Fischer.

Liszka, James Jakob. 1989. *The Semiotic of Myth: A Critical Study of the Symbol*. Bloomington: Indiana University Press.

Littlefield, Richard. 2001. *Frames and Framing*. Imatra, Finland: International Semiotics Institute.

Lobanova, Marino. 2002. *György Ligeti: Style, Ideas, Poetics*. Trans. Mark Shuttleworth. Berlin: Verlag Ernst Kuhn.

Lochhead, Judy. 1979. "The Temporal in Beethoven's Opus 135: When Are Ends Beginnings?" *In Theory Only* 4.7: 3–30.

Locke, Ralph. 1991. "Constructing the Oriental 'Other': Saint-Saëns's *Samson et Dalila*." *Cambridge Opera Journal* (3 Nov.): 261–302.

Longfellow, Henry Wadsworth. 1904. *Prose Works*. Vol. 1, *Outre-Mer*. New York: Houghton Mifflin.

Lyall, Harry Robert. 1975. "A French Music Aesthetic of the Eighteenth Century: A Translation and Commentary on Michel Paul Gui de Chabanon's *Musique considérée en elle-même et dans ses rapports avec la parole, les langues, la poésie, et la théâtre*." Ph.D. dissertation, North Texas State University.

de Man, Paul. 1986. *The Resistance to Theory*. Minneapolis: University of Minnesota Press.

Martin, Peter J. 1995. *Sounds and Society: Themes in the Sociology of Music*. Manchester: Manchester University Press.

Martner, Knud, ed. 1979. *Selected Letters of Gustav Mahler*. Trans. Eithne Wilkins, Ernst Kaiser, and Bill Hopkins. New York: Faber and Faber.

Matthews, J. H. 1977. *The Imagery of Surrealism*. Syracuse, N.Y.: Syracuse University Press.

Maus, Fred Everett. 1988. "Music as Drama." *Music Theory Spectrum* 10: 56–73.

———. 1991. "Music as Narrative." *Indiana Theory Review* 12: 1–34.

McClary, Susan. 1991. *Feminine Endings: Music, Gender, and Sexuality*. Minneapolis: University of Minnesota Press.

———. 1992. *Georges Bizet's Carmen*. Cambridge: Cambridge University Press.

———. 1998. *Rap, Minimalism, and Structures of Time in Late Twentieth-Century Culture*. Geske Lectures, College of Fine and Performing Arts, University of Nebraska–Lincoln.

———. 2000. *Conventional Wisdom: The Content of Musical Form*. Berkeley: University of California Press.

Melrose, Susan. 1994. *A Semiotics of the Dramatic Text*. London: Macmillan.

Metzer, David. 2003. *Quotation and Cultural Meaning in Twentieth-Century Music*. Cambridge: Cambridge University Press.

Meyer, Leonard B. 1956. *Emotion and Meaning in Music*. Chicago: University of Chicago Press.

———. 1967. *Music, the Arts, and Ideas: Patterns and Predictions in Twentieth-Century Culture*. Chicago: University of Chicago Press.

———. 1973. *Explaining Music: Essays and Explorations*. Berkeley: University of California Press.

Micznik, Vera. 2001. "Music and Narrative Revisited: Degrees of Narrativity in Beethoven and Mahler." *Journal of the Royal Musical Association* 126: 193–249.

Miller, Daniel. 1987. *Material Culture and Mass Consumption*. Oxford: Blackwell.

Mitchell, Donald. 1995. *Gustav Mahler: The Wunderhorn Years*. Rev. ed. London: Faber and Faber.

Monelle, Raymond. 1992. *Linguistics and Semiotics in Music*. Philadelphia: Harwood Academic.

———. 2000. *The Sense of Music: Semiotic Essays*. Princeton, N.J.: Princeton University Press.

Narmour, Eugene. 1977. *Beyond Schenkerism: The Need for Alternatives in Music Analysis*. Chicago: University of Chicago Press.

———. 1992. *The Analysis and Cognition of Melodic Complexity: The Implication-Realization Model*. Chicago: University of Chicago Press.

Nattiez, Jean-Jacques. 1990a. "Can One Speak of Narrativity in Music?" Trans. Katharine Ellis. *Journal of the Royal Musical Association* 115: 240–57.

———. 1990b. *Music and Discourse: Toward a Semiology of Music*. Trans. Carolyn Abbate. Princeton, N.J.: Princeton University Press.

New Grove Dictionary of Music Online. 2003. Ed. L. Macy. http://www.grovemusic.com; accessed 16 Sept. 2003.

Newcomb, Anthony. 1987. "Schumann and Late Eighteenth-Century Narrative Strategies." *19th-Century Music* 11.2: 164–74.

Nicolas, François. 2000. "La puissance et la gloire de la transcription (De la confrontation Schoenberg-Busoni)." In Peter Szendy (ed.), *Arrangements, dérangements. La transcription musicale d'aujourd'hui*, 45–60. Paris: L'Harmattan.

Nietzsche, Friedrich W. 1958. *Thus Spake Zarathustra*. Trans. A. Tille. Rev. M. M. Bozman. London: J. M. Dent; New York: E. P. Dutton.

Noël, Edouard, and Edmond Stoullig. 1892. *Les Annales du théâtre et de la musique*. Paris: Charpentier.

Nora, Pierre. 1984. "Présentation." In Pierre Nora (ed.), *Les lieux de mémoire. I. La république,* vii–xiii. Paris: Gallimard.

Pasler, Jann. 2004. "Material Culture and Postmodern Positivism: Rethinking the 'Popular' in Late 19th c. French Music." In Roberta Marvin, Michael Marissen, and Stephen Crist (eds.), *Historical Musicology: Sources, Methods, Interpretations*, 356–87. Rochester, N.Y.: University of Rochester Press.

———. Forthcoming. *Useful Music, or Why Music Mattered in Third Republic France*. Berkeley: University of California Press.

Pauset, Brice. 2000. "La transcription comme composition de l'écoute." In Peter Szendy (ed.), *Arrangements, dérangements. La transcription musicale d'aujourd'hui*, 131–40. Paris: L'Harmattan.

Pearsall, Edward. 2003. "The Structure of Conflict: Dialectics and the Play of Personae in Chopin's Op. 27, No. 2." *Indiana Theory Review* 24.1 (Special Issue on Analysis and Performance): 107–27.

Pearson, Charls, and Robert S. Hatten. Forthcoming. "The Semiotic Theory of Aspect Aids in the Discovery of Musical Aspect." Proceedings of the Seventh International Congress on Musical Signification, Imatra, Finland, 2001.

Pedroza, Ludim. 2002. "The Ritual of Music Contemplation: An Anthropological Study of the Solo Piano Recital." Ph.D. dissertation, Texas Tech University, Lubbock.

Pierre, Constant. 1899. *Musique des fêtes et cérémonies de la Révolution française*. Paris: Imprimerie Nationale.

Pople, Anthony, ed. 1995. *Theory, Analysis, and Meaning in Music*. Cambridge: Cambridge University Press.

Raffman, Diana. 1993. *Language, Music, and Mind*. Cambridge, Mass.: MIT Press.

Ramey, Phillip. 1988. Liner Notes to *Copland Conducts Copland*. New York: CBS Records Masterworks MK 42430.

Ratner, Leonard G. 1980. *Classic Music: Expression, Form and Style*. New York: Schirmer Books.

Ratner, Sabina. 1985. "La Genèse et la fortune de 'Samson et Dalila.'" *Cahiers Ivan Tourguéniev, Pauline Viardot, Maria Malibran* 9: 109–21.

———. 1997. "Saint-Saëns's Self-Borrowings." In Marie-Claire Mussat, Jean Montgrédien, Jean-Michel Nectoux (eds.), *Echos de France et d'Italie: Liber Amicorum Yves Gérard*, 243–56. Paris: Buchet/Chastel.

———. 2002. *Camille Saint-Saëns, 1835–1921: A Thematic Catalogue of His Complete Works*. New York: Oxford University Press.

Rees, Brian. 1999. *Camille Saint-Saëns: A Life.* London: Chatto and Windus.

Riemann, Hugo. 1877. *Musikalische Syntaxis: Grundriss einer harmonischen Satzbildungslehre.* Leipzig: Breitkopf und Härtel.

Ringer, Alexander L. 1988. "'Lieder eines fahrenden Gesellen': Allusion und Zitat in der musikalischen Erzählung Gustav Mahlers." In Hermann Danuser et al. (eds.), *Das musikalische Kunstwerk: Geschichte, Ästhetik, Theorie: Festschrift Carl Dahlhaus zum 60. Geburtstag,* 589–602. Laaber: Laaber-Verlag.

Robinson, Jenefer, ed. 1997. *Music and Meaning.* Ithaca, N.Y.: Cornell University Press.

Robinson, Paul A. 1985. *Opera and Ideas: From Mozart to Strauss.* New York: Harper and Row.

Rosen, Charles. 1994. *The Frontiers of Meaning: Three Informal Lectures on Music.* New York: Hill and Wang.

———. 1997 [1971]. *The Classical Style: Haydn, Mozart, Beethoven.* New York and London: W. W. Norton.

Rousseau, Jean-Jacques. 1981 [1825]. *Essai sur l'origine des langues* [excerpts]. In Peter le Huray and James Day (eds.), *Music and Aesthetics in the Eighteenth and Early Nineteenth Centuries,* 92–105. Cambridge: Cambridge University Press.

Rowell, Lewis. 1985. "The Temporal Spectrum." *Music Theory Spectrum* 7: 1–6.

———. 1996. "The Study of Time in Music: A Quarter-Century Perspective." *Indiana Theory Review* 17.2: 63–92.

Samarotto, Frank. 1999. "A Theory of Temporal Plasticity in Tonal Music: An Extension of the Schenkerian Approach to Rhythm with Special Reference to Beethoven's Late Music." Ph.D. dissertation, Graduate Center, City University of New York.

Santaniello, Weaver. 1994. *Nietzsche, God, and the Jews: His Critique of Judeo-Christianity in Relation to the Nazi Myth.* Albany: State University of New York Press.

Schenker, Heinrich. 1954 [1906]. *Harmony.* Ed. Oswald Jonas. Trans. Elizabeth Mann Borgese. Chicago: University of Chicago Press. Originally published as *Harmonielehre,* 1906.

———. 1979. *Free Composition (Der freie Satz).* Ed. and trans. Ernst Oster. 2 vols. New York: Longman.

Schmalfeldt, Janet. 1991. "Berg's Path to Atonality: The Piano Sonata, Op. 1." In David Gable and Robert P. Morgan (eds.), *Alban Berg: Historical and Analytical Perspectives,* 79–109. Oxford: Clarendon.

Schneede, Uwe. 1972. *The Essential Max Ernst.* Trans. R. W. Last. London: Thames and Hudson.

Schopenhauer, Arthur. 1883. *The World as Will and Idea.* 2 vols. Trans. R. B. Haldane and J. Kemp. London: Routledge and Kegan Paul.

Scruton, Roger. 1997. *The Aesthetics of Music.* Oxford: Clarendon.

Service, Tom. 2004. "Playing a New Game of Analysis: Performance, Postmodernism, and the Music of John Zorn." Ph.D. dissertation, University of Southampton, U.K.

Servières, Georges. 1930. *Saint-Saëns.* Paris: Alcan.

Sessions, Roger. 1970. *Questions about Music.* New York: Norton.

Silverman, Debora. 1989. *Art Nouveau in Fin-de-Siècle France: Politics, Psychology, and Style.* Berkeley: University of California Press.

Silverman, Kaja. 1983. *The Subject of Semiotics.* New York: Oxford University Press.

Simmel, Georg. 1904. "Fashion." *International Quarterly* 10: 130–55.

Solomon, Eldra Pearl, and William P. Davis. 1983. *Human Anatomy and Physiology.* Philadelphia: CBS College Publishing.

Sontag, Susan. 1966. "The Aesthetics of Silence." In *Styles of Radical Will,* 3–34. New York: Farrar, Straus and Giroux.

Sousa, John Philip, ed. 1886. *A Book of Instruction for the Field-Trumpet and Drum.* New York: Carl Fischer.

Spuller, Eugène. 1888. "Inauguration du Lycée Racine à Paris (19 octobre)." In *Au Ministère de l'Instruction publique, 1887, Discours, allocutions, circulaires,* 242–50. Paris: Hachette.

———. 1895. "Inauguration du Lycée des jeunes filles à Versailles (1 avril 1894)." In *Au Ministère de l'Instruction publique, 1893–94, Discours, allocutions, circulaires,* 2 série, 88–97. Paris: Hachette.

Stam, Robert, Robert Burgoyne, and Sandy Flitterman-Lewis. 1992. *New Vocabularies in Film Semiotics: Structuralism, Post-structuralism, and Beyond.* London: Routledge.

Stefani, Gino, Eero Tarasti, and Luca Marconi, eds. 1998. *Musical Signification, Between Rhetoric and Pragmatics: Proceedings of the 5th International Congress on Musical Signification.* Bologna: Cooperativa Libraria Universitaria Editrice Bologna.

Straus, Joseph N. 1990. *Remaking the Past: Musical Modernism and the Influence of the Tonal Tradition.* Cambridge, Mass.: Harvard University Press.

Swain, Joseph P. 1994. "Musical Communities and Music Perception." *Music Perception* 11: 307–20.

———. 1997. *Musical Languages.* New York: Norton.

Szendy, Peter. 2000a. "L'arrangement dérange . . . " In Peter Szendy (ed.), *Arrangements, dérangements. La transcription musicale d'aujourd'hui,* 7–15. Paris: L'Harmattan.

———, ed. 2000b. *Arrangements, dérangements. La transcription musicale d'aujourd'hui.* Paris: L'Harmattan.

———. 2001. *Ecoute—une histoire de nos oreilles.* Paris: Minuit.

Takemitsu, Toru. 1995. *Confronting Silence: Selected Writings.* Ed. and trans. Yoshiko Kakudo and Glenn Glasow. Berkeley, Calif.: Fallen Leaf.

Tarasti, Eero. 1994. *A Theory of Musical Semiotics.* Bloomington: Indiana University Press.

———, ed. 1995. *Musical Signification: Essays in the Semiotic Theory and Analysis of Music.* New York: Mouton de Gruyter.

Taruskin, Richard. 1995. *Text and Act.* New York: Oxford University Press.

Tavener, John. 1999. *The Music of Silence: A Composer's Testament.* Ed. Brian Keeble. London: Faber and Faber.

Todorov, Tzvetan. 1982 [1977]. *Theories of the Symbol.* Trans. Catherine Porter. Ithaca, N.Y.: Cornell University Press.

Velmar-Janković, Svetlana. 2002 [1990]. *Dungeon.* Trans. Celia Hawkesworth. Belgrade: Dereta.

Vergo, Peter. 1989. "The Reticent Object." In Peter Vergo (ed.), *The New Museology,* 41–59. London: Reaktion Books.

Vernallis, Carol. 2004. *Experiencing Music Video: Aesthetics and Cultural Context.* New York: Columbia University Press.

Waldberg, Patrick. 1965. *Surrealism.* London: Thames and Hudson.

Watkins, Glenn. 1994. *Pyramids at the Louvre: Music, Culture, and Collage from Stravinsky to the Postmodernists.* Cambridge, Mass.: Harvard University Press.

Whitlock, Greg. 1990. *Returning to Sils-Maria: A Commentary to Nietzsche's "Also sprach Zarathustra."* New York: Peter Lang.

Whittock, Trevor. 1990. *Metaphor and Film*. Cambridge: Cambridge University Press.
Youens, Susan. 1986. "Schubert, Mahler, and the Weight of the Past: *Lieder eines fahren-den Gesellen* und *Winterreise*." *Music and Letters* 67.3 (winter): 256-68.
Yudkin, Jeremy. 1992. "Beethoven's Mozart Quartet." *Journal of the American Musicological Society* 45: 30-74.
Zender, Hans. 2002. "Notes sur mon interprétation composée du *Voyage d'hiver* de Schu-bert." In *Cité de la musique, Saison 2002–2003*. Paris: Cité de la musique.
Žižek, S. 1989. *The Sublime Object of Ideology*. London: Verso.

Contributors

Byron Almén is Assistant Professor of Music Theory at the University of Texas at Austin. He is the author of several articles on narrative theory, the music of Gustav Mahler, music and psychology, early-twentieth-century Germanic culture, and music pedagogy. He is also an accomplished pianist and organist.

J. Peter Burkholder is Distinguished Professor of Music at Indiana University. His research interests include twentieth-century music, Charles Ives, American music, musical borrowing, and musical meaning and analysis. Professor Burkholder has received the Alfred Einstein Award from the American Musicological Society, the Irving Lowens Award from the Society for American Music, and an ASCAP–Deems Taylor Award.

Nicholas Cook is Professorial Research Fellow in Music at Royal Holloway, University of London, where he directs the AHRC Research Centre for the History and Analysis of Recorded Music (CHARM). He is the author of articles and books on a wide variety of musicological and theoretical subjects (*Music: A Very Short Introduction* has been translated into ten languages). His most recent book is a forthcoming study of the music theorist Heinrich Schenker in the context of fin de siècle Vienna. He was elected Fellow of the British Academy in 2001.

Robert S. Hatten, editor of the series "Musical Meaning and Interpretation," is Professor of Music Theory at Indiana University. He is author of *Musical Meaning in Beethoven* (Indiana University Press, 1994, paperback 2004—co-recipient of the Wallace Berry Publication Award from the Society for Music Theory in 1997) and *Interpreting Musical Gestures, Topics, and Tropes: Mozart, Beethoven, Schubert* (Indiana University Press, 2004).

Patrick McCreless is Professor of Music Theory and Chair of the Department of Music at Yale University. He has also taught at the Eastman School of Music and the University of Texas at Austin. He has published work on the operas of Wagner (*Tristan,* the *Ring,* and *Parsifal*), including a monograph, *Wagner's Siegfried: Its Drama, Its History, and Its Music.* He has also published essays or book chapters on the theory and analysis of chromatic music in the nineteenth century; Schenkerian theory; literary theory and music; the music of Shostakovich; and the history of music theory.

Jann Pasler is Professor of Music at the University of California, San Diego, and founder/director of its Critical Studies and Experimental Practices graduate program. Musicologist, pianist, and documentary filmmaker, Pasler has published widely on contemporary American and French music, modernism, postmodernism, colonialism, and especially the music culture of fin de siècle Paris. In 2005 she received the Colin Slim award from the American Musicological Society. Her *Useful Music, or Why Music Mattered in Third Republic France,* volume 1, is forthcoming from the University of California Press.

Edward Pearsall is Associate Professor of Music at the University of Texas at Austin. He is known internationally as a performer, composer, and scholar and has published numerous articles on subjects ranging from prolongation in tonal and post-tonal music to theories of rhythm, interpretation and performance, and biological approaches to the study of music and the mind.

Index

Boulez, Pierre, 210n28; *douze notations, No. 2,* 37, *39,* 39–40
bourgeois worldview, 121
Brahms, Johannes: Fourth Symphony, 63; Violin Sonata in G, Op. 78, *64,* 64–65
Breton, André, 119, 124, 131
brilliant style, 93
Brooks, Jeanice, 116
bugle, 81
Bull, Georges, 192, 194
Bürger, Peter, 171
Burgoyne, Robert, 133n5
Burke, Richard, 128
Burkholder, J. Peter, 6, 7–8, 66, 144
Busoni, Ferruccio, 190
Butler, Judith, 134n34

cadence, four-part melodic idea and, 19–20, *20–25,* 26–29
Cage, John, 43, 59n7
Campbell, Joseph, 143, 169nn28,30
Caplin, William, 49
Carnaval (Schumann), 111
causality, interpretation and, 112, 113
Chabanon, Michel-Paul-Gui de, 104n6
Chants de Maldoror, Les (Lautréamont), 118
"Chapeaux de gaze" (Breton), 119, 124
Chatman, Seymour, 72, 112
Chevalier, Jean, 146
Chopin, Frédéric: arpeggiated figure in cadence, 19–20, 26; Ballade in A♭ Major, Op. 47, 19, *21,* 26, *28;* Ballade in F Minor, Op. 52, 20, *23;* Beethoven's influence on, 14–19; Etude in A Minor, Op. 25, No. 10, 19–20, *22,* 23; gestural elements, comparison of, 26–29, *28;* Prelude in D Minor, Op. 28, No. 24, 20–26, *24–25, 28;* Sonata in B Minor, Op. 58, 14, *16;* Waltz in A♭ Major, Op. 64, No. 3, 18, *20;* Waltz in E Minor, Op. posth., 14, *15*
chord of nature, 112
Cincinnati Symphony Orchestra, 88
classical tradition, 136–139, 141–142, 153, 158
Clifton, Thomas, 110, 114
closural gesture, 7; used as opening theme, 64–66, 72
coda, four-part melodic idea and, *21, 25,* 26–29
codetermination, 128–129
cogency, 114–115, 126–127
cognitive linguistics, 124
Cohan, George M., 83–85
coherence, 109, 110
Coker, Wilson, 101
collage, 8, 10, 118; musicological approaches to, 119–121, 123. *See also* montage

Colonne, Edouard, 185–186
comic mythos, 160–165, 168n8
common man, concept of, 88
communication, 57, 77; associative meaning and, 103–104
community of listeners, 101, 106n40
composer: effect of transcriptions on, 207–208; factors outside of control of, 9–10; listeners and, 43–44, 59n10, 201; meanings attached to, by analyst, 8–9; musical personae and, 43, 59n12
concatenationism, 113–115, 123, 127, 181
concerts: context of, 173; programming, 185–187, 211n54
Concerts Lamoureux, 195
Concerts Pasdeloup, 185
conductors, 185–186, 210n28
Cone, Edward T., 59nn6,12
connotation, 60n22, 77, 101, 102, 130, 136
contemplative approach, 43, 59n11
context: associative meaning and, 102–103; of interpretive act, 45–47, 60n19; political, 173, 174, 179–180
continuity, 5, 44–45. *See also* discontinuity
contrast, 110
Cook, Nicholas, 8, 10, 60n18, 77, 138
Copland, Aaron, 76, 83–88, 99; Piano Fantasy, 35, 37, *38;* possible invocation of Strauss, 89–93, 103. *See also* Fanfare for the Common Man
counterpoint: in *Hammerklavier* Piano Sonata, 66–68, *67;* silence and, 54–57, *55, 56*
Courage, Alexander, 102
Cox, Arnie, 100
Cramer, Henri, 188, 190, 192
Creston, Paul, 88
cuckoo, symbol of, *141,* 141–142
cumulative form, 7, 66
cumulative setting, 144

Dalila (Feuillet), 176, 209n11
dance music, as socially constructed, 158–159
"Dance of the Priestesses" (arr. Roquet), 205
"Dance of the Priestesses" (Saint-Saëns), transcriptions of, 188, *189,* 205
Danse macabre (Saint-Saëns), transcriptions of, 210nn38,43
Dante Alighieri, 147, 152, 160
Dante Symphony (Liszt), 147
Dauenhauer, Bernard P., 43, 60nn15,20
Davidovsky, Mario, 11–14, 35, 39–40
de Man, Paul, 172–173, 209n5
Debussy, Claude, *50,* 51, 58, 61n25, 208, 213n78
Decoration Day (Ives), 83, *84*
defamiliarization, 121, *122*

tensification), 11–13, 26–28, 35, 37, 39; history of, in familiar repertoires, 14–19; in jazz music, 34–35; large-scale dynamic shape, 11, *12;* low-register "thud," 11–13, 35, 37, 39; physicality of gestures, 13, 19; plunge to low register, 11–13, 26, 28, 29, 32, 35, 37, 39; rebound to middle register, 11–13, 26, 32, 35, 37, 39; surface features, 27, 29

framing level of discourse, 65

France: Constitution, 174; essentialist thinking about race and gender, 178–179; exotic, interest in, 179, 191–194, 206; genres available to public, 181–185, *182–184,* 207; Paris Commune, 179; political context, 191; Republican concerns, 174; Third Republic, 179; women as allegories, 179–180

Franco-Prussian War, 179

Freud, Sigmund, 131

fruit, symbol of, 139–140

Frye, Northrop, 138, 153, 160, 167nn3,5, 168nn8,9

Fulcher, Jane F., 99

functional categories, 44–45, 59n14

Garde Républicaine, 205, 207

gender: masculine and feminine themes, 181, 192–195; nineteenth-century French views, 178–179

generalization, 118, 121–123, 129

Genette, Girard, 7

gesture, 5–7; physicality of, 5, 13, 19; tragic, 64–66, 72

Gheerbrant, Alain, 146

Gide, André, 23, 26

Gilbert and Sullivan, 126

Girard, René, 137, 154

Goethe, Johann Wolfgang von, 140

Goossens, Eugene, 88

Gossec, François-Joseph, 174

Gould, Eric, 140

"Grain of the Voice, The" (Barthes), 131–132

Guiraud, Ernest, 188, 210n43

Gurney, Edmund, 113–114, 181

Gustav Mahler (Floros), 135

habituation, 60n23

Halanzier, Olivier, 180

Hammerklavier Piano Sonata, Op. 106 (Beethoven), 66–68, *67*

Handel, George Frideric, 174, 187

Hanslick, Eduard, 45, 60n18, 101

Hanson, Howard, 88

Harmonielehre (Schenker), 107–109

harmony, 46–47; four-part melodic idea, in Chopin, 26, 27, 29; non-discursive events, 51–53

Hatten, Robert S., 6–7, 8, 9, 99, 143, 212n62

Haydn, Franz Joseph, 66

Heile, Björn, 117

hero: as agent of re-creation, 164–165; call to adventure, 143; emergence of social persona, 140, 144–145, 148; existential doubt of, 147–148; future salvation of, 161; initiation of quest, 145–146; as internal threat, 153–154; pre-cultural manifestation of, 139, 143–144, 148; quest from without, 160; redemption of, *156,* 162; as representative of forces of good, 148; romance mythos and, 138–153; as scapegoat, 137, 153–157; stages in development of, 151–152

Hérodiade (Massenet), 207

Hertz, David Michael, 99

historical meanings, 136

History of Photography in Sound (Finnissy), 128

Holmès, Augusta, 178, 180

Hooper-Greenhill, Eilean, 116–117

horizon of expectation, 172, 173, 207, 209n5

Howards End (Forster), 170–172, 208nn1,2

"Hunter's Funeral Procession, The" (von Schwind), 147

Husserl, Edmund, 59n5, 110, 114, 209n5

Iberia (Debussy), *50,* 51, 58, 61n25

Illustrations (Roques), 192

images, language of, 130

implication-realization model, 5

Incoronazione di Poppea, L' (Monteverdi), 100

individual, 137–138, 178; emergence of, 140, 144–145, 148

ineffability of music, 129–130, 131, 134n36

influence theory, 99

instrumentation, 14, 17, 46–47

intellectual montage, 124, 132

inter-essay approach, 3–4

interpretation: associative perception, 7–8; causality and, 112, 113; context of, 45–47, 60n19; dialectical process, 45–46, 60nn19,20; effect of performative silence on, 43–44; of re-ordered events, 63–64; subjectivity of, 47, 60n22. *See also* associative meaning; listeners; music analysis

interpretive community, 106n40

interruptive gesture, 68–71

intertextuality, 8, 99

intervallic saturation, 44

ironic mythos, 157–160

McCreless, Patrick, 5–6, 7, 9

meaning, as term, 1. *See also* musical meaning

medieval Romance tradition, 136, 145

Meister, Georges, 196–204, *198, 202,* 211n62

melodic gesture, 4–7, 29, 44–45. *See also* four-part melodic idea

Melrose, Susan, 136

memory, 7

Mercury, Freddie, 125–127

Messe de la Pentecôte (Messiaen), 35

Messiaen, Olivier: "Sortie" (*Messe de la Pentecôte*), 35; *Vingt Regards sur l'Enfant-Jésus,* 35, *36*

Metamorphoses (Ovid), 164

metaphor, 124; language as, 44, 76–78, 117

Metzer, David, 117

Meyer, Leonard B., 5, 41, 42, 44–45, 64, 100

Micznik, Vera, 7, 113, 122, 128

military bands, 212nn68,75; soldiers as performers, 204; transcriptions for, 196–204, *198, 200, 202*

military calls, 81–83, *82,* 102, 105n8; arbitrary encoding of, 81; *Assembly,* 81; instruments used, 81; in Mahler, 142–143; performance and, 81–83; quotation of, 83; *Reveille,* 81, 87; social orientation, 142–143; stylistic allusion to, 83–85; *Taps,* 81–83, 87; timbre of, associative meaning and, 85–88. *See also* fanfares

Miller, Daniel, 117, 130, 131, 133n10

"Miserere" from *Il Trovatore* (Liszt), 29, *30*

modernism, 208

moment-to-moment process, 7, 108–110, 113–114, 181

Mon, Franz, 118

Monelle, Raymond, 45, 58n1, 60n17, 99

montage: differential replacement, 122, 123, 125, 127; film, 13, 121–125; intellectual, 124; music as, 125–128; as musical, 132; shot-to-shot editing, 122–123; vertical, 122, 130, 132. *See also* collage

Monteverdi, Claudio, 100

Mozart, Wolfgang Amadeus, 49–51, *50,* 58; Piano Concerto in B♭, K. 595, 105n24; Piano Sonata in B♭, K. 281, 71; Piano Sonata in D Major, K. 576, 93–95, *94, 95;* Symphony in G Minor, 49–51, *50,* 58

multidimensional approach, 4–9

museum, 115–117

music: as form of communication, 77, 172; ineffability of, 129–130, 131, 134n36; as montage, 125–128; as paradigm case of uncanny, 132; process-oriented aspects of, 2, 44–45, 63, 181; resistance to authority, 171; socially constructed character of, 158–159; terminology

of language used to describe, 44, 117. *See also* non-discursive music

music analysis: conventional structuralist analysis, 111; divining rod analogy, 1–2; emphasis on non-obvious elements, 109–110; explaining away discontinuity, 107–108; multidimensional approach, 4–9; mythic readings, usefulness of, 167; narratological approach, 110–115; origins in Beethoven criticism, 109–110; phenomenological approach, 110, 114

Music in the Moment (Levinson), 181

musical meaning: changes over time, 173–174; contextual associations, 3–4; as contingent, 9–10; conveyed by silence, 43–44, 47–49; created through juxtaposition, 116–117; denotive vs. connotative, 60n22; differential replacement and, 122; discursive vs. non-discursive interpretations of, 45–47, 58n4; emergent, 66, 119–120, 124; excerpts and, 180–188; factors outside composer's control, 9–10; language metaphor for, 44, 76–78, 117; melodic gesture and, 4–7, 29, 44–45; nineteenth-century listener and, 171–172; obtuse, 131; overt, 131; syntactic features of music, 45, 58n1, 60n17, 77, 97–98; temporal succession and, 113, 127, 133n22, 181; textual, 116–117; transcriptions and, 188–195. *See also* associative meaning; context; melodic gesture; troping of temporality

musicals, evocation of, 126

musikalische Gedanke, 5

mystification of musical meaning, 1–2

myth, 137. *See also* mythoi

Mythic Intentions in Modern Literature (Gould), 140

mythoi, 167n5; comic, 160–165, 168n8; ironic, 157–160; romance, 138–153, 165; tragic, 153–157, 168n8

Narmour, Eugene, 5, 100

narrative, 9, 78; two distinct times in, 111, 115

narrative cycle, 136–137, 153. *See also* mythoi

narrativity, degrees of, 113, 122, 128

narratological approach, 110–115; limitations of, 112–113

Nattiez, Jean-Jacques, 45–46, 106n41, 112, 127

Nearer My God, to Thee, 83

New Museology, The (Vergo), 117

"New" musicologists, 129

Newcomb, Anthony, 65, 111–112, 132nn1,4

Nietzsche, Friedrich, 89–92

Night at the Opera, A (Queen), 125–127

noctis avis, 164

Noel, Edouard, 196
non-discursive music, 41–42; aesthetic categories compared, 44, 59n14; attributes, 44, 60n16; concurrent with discursive events, 47–49, 58n4; context of, 45–47, 60n19; intermittent, 49–53; in music before twentieth century, 49–51; pervasive, 53–57; properties of, 44–45; random pitch, 54; as silent, 42–43; structure and, 42–43; thick texture, 53–54
non-durative process, 63
nonlinear music. *See* non-discursive music
nonverbal, limitations of language to explain, 129–130
Nora, Pierre, 206–207
Nougé, Paul, 119, 122, 124
Novalis, 139

obtuse meaning, 131
October (Eisenstein), 124, 132
ongoing present, 6–7, 62
Opéra, 180
opera, genres available to French public, 181–185, *182–184,* 207
organ music, 35, *37*
Orient et occident (Saint-Saëns), 199
Over There (Cohan), 83–85
Ovid, 164

Pace, Ian, 128
Panzéra, Charles, 131
paradigmatic plot, 111–112, 128, 132n1
Paris Commune, 179
Paris Conservatoire, 174, 191
Parsifal (Wagner), 126, 145–146, 151, 168n15
Pasler, Jann, 8, 9
passacaglia, 63
Paul, Jean, 138, 139
Pearsall, Edward, 6, 8, 9
Pearson, Charles, 62
Pedroza, Ludim, 59n11
perfective process, 63
performance, 9; all items as relevant to, 121, 133n21; associative meaning and, 81–83
performative silence, 43–44, 51, 57–58, 59n7
personae, musical, 43, 59n12
Petit poucet, Le, 205, 207
physicality of gestures, 5, 13, 19
pianists, 14, 190
piano: Romantic era instruments, 14; Romantic era music, four-part melodic idea in, 14–19; transcriptions for, 188–195; twentieth-century music, 34–40
Piano Concerto in B♭, K. 595 (Mozart), 105n24

Piano Concerto in G Major (Fourth) (Beethoven), 107–109, 114–115, 127, 128–129
Piano Fantasy (Copland), 35, 37, *38*
Piano Sonata, Op. 1 (Berg), *65,* 65–66, *96,* 96–98, 106n26
Piano Sonata in A Major, D. 959 (Schubert), 68–71, *69*
Piano Sonata in A Minor, D. 845 (Schubert), 70, *71*
Piano Sonata in B♭, D. 960 (Schubert), 71, *72*
Piano Sonata in B♭, K. 281 (Mozart), 71
Piano Sonata in C Minor, D. 958 (Schubert), 71–72, *73*
Piano Sonata in D Major, K. 576 (Mozart), 93–95, *94, 95*
Piano Sonata in E, Op. 109 (Beethoven), 75nn7,8
Piotrovsky, Adrien, 122
Piston, Walter, 88
pitch, random, 54
postmodernism, 7
Pougin, Arthur, 196
Poulenc, Francis, 116
Power of Sound, The (Gurney), 113–114
Prelude to the Afternoon of a Faun (Debussy), 208
premodalization, 143, 168n14
present, ongoing, 6–7, 62
present now of consciousness, 42, 59n5
Prix de Rome competition, 176, 191
process-oriented aspects of music, 2, 44–45, 62, 181
programmatic music, associative meaning and, 83–93
progressive process, 63
psychological effects, associative meaning and, 5, 99–100
psychopomp, 147
Pudovkin, Vsevolod, 123
Pyramids at the Louvre: Music, Culture, and Collage from Stravinsky to the Postmodernists (Watkins), 117–118

Quartet in E♭, Op. 33, No. 2 ("Joke" Quartet) (Haydn), 66
Queen, 125–127, 128, 133n30
Queen 2, 126
quotation, 7, 83

Raffman, Diana, 134n36
Rameau, Jean-Philippe, 174
rarefied excellences, 114, 127
Ratner, Leonard G., 93, 99, 105n20, 143
Ratner, Sabina, 179, 190, 212n64

retrospective (codas), 62–63, 68, 72; reordering of events, 62–64
Tynyanov, Yuri, 121, 122, 123, 127–128, 132, 133n22

Unanswered Question (Ives), *46*, 46–47, 58
uncanny, 107, 129, 131–132
universal language concept, 77, 104n6

Vaughan Williams, Ralph, 47–49, *48–49*, 58
Velmar-Janković, Svetlana, 74
Verdi, Giuseppe, 176
Vergo, Peter, 116, 117, 123
Verhurt, Henry, 195
vertical montage, 122, 130, 132
Viardot, Pauline, 178, 180
video, music, 125–127, 133n30
Vingt Regards sur l'Enfant-Jésus (Messiaen), 35, *36*
Violin Sonata in G, Op. 78 (Brahms), 64–65, *64*
Voltaire, 174, 176, 179
Vom Musikalische-Schönen (Hanslick), 60n18

Wagner, Richard, 126; in concerts of excerpts, 188; *Flying Dutchman,* 146; *Lohengrin,* 207; *Parsifal,* 126, 145–146, 151, 168n15
Wallace, Henry, 88
Watkins, Glenn, 117–118
Whittock, Trevor, 122, 124
Williams, John, 102
wind-band transcriptions, 196–204, *198, 200, 202,* 211n62; of female vocal solos, 201
Witz, 111
women, transcriptions and, 194–195. *See also* gender
World War II era, 88
Wunderhorn: First Symphony (Mahler), 166; first movement, 139–146; second movement, 146; third movement, 146–147, 152–153, 157; "Aground," 146–147; *Blumine* movement, 139, 168n16; breakthrough harmony, 145–146, 152; *Bruder Martin* variant, 147; *cantabile* cello theme, 141, *142,* 144–145, *145,* 148, 151; chorale topics in, 152, 161; Cross/Grail motive, 145–146, *145,* 147, 148, *149–150;* cuckoo imagery, 141–142, *141,* 164; "Dall' Inferno al Paradiso," 147, 153; development section, 144; dysphoric elements in, 147, 148–149, 151–152; fanfare motive, *141,* 153; finale, 147–148; first movement, 139–140; funeral-March material, 147; *Gesellen* song, 144; "Ging heut Morgen uber's Feld," 141, *142,* 143, 146; Hamburg concert notes, 139, 140; horn call, *141,* 142–143; "In Full Sail," 146;

Infernal triplet motive, 147, 148, *149–150,* 152; irony in, 146–147, 157; "Lieder eines fahrenden Gesellen," 147, 168n19; natural world in, 140, 141–144; outcry motive, 148, *149–150,* 151, 152; programmatic titles, 139–140, 140, 146–147, 153; recapitulation, 151–152; redemptive element in, 148; spring, imagery of, 139–140, 168n9; "Spring and No End," 140; "Theme of Fourths," 140, *141,* 148, 152, 153; "Tirili" motive, 144, *144,* 146; "Titan" as title for, 138–139; Victorious theme, *151,* 152; von Schwind woodcut as inspiration in, 146, 147; "Weh" motive, 148, 151, *151*
Wunderhorn: Second Symphony (Mahler), 166; first movement, 153–157, *156;* second movement, 158; third movement, 158–159; fourth movement, 160–161; fifth movement, 161–165, *162;* ascension motive, *162;* "Bird of the Night," 142, *162;* Caller motive, 162, *162,* 163; chorale topics, 161, *162,* 163; Cross/Grail variant in, 154–155, *155, 156;* dance topics in, 158–159; *Dies Irae* in, *156,* 157, 162, *162,* 163; Entreaty motive, 162–163; Eternity motive, *156, 162;* fanfare motive, 155; fanfare of the Apocalypse, 162–163, *162;* fear motive, *162;* fish symbolism, 158–160; fright fanfare, 161, *162;* funereal themes, 154, 155, *156;* Gesellen song, *156;* heroic theme, *156;* Infernal triplets, 155, *156;* Judgment music, 143; Last Judgment section, 161–165, *162;* march music, *156, 162;* narrative summary, 155–157, *156;* opening "decree," *156,* 163; outcry motive, 162; pastorale, 155, *156;* Prophecy/Annunciation section, 161–165, *162;* Resurrection section, 161–165, *162;* sigh motive, *156, 162;* "Theme of Fourths," 155; *Todtenfeier* movement, 154–155; triplet motives, *162;* *Urlicht* movement, 160–161
Wunderhorn: Third Symphony (Mahler), 165–166, *166;* "Bird of the Night," 164; cuckoo theme, 142; *Mitternacht* movement, 164
Wunderhorn: Fourth Symphony (Mahler), 139–140, 142, 165–166, *166*
Wunderhorn: Fifth Symphony (Mahler), 166–167
Wunderhorn symphonies (Mahler), 136, 160–165; biblical tradition in, 140, 143, 153–154, 158–160, 161; bird imagery in, 141–142, 164; child, imagery of, 166; classical tradition in, 136–139, 141–142, 153, 158; *creative mythopoesis* in, 135, 161; critique of relationship between individual and society, 137–138; cyclic narrative structure, 136–137, 153; ironic mythos in, 157–160; medieval Romance tradi-